ALSO BY JASON M. BARR

*Building the Skyline: The Birth and Growth
of Manhattan's Skyscrapers*

CITIES IN THE SKY

THE QUEST TO BUILD
THE WORLD'S TALLEST
SKYSCRAPERS

JASON M. BARR

SCRIBNER

NEW YORK LONDON TORONTO SYDNEY NEW DELHI

Scribner
An Imprint of Simon & Schuster, LLC
1230 Avenue of the Americas
New York, NY 10020

First Scribner hardcover edition May 2024

SCRIBNER and design are trademarks of Simon & Schuster, LLC.

Simon & Schuster: Celebrating 100 Years of Publishing in 2024

For information about special discounts for bulk purchases,
please contact Simon & Schuster Special Sales at 1-866-506-1949
or business@simonandschuster.com.

The Simon & Schuster Speakers Bureau can bring authors to
your live event. For more information or to book an event,
contact the Simon & Schuster Speakers Bureau at 1-866-248-3049
or visit our website at www.simonspeakers.com.

Interior design by Kyle Kabel

Manufactured in the United States of America

1   3   5   7   9   10   8   6   4   2

Library of Congress Cataloging-in-Publication Data

Names: Barr, Jason M., author. Title: Cities in the sky : the quest to build the
world's tallest skyscrapers / Jason M. Barr. Description: First Scribner hardcover edition. |
New York : Scribner, 2024. | Includes bibliographical references and index.
Identifiers: LCCN 2023056186 (print) | LCCN 2023056187 (ebook) |
ISBN 9781982174217 (hardcover) | ISBN 9781982174231 (ebook) Subjects: LCSH: Skyscrapers. |
Supertall buildings. | City planning. | Sociology, Urban. | BISAC: ARCHITECTURE /
Buildings / Public, Commercial & Industrial | SOCIAL SCIENCE / Sociology /
Urban Classification: LCC NA9053.S4 B37 2024 (print) | LCC NA9053.S4 (ebook) |
DDC 720/.483—dc23/eng/20240117
LC record available at https://lccn.loc.gov/2023056186
LC ebook record available at https://lccn.loc.gov/2023056187

ISBN 978-1-9821-7421-7
ISBN 978-1-9821-7423-1 (ebook)

To Kathy and Will
and the memory of my father, Sheldon P. Barr

Contents

CITIES IN THE SKY

A hypothetical mooring of an airship to the mast
atop the Empire State Building, ca. 1930.

Introduction

THE OBSERVATION DECK was an afterthought.

The initial plans for the Empire State Building, produced in August 1929, called for a workaday, but tall, 1,000-foot (305 m), eighty-story office building to house Gotham's energetic business community. A couple of months later, the developers purchased a lot next door, which enabled them to add five stories while remaining within the city's building regulations. But more importantly, the tower could now rise taller than Walter Chrysler's building at 1,046 feet (319 m), under construction ten blocks to the north.

Not content to just beat Chrysler by a hair, the developers decided to go the extra mile, so to speak, by adding a 200-foot (61 m) mooring mast for airships, which, prior to the Hindenburg tragedy in 1937, were a fashionable means of international travel.

At the announcement of the mast's addition, on December 12, 1929, former New York governor Al Smith, the president of the company erecting the building, addressed its legitimacy, telling the world:

> The directors of the Empire State, Inc., believe . . . that in a comparatively short time the Zeppelin airships will establish transatlantic, transcontinental and transpacific lines, and possibly a route to South America from the port of New York.

Building with an eye to the future, it has been determined to erect this mooring tower with elevator facilities through the tower to land people directly on Thirty-fourth Street and Fifth Avenue after their ocean trip, seven minutes after the airship connects with the mast.

History does not record if Smith ever believed that the structure would be a functional airship gate. But with the first test run, any illusions quickly evaporated. The perilous, and ultimately futile, task was reported in the *New York Times*:

> A stiff wind was blowing as the dirigible hovered with throttled engines and approached the high tower and superstructure of the new building. In the cabin of the airship Lieutenant S. M. Bailey, the commander, kept his hands on the controls and ballast releases in case a gust threw him too close to the near-by buildings.

After thirty minutes, Bailey gave up and went home. Nonetheless, what became an overengineered decorative tower sitting on an office building roof serendipitously morphed into opportunity—an observation deck 1,050 feet (320 m) in the air.

Not only does that deck draw millions of tourists, but it was also the serendipity that helped the owners keep from losing their building during the Great Depression. The observatory was a cash cow that, in the first full year of operation, brought in nearly $800,000 in revenue, while the building's offices generated $1 million. In hindsight, the Empire State Building is a more elegant structure not despite the height competition, but because of it.

Today some might call the mooring mast simply vanity height. But every night it is lit up in a different color as a kind of communal lighthouse. On July Fourth, Independence Day, it glows red, white, and blue. On St. Patrick's Day, it is lit up in green, and on Pride Day, it displays the rainbow. While the Empire State Building was erected from a cocktail of economics and ego, all New Yorkers would agree that it is the prince of the city—a well-dressed, benevolent guardian, waving at passersby. Gotham officially conferred its knightly status on May 19, 1981, by declaring it a landmark—making it *Sir* Empire State Building.

This history, perhaps more than any other, shows the wondrous accidents that we sometimes get from our skyscrapers. But ultimately, their success depends on the dollars, loonies, euros, shekels, pesos, or yuan that flow into their coffers. And though the Empire State Building got off to a rocky start during the Great Depression, some ninety years later it is both beloved and a moneymaker, having averaged an annual inflation-adjusted 5 percent growth rate in its market value. The once-dubbed Empty State Building is now the pride and profit of Gotham.

The skyscraper's iconic form also has become a global beacon for American entrepreneurial and engineering prowess. The Empire State Building is the ultimate symbol of a city of strivers, and other cities seek to imitate its magic by erecting their own version, be it the Shanghai Tower, the Burj Khalifa, or Taipei 101. Nothing says "we have arrived on the global scene" more than having the world's tallest building. The Empire State Building, with its combination of grandeur, simplicity of design, and quiet elegance, paved the way to the future.

And, from time to time, when I go up to the observation deck and look around, I see the hum and flow of the world below. Looking farther afield, I can glimpse my past beyond Manhattan Island. If you squint to the east, you can see the borough of Queens, and though too far to see with the naked eye, there lies my hometown of Baldwin, seven miles east of the New York City border.

Past the great brick ridges and blacktop valleys of Manhattan lie vast suburban plains with mile after mile of single-family homes surrounded by moats of lawn. Each workday, commuters emerge from their front doors to sluice their way to the business districts. The bridge-and-tunnel day-trippers come in for gourmet muffins, Broadway shows, or all-night clubbing. The international immigrants arrive with their taxicabs, food trucks, and work tools. The global tourists bumble and gawk their way through Times Square. Together, the center becomes a chaotic yet controlled sociological soup: the mix of the mundane with the mighty. Looking down from the Empire State Building, I can see it all.

The mysticism of the human-created city, whose whole is so much greater than the sum of its parts, combined with the uneasy feeling as a youth of being an urbanite trapped in a suburban body, produced my fascination with cities and skyscrapers. Over my professional career as an economist, I have come to see that skyscrapers and cities each need the other and, for the most part, exist in symbiotic harmony. All the books, articles, and TV shows about tall buildings—their architectural designs, their engineering feats, and their acts of hubris—miss this bigger, more important picture. To really understand skyscrapers requires us to also see the urban environment that created them.

When we look around the world, we see that skyscrapers are steadily sprouting upward, even as economics, politics, city patterns, and technology change. In 2018, for example, 308 buildings of 492 feet (150 m) or taller were built worldwide. Laid end to end, they would run nearly 40 miles (64 km) long. If we go back to the year 2000, the number of completions was a mere seventy-eight, meaning a quadrupling in less than two decades. In fact, nearly seven times more skyscrapers were erected in the first two decades of the new millennium than during the entire twentieth century. While the COVID pandemic put the brakes on for a spell, the world has resumed its building spree.

Focusing on the decade from 2010 to 2019, we can get a sense of where new buildings are rising. Nearly half were built in mainland China alone, and rounding out the top five were South Korea with 11 percent, Malaysia with 7 percent, the United Arab Emirates with 4 percent, and the United States with 3 percent. But all told, Asia was responsible for a whopping 90 percent of the world's skyscrapers constructed in this period.

Looking at the tallest one hundred structures around the world tells an equally impressive story. Earning a spot in this club requires at least fifty-four stories. But to make it into the top twenty requires at least eighty-one stories and a minimum of 1,476 feet (450 m). In other words, the Empire State Building, at 1,250 feet tall, is decidedly second class and, I'm sorry to say, an old man. Nine of the ten tallest buildings in the world are in Asia, with five in mainland China.

Only one tower in the United States, One World Trade Center (2014), makes it to the top ten, thanks to its long spire. If we were merely counting floors, the tower would get bumped down to twenty-seven. Nowadays, if you want to make your mark, you need at least 100 floors, with twenty buildings having that many or more. And if you're going to be really, really tall, you need at least 115 floors, of which there are six, and all in Asia. The world's tallest building has 163 stories.

What is driving this global quest for skyscrapers and skylines? The answer boils down to one simple answer: We want and need them. And yes, that includes you and me. We create the skylines of the world. You may not directly ask for them, but we are all part of the larger system of networks and nodes of trade and urbanization that gives rise to tall buildings.

Our desire to get on with our lives—to work, live, and play—and do it in cities generates a kind of natural order, of steel, concrete, glass, and brick rising out of the ground, in the way that ants build mounds, or bees their hives.

Cities, by definition, are large, dense clusters of humans and the institutions that support them. Ultimately, skyscrapers are the solution to a geography problem—how to allow many people to be in the same place at the same time. Skyscrapers pinch geography by creating land in the sky.

This book is about how the trajectories of globalization and urbanization, and our evolving tastes and needs, have created the world's skylines. The changing nature of work, living, and playing is, in fact, making the tall building more important than ever.

The vast webs of interconnected computer-based technologies—the internet, social media, email, and Zoom—were "supposed" to make cities obsolete. But computers have, ironically, made cities more important. They have created new kinds of jobs that are more socialized. They have given us vast wealth, much of which we spend on things in big cities. And, as a collective whole, skylines help forge our identities and give us pride of place.

In the process, they contribute to another, perhaps unintended, consequence. They move us that much closer to what can be termed Terranism—one global human society. The skyscraper is the lingua franca of urban real estate. It is arguably the one building form that brings us together, literally because so many people can be inside at the same time, and because of what each represents—the triumph of our universal aspirations.

Skyscraper chroniclers Earle Shultz and Walter Simmons summarized this idea nicely in 1959 when they wrote: "The character and quality of any city can be told from a great distance by its skyline, but these buildings do more than advertise a city. They show the faith of many in its destiny, and they create a like faith in others."

This is not to say that skyscrapers are always benign or they never create negative unintended consequences, but they are now, more than ever, engines that power our modern world. And there's nothing in the history of society or technology that was ever gotten right on the first try. Rather, humanity is in a constant process—struggle even—of trial and error and success. The skyscraper is part of the larger attempt to "get society right." The lessons of its many failures have been learned, and tall buildings have adapted and will adapt accordingly. As new problems arise, developers will alter building forms and technologies to cater to the needs of the day.

But just as importantly, I want to stress, we do not need, nor should we have, skyscrapers everywhere and in all cities, or in all places and at all times. But when constructed in the right places at the right time—of which the vast majority are—they facilitate the things we want to have and do. The word "metropolis" is from the Greek for "mother city." If the city-as-mother is to succeed, it needs nests for its hatchlings and room for the family. The skyscraper is a home that allows the species to thrive.

Now, perhaps you say, "I'm one of those who hate tall buildings and I actively work to prevent them." Yet you, too, are helping to produce them. If barriers are created to make something artificially scarce, it raises the stakes and suppliers will find a way to game the system to cater to the demand. When you try eliminating something people want, you wind up generating more unintended consequences than if you created a more rational and reasonable policy that better balanced the trade-offs. When cities try to limit needed skyscrapers, they get higher real estate prices, more inequality, fewer employment opportunities, and more automobile-based sprawl. Often we blame the skyscraper for these problems when, in fact, as I will discuss throughout the book, the skyscraper can mitigate them.

Indeed, without the desire for people to be inside these lofty structures, there would be no soaring architectural gems, no height competition, no icons, no engineering feats, no coffee table books or History Channel documentaries. Yet if you watch any TV show on the subject, there is usually some perfunctory remark about how urbanization is driving the rise of skylines, and from there the narrator proceeds to launch into images of steel riveters from the 1920s or reenactments of car moguls fighting to have the world's tallest building. In this way, the demand side—the real story—is barely mentioned.

It also seems strange to me the oft-repeated idea that skyscrapers are bad or too tall because developers have big egos. When we vilify narcissistic developers, we oversimplify and lose awareness in the process—the city is the product of millions of people and millions of decisions; we all play a part. Ego and optimism power the world.

And if ego alone was, in fact, the key driver of skyscraper heights, the world would have had many more record breakers. The fact that we've only had twelve since 1890 shows that it takes many planets to align before a new record-breaking building emerges. The road to the world's tallest building is paved with the ego-drenched renderings of the starry-eyed dreamer.

But whose ego? Whose dreams? When you ask an architect, an engineer, or a general contractor who "the client" is, they will say it's the lead developer — the person or group in charge that raises the money and makes sure the structure gets built. In this sense of the word, the architect is hired by "the client," the person paying for the services.

But to me, this use of the word "client" is the opposite of how we should understand it. In my view, the developer is a patron and the architect is a client. The developer is, however, just one link in a series of client-patron relationships. The architects and engineers are hired by the developer, but the developer is often beholden to the bank or investors. So, in this context, the developer is the client and the investors are the patrons.

But the aim of the developer is to create land in the sky and make money in the process — so the developer is also the client of the occupant "patrons," who pay money because they want to be inside the building. But the structure exists within the fabric of the larger city. Its construction and operation are governed by rules, regulations, and policies. So here the city acts as the patron and the developers are the clients of the city-as-corporate entity. More broadly, skyscrapers emerge within the wider society that sanctions them. Skyscrapers can only be built when the culture, beliefs, and mores about them mean that society thinks they are useful. In this sense, society is the patron and the city that builds them is the client.

As an example, we can look at the Shard, completed in London in 2012 and rising to 1,016 feet (310 m). The lead developer, Irvine Sellar, hired Renzo Piano, a world-famous architect, to design his structure. Here Sellar was the patron and Piano the client.

Sellar did not have the money to build the $2 billion structure himself, so he turned to investors. When the 2007–2008 financial crisis hit, he lost his main backer, Credit Suisse. In its place, he found the Qatari government, which stepped in with the funds. In this way, the State of Qatar was the patron and Sellar was the client. Qatar has made its fortune from the sale of crude oil, which eventually winds up in your car's gas tank. So that makes you a patron, as well.

But even with Piano's elegant design, British officials still demanded it go through a rigorous approval process, the outcome of which was highly uncertain. British officials now became the patron, who had to bestow their approval on Piano and Sellar.

Nonetheless, the venture's success depended on the income that would be generated. The building had to be filled with revenue-producing tenants and visitors. Here the "patrons" are the occupants who make the building pay. Sellar inked a deal with the Shangri-La Hotel to occupy eighteen stories, and the top floors house the observatory. Between the hotel and the observatory are rented apartments. The bottom thirty-one floors are offices, whose occupants include Tiffany & Co., Al-Jazeera, and the Warwick Business School.

Now that the Shard is open for business and humming away, London has embraced it. The nickname also adds value to the London brand of skyscraper. The building is featured in postcards, social media, and documentaries and is part of the soul of modern London. In this way, London has become *the client* of the Shard, which stands as a crystal prince, a knight in the city.

It is through the client-patron relationships that we can also get a glimpse into how skyscraper technology evolves. The technology and design are not just for building height alone but also used to create productive spaces. For skyscrapers to work, they must satisfy a hierarchy of needs. First, they must be safe from fire, wind, or collapse. Second, they must be occupiable—the interior spaces need to be comfortable and contain modern conveniences. Lastly, they must adequately project our desires and what we wish to communicate to the outside world, as they help define our identities. And all this must be done at a cost that is below the income the occupants generate.

Without efficient and economic solutions to these problems, a building's height is irrelevant. But these problems can be solved because of the companies and institutions that have arisen to help the developer provide a tall building in a relatively low-cost manner. At the end of the day, building height and better buildings are two sides of the same coin. Rising heights emerge out of the evolving needs and tastes of urban residents, as much as from the dreams of the developer. In this way, the technology that produces towering achievements is not separate from the economics and the incentives that turn them into reality.

But because tall buildings are so large and so mysterious—spiritual even—we tell ourselves stories about them: How they were produced from battles between powerful godlike tycoons, architects, and engineers. Such narratives are designed to shrink skyscrapers down to a more manageable psychological size. "Ego" is easy to understand. A height competition between robber barons is easy to understand. An engineer who says he invented the skyscraper after seeing a birdcage is easy to understand. But they are gross oversimplifications (and sometimes outright fabrications), and they contribute to the widespread misunderstanding of the skyscraper's purpose.

By examining how human demand drives the rise of skyscrapers, we can more easily clear away the myths and misconceptions, which all too often arise because of the focus on the supply side. The goal is not just to tell stories about specific buildings but also to see how and why these buildings, and countless others, are being brought forth and how they change our lives.

Now we may begin our account of the quest for the world's tallest skyscrapers. First stop: Chicago, 1883.

PART I

AMERICA

CHAPTER I

Chicago

From Dismal Swamp to Second City

Home Insurance Building (1885)

THE ARCHITECT

Early one morning in the fall of 1883, executives from an influential and profitable insurance company assemble in a conference room twelve years after a fire has consumed much of Chicago. They have arrived after a long train ride from a city hundreds of miles away. They have commissioned an architect to build a new local headquarters and are eager to hear his ideas.

Dressed in black suits and bowler hats, the men take their seats as the room fills with cigar smoke. They chatter among themselves, speculating on what kind of building they are going to get. Their main request was that their offices be as accommodating as possible. The sun must spill far into the interior. The structure must exude comfort and stand as a beacon of commerce while also providing a satisfactory profit. And, of course, it must be fireproof.

As the executives take their seats, the architect enters. He is a serious, stocky man of about fifty. His hairline is deeply receded, and a bushy Vandyke beard clings to his face, while thick bags sag below his eyes. The men hush and turn to him.

Slowly and methodically, sheet by sheet, he goes through his drawings. He starts with the size and shape of the building—a nine-story cube. Then he turns to the façade. The first story and basement will be rose granite, followed by eight stories of red-pressed brick. Next, he turns to the floor plans and shows them how every office will have ample sunlight. Until now, there is nothing controversial—a standard office building by every measure.

But then, he turns to the structural design—showing how the building will stand up—and here, the executives become uneasy. The company president speaks up, "Where else is there such a building?"

"This will be the first," the architect responds. And they think to themselves, "This man must be mad! As if the recent fires were not bad enough, now he wants our building to collapse!" The president responds, "How do we know if this building is any good?"

Bristling with indignation, the architect retorts, "I will submit all my designs and calculations to one or more bridge engineers of distinction, as the company might select, to review my designs for the skeleton building resembling in many respects iron railroad bridges standing on end, side by side."

The managers grumble. Then suddenly an individual rises—the Civil War hero Brigadier General Arthur Charles Ducat. He stamps out his cigar and addresses the room. Ducat is their business agent in this city, and they trust him implicitly. The room becomes quiet. "Before I was in the insurance business, I was an engineer," he begins. "I have carefully studied the architect's designs and the data for his calculations. I approve of what he has done, both from an engineering and economic point of view. Gentlemen, you can rest assured—this building will stand. Now, I request a motion to commence construction at the earliest date possible." Looking around with relief and self-satisfaction, the officers of the Home Insurance Company unanimously approved the motion.

Thus goes the tale. Since the end of the nineteenth century, the Home Insurance Building in Chicago has been considered by the public as the world's first skyscraper, and architect William Le Baron Jenney is hailed as its inventor. It is a yarn deeply embedded in skyscraper folklore. But the truth is this: Jenney did not invent the skyscraper and the Home Insurance Building was not the first one. Rather, its designation as such emerged out of a public relations campaign by Jenney, his protégés, and colleagues. The story was disseminated for that purpose.

Jenney's friends helped him sell the idea because they loved the man and respected his engineering prowess. They sought to earn him a place in American architectural and technological history, which he no doubt deserved for his lifetime of achievements. By the end of the nineteenth century, arguments about who "invented" the skyscraper were swirling in the media and professional journals. Chicagoans circled the wagons around their man Jenney.

This "Battle for the First" was fundamentally about the framing of the building—its structural design—and the combatants cared little about its height; and, in this regard, the Home Insurance was second-rate. So, let us pause and define what we mean by a "skyscraper" when trying to parse the sequence of events.

The word "skyscraper" for buildings predated the Home Insurance by a wide margin. For example, the *Chicago Tribune* on February 25, 1883, reported in its "New York Gossip" column about the "high-building craze," which included a discussion of Gotham's "sky-scrapers," mentioning that city's Tribune Building (1875, nine floors) and the Western Union Building (1875, ten floors). From the perspective of the press and public, a "sky-scraper" was so named by its height, and not its design or construction. Prior to its application to buildings, the word referenced nearly any tall or high thing, including big horses, sailing ship masts, fly balls in baseball, and ladies' flowery hats.

Since time immemorial, the tallest buildings in cities were rarely more than five stories. Church spires or clock towers were the exceptions that proved the rule. The original thirteenth-century spire of Notre Dame de Paris was 256 feet (78 m) high, while the Great Clock of Westminster, aka Big Ben, completed in 1859, rises to 316 feet (96 m). But when it came to living and working, few were willing to climb more than five stories or 50 vertical feet, and space on the top floors had the lowest value. The elevator, along with other innovations, flipped the profitability of renting out higher floors. As a result, developers now had an incentive to go taller, and taller they went, starting in New York in the early 1870s and then in other major cities throughout the United States. This growth spurt was nothing short of revolutionary, like the introduction of the iPhone in 2007.

The first office building in Chicago to reach ten stories was the Montauk Block completed in 1882, designed by Burnham & Root as a speculative venture for Boston brothers Peter and Shepherd Brooks. In 1885, when the Home Insurance was opened, at least three other completed buildings that year were nine stories or taller.

But the real focus of Jenney's building is on the structural elements—its framing. In this regard, the true structural birth of the Skyscraper Revolution can be defined as when several technological elements came together, circa 1890. Not only did these elements have to be readily obtained in a cost-effective manner, but also the builders needed to understand the methods behind using them and the physics of skyscrapers. These elements formed at least a half decade after the Home Insurance Building, and not because of it, either.

The modern "true" skyscraper after 1890 was a relatively tall structure that contained four key components. First, it required an all-steel frame of columns, beams, and girders. Second, these steel members had to be riveted together to form one continuous latticework. Third, the structure needed extra steel for the sole purpose of wind bracing (and in some cases against seismic activity). Lastly, the façade itself was to be a mere curtain. That is, it served no structural purpose, and its primary functions were to keep out the elements, allow for access to sunlight, and offer the viewer a pleasing architectural statement. This true skyscraper, as described here, is what finally broke the height barrier, in the sense that buildings could rise as high as developers wanted in a way that was safe, comfortable, and profitable.

Against this standard, the Home Insurance Building fails in all four categories. First, only the two street-facing exterior walls had *iron* columns, which were embedded in the masonry piers. The iron was used to reduce the thickness of the exterior walls, and Jenney himself knew that the iron and masonry would share the load since the iron columns were built into the surrounding brick piers. In addition, the rear two façades were standard load-bearing masonry. The totality of the structure was a mix of old and new materials and methods. Further, the iron beams and columns were not riveted but were loosely connected with iron rods, since iron was too brittle to be riveted. And finally, the building contained no additional materials for wind bracing. In short, the Home Insurance Building was not a pure skeletal structure.

Jenney's design, rather, was an incremental change from what preceded it, and what followed were also incremental adjustments. There were no tipping points involved. If Jenney had not built the Home Insurance Building, the skyscraper would have been created all the same.

When his building was completed, neither Jenney nor the wider architectural and engineering community took note. In fact, when Jenney wrote about his building in the journal *The Sanitary Engineer* in December 1885—an expansion of an address he gave at the meeting of the American Institute of Architects—the accomplishment of which he was most proud was that he had successfully employed a foundation design to prevent the structure from settling in an uneven manner.

Only in the second half of the article does he turn to its structural design, where he discusses how he implanted iron columns into the load-bearing walls and connected them to expanded iron lintels. Nowhere in his article does he mention the word "steel." And nowhere does he try to argue that he invented the first fully metal-framed building.

Interestingly, he uses the word "skeleton" to describe the framing, but this word meant little in 1885; it was just a shorthand way of saying that iron columns were connected to iron beams and girders. One could read this article and falsely conclude that his building had a modern skeletal frame.

When we revisit the old black-and-white photos of the steel frame of the Empire State or Chrysler Buildings being riveted together by the fearless riveting gangs, we think of elegance and simplicity of design, an Erector Set writ large rising in the world's great metropolises. But those towering towers were not the direct offshoots of Jenney's building. Looking back from the twenty-first century, the Home Insurance Building was a hybrid, one of the many transitional buildings moving away from the past and toward the future.

Jenney had an innovative architectural career to be sure, and he was willing to substitute new materials when the opportunity presented itself. Ironically, Jenney would, in fact, design one of the first true skyscrapers in 1891, the Manhattan Building in Chicago. And this building, more than any other, deserves credit in this regard, as it brought all the structural elements together.

A key problem with the debate about the first skyscrapers, however, is that of definition. Defining the first is what architectural historian

The steel frame and curtain wall façade of the Chrysler Building in 1929.
(© Walker Evans Archive, The Metropolitan Museum of Art.
Image source: Art Resource, NY)

Thomas Leslie says is akin to defining the first fish. As he told me, "The evolution of the 'fish' happened very gradually. Only in hindsight can we look back at the fossil record and say, 'that looks like a fish,' long after the defining characteristics have established themselves."

At the time, architects and engineers were not trying to invent the "skyscraper" per se; rather, they were trying to solve the problem of how to provide more functional and taller office buildings. As architectural historian Gerald R. Larson notes, the reason for the gradual transition from the masonry building to the steel skeleton is that "buildings fall down." No one was willing to create a building that had a full steel skeletal frame all in one clip. Builders did not have the materials, the knowledge, or the complicity of the wider society. No developer would hire an engineer pushing radical changes to a structure that was meant to be a house of commerce. Confidence was the key. And that took time.

In Chicago, each problem was solved as it cropped up. As buildings got heavier, foundation methods were needed to overcome Chicago's unhelpful "jelly cake" geology, with alternating layers of soft and hard clays. Many an architect watched in fear as their buildings slowly sank and cracked as the clay was compressed.

One of the worst cases was the Board of Trade Building. Completed in 1885, it was ten stories with a 303-foot-tall (92 m) tower. The building's weight of nearly 70 million pounds (318 million kg) was unevenly distributed. The tower quickly sank over ten inches (25 cm), while the rest settled by only five (13 cm), causing the tower to separate nearly a foot from the structure.

As the geologist Ralph Peck recounts, "Within five years after the structure was completed, its settlement had become so alarming that the owners retained General William Sooy Smith, one of the foremost foundation engineers of the day . . . to study the problem." Smith proposed costly repairs, but the owners balked. They simply removed the heavy cast-iron lantern from the tower and employed steel rods to hold the walls together. The structure stood until 1929, when it was cleared to make way for a new Board of Trade Building. At the time of its demolition, parts of the building had sunk nearly two feet (53 cm).

To lighten their buildings, and gain access to more sunlight and fire protection, architects substituted iron for wood or stone. But when exposed iron revealed it could succumb to fire, buildings required materials that could thwart extreme heat; the most popular solution was to enclose the iron in terra-cotta tiles.

Next came the need for wind bracing. During the "cage construction" period of the 1880s, with load-bearing masonry walls and internal iron framing, architects did not worry about the wind because the heavy masonry façades did most of the work. Proper wind bracing became

necessary—and possible—when steel members were available because
they could be riveted together to produce buildings that could rise
high into the sky.

THE REAL STORY

The argument about whether the Home Insurance Building was the
first skyscraper or not prevents us from understanding the larger significance of Chicago in world history. Chicago's skyline erupted from the
fortuitous confluence of economic, technological, and social conditions
that were present in the early decades of the United States. Chicago's
true legacy is not only the supply side—the design and construction of
skyscrapers—but what drove the demand.

Thus, the real story is that Chicago had, unwittingly, produced a
fertile and dynamic environment where developers could bring forth
a new building type to satisfy the needs of Chicago's business community. So, what were these magic ingredients? First and foremost was its
central location within the American continent. Before the first brick
was even laid, Chicago's greatness was nearly a foregone conclusion.
As the economist Homer Hoyt relays:

> The pioneers of empire hunted for such a spot before they had ever
> seen it, and during the many decades that intervened between its first
> discovery and its actual settlement the advantages of its site entered into
> the calculations of ministers in the capitals of Europe. Its location was
> carefully marked on the maps of North America as a place of strategic
> importance by those who never caught a glimpse of the dismal swamp
> that seemed to belie all promise of its future greatness.

Chicago was the lowest point in a barrier between three water-based
highway systems. To the west were the mighty Mississippi River and all
its tributaries. To the east were the Great Lakes and the St. Lawrence

River. And in 1825, New York completed the Erie Canal, which connected the Hudson River to the Great Lakes. Chicago was thus a node that united a growing nation.

In 1827, Congress approved land grants for a canal to link Lake Michigan to the Illinois River, which drains into the Mississippi. In 1830, Chicago was mapped and platted, and in 1833 it was incorporated. In 1836, the state of Illinois authorized the canal's construction. The once and future Metropolis-on-the-Prairie was born. But a city could not be created simply from charters and blueprints. Investments needed to be made. Buildings needed to be built. Roads needed to be laid. Labor needed to arrive. And marketplaces needed to emerge.

And so, the army of would-be capitalists marched forth from the East to build—and finance—Chicago. The bankers supplied the money, the ambitious supplied the talent, and the penniless immigrant supplied the labor. The great nexus of trade and commercial flows was born.

The canal was finally completed in 1848. But, in an unexpected twist of fate, while the canal created *the idea* of Chicago, it was the railroad that made it so. The first road, also completed in 1848, was a short experimental line eight miles west of the Loop. After that, lines began to expand out from the center into a dense transportation web.

Just as important in this centrality was the boundless hinterland, which funneled cheap resources and commodities into Chicago, where they were processed, marketed, and distributed far and wide. The Union Stock Yards, for example, established just after the Civil War, were annually processing about 2 million head of cattle and about one hundred thousand hogs by 1875. Two decades later, that figure was up to 6 million and 2.5 million, respectively.

The forests of Minnesota and Wisconsin produced an immense wood supply, and by 1890, 2.9 million tons of timber entered Chicago's port, and 2 million tons of grain arrived from the hinterland. As one geographer put it, Chicago was "a colossal hopper into which the grain fields of the whole West pour their harvests, and made of the lake route one of the great delivery chutes to the densely populated industrial regions of the United States and Europe."

This centrality produced, arguably, the fastest growth of any city in human history. In 1830, Chicago comprised twelve huts. Four decades later, it was the fourth-largest city in the country; twenty years after that it was officially the Second City.

And just as Chicago was getting its economic groove, in October 1871, Mrs. O'Leary's cow, as legend would have it, unwittingly ignited a massive conflagration that destroyed much of the city. But Chicago was reborn—literally and figuratively—from its ashes. The burned material was used to raise the city's grade several feet to lift itself out of its own "dismal swamp." And because of the clearing away of the old, dilapidated rookeries, new polished office buildings, like the Rookery (1888), could rise in their place.

The Great Chicago Fire (1871)

The need to organize the importing, processing, marketing, and exporting of the tremendous quantity of commodities gave rise to an industrial bureaucracy. Banks were financing corporations; insurance companies were reducing risk; and headquarters were overseeing their operations.

To facilitate marketing, the Chicago Board of Trade became a powerful boost to the city's economy. Over time, the Board helped establish standards for the inspection of flour, pork, and lumber and eventually became the most important commodities futures exchange in the nation. In 1885, the Board completed its ten-story skyscraper in the Loop with a massive trading hall and its sinking supertall clock tower.

The history of Cyrus McCormick's mechanical grain reaper works also illustrates the symbiotic relationship between manufacturing and office space. In the 1850s, McCormick worked with only two clerks inside the factory. In 1863, business was booming, and McCormick created a separate office within the plant's grounds, though, as he wrote to his brother, this space was "little and dusty . . . unpleasant and unhealthy for so many men & boys as are generally in it. Agents come in and it's full. Vault altogether insufficient . . . Now we face the foundry & some days dust and smoke come into our windows."

By the late 1870s, with the workforce expanding and the increasing separation between those who did the manufacturing and those who dealt with finance, legal, marketing, and operations, the company rented office space in the Loop and "kept in contact with the factory using telegraphs, telephones, and express wagons."

McCormick's company was just one example. Between 1870 and 1890, the number of clerical workers in Chicago—including bookkeepers, stenographers, typewriters, bill collectors, and telephone and telegraph operators—increased from 6,400 to nearly 54,000. By 1890, the Illinois Central Railroad alone employed 800 of these clerks to help run its operation. Greater business activity also necessitated more lawyers for legal advice and business contracts. In the twenty-year period from 1870 to 1890, the number of Chicago attorneys rose from 629 to 4,421. These people needed somewhere to sit.

The depression following the Financial Panic of 1873, however, sent Chicago's economy into a lull. When commerce finally began to pick up in 1879, there was a great office shortage, as much of it had disappeared in the Great Fire. That the Loop was hemmed in at first by the Chicago River and Lake Michigan and then by the elevated railroad and railyards meant tremendous pressure on the market price of its soil, which incentivized the construction of tall buildings.

Thus, the real story of Chicago was not that Jenney put iron columns inside the façade of the Home Insurance Building or that he used steel beams on the upper floors, but rather that the Home Insurance Company wanted a Chicago headquarters in which to provide fire insurance for its customers.

In the historiography of skyscrapers, however, the architects get all the credit, while the developers are the villains. Developers, on the one hand, are portrayed as greedy, ego-driven tycoons who exploit labor, rip off investors, filch the commonweal, and build oversized monuments to themselves. (Donald Trump's actions have done nothing to diminish these perceptions.) Architects, on the other hand, are the masters of the art. They give birth to beauty, levity, and soaringness. The engineers are, more or less, ignored.

But the truth is that without the developers there would be no Chicago. They were the Cyrus McCormicks, the George Pullmans, and the Philip Armours of the real estate world, and it was their entrepreneurial activity—their matching of the demand for office space with its supply—that created the skyline. They were responding to the rapid economic growth and rise in land values, and they hired architects and builders to do their bidding.

This is not to say that all developers were morally upright, but it is to say that the requests of the developers had, and have, been the driving force of what the architects provide to humanity. Architects' philosophical musings and aesthetic viewpoints are vital, of course. They have sought to isolate the eternal elements of art and meaning, but they can only do it from the money that flows in from billable hours. Thought without practice is a vacant lot.

If you read the writings of the architects who created the Chicago School of Architecture, their aesthetics—including the rejection of ornamentation—were based on what would work economically and were less bound by the dictates of the European architectural scene. Far off in the prairie where practicality and speed ruled the day, the Chicago architects set themselves to the task of creating a new architecture.

The famous dictate of Louis Sullivan, the quintessential creator of the Chicago School of Architecture, "that form ever follows function" was an artistic rationalization of real estate development—architectural realpolitik. Sullivan's words were a direct admission that beauty had to be born from the economic realities of modern office space, where layout, access to light, and provision of creature comforts were paramount.

This idea was revolutionary because ever since the Renaissance "true" architecture was for monumental structures: palaces and government buildings, houses of worship, mansions, or other public buildings such as libraries or concert halls. There was never a sense that architecture should be applied to a place where people merely worked.

For countless years, "work"—that which the "leisure class" did not do—was dirty, lowly, and for the commoner. The merchant classes throughout the world were considered second-class citizens, such as the Jews in Europe and the hongs in China. In rare cases, where the stigma of trade was not so great, the traders came to run their city-states, such as the Medici of Florence or the merchants of Amsterdam. But in most cases, the locals exchanged with traders while holding their noses.

Profit was tolerated not because it was good (as Adam Smith would argue at the dawn of the Industrial Revolution), but because it was a necessary evil if one was to enjoy wine, silk, sugar, coffee, tobacco, or spices.

Only by the mid-nineteenth century did it dawn on society that the *business community* was worthy of architecture. At first, it was given what architects believed was architecture: versions of European Renaissance, Gothic, or classical. Banks had Roman and Greek styles to telegraph their soundness and stability. Insurance companies built their headquarters in Second Empire French or Italian Renaissance styles.

Then the Chicago architects came along and—radically and shockingly—said that business deserves its own aesthetic. Catholic bishops got the Notre Dame de Paris. The Ming emperors got the Forbidden City. And the Home Insurance Company got its offices in Chicago. This was because Chicago developers demanded something new from the designers they hired. New corporations doing new types of work wanted new buildings to be comfortable both on the inside and out and to reflect their values and ambitions. The history of the skyscraper is summed up nicely by architectural and engineering historian Carl W. Condit:

> The utilitarian advantages of iron and steel framing were enormous and immediately obvious to architects, builders and owners. First was the possibility of getting rid of a supporting wall, with a consequent reduction in weight and an immense increase in height. The steel necessary to carry a tall building weighs only one-third as much as bearing masonry for an equal number of stories. The virtually unlimited increase in glass area, up to 100 per cent of coverage, allowed for maximum admission of natural light. The slender columns and wide bays offered generally increased freedom in the disposition of interior partitions. Economy in the cost of materials together with speed and efficiency of construction convinced even the most skeptical builders of the superiority of steel and iron framing.

The conventional wisdom that the Chicago School was an architecture of simplicity is misleading, however. Chicago architects did not

abandon ornamentation. Rather, the business community was focused
on having lavish, artistically decorated lobbies, banking halls, and office
spaces. The reduction of exterior ornamentation thus freed up money
for the interiors.

The Rookery's (1888) lavish interior

Many lobbies had grand marble staircases under a canopy of vaulted
arches and ornate mosaics. Gold-leafed and silver chandeliers dangled
from the ceilings. Large meeting halls were lined with Corinthian columns having finely carved capitals. The stairways had ornamental iron
balusters, and central courtyards were covered in gossamer skins of glass
and wrought iron. Elevators were enclosed in highly detailed screens
with floral patterns. No expense was spared to make the visitor feel special and to signal that important work was being done in these spaces.

Ironically, most of the books and websites on Chicago skyscrapers are
about the architects who invented the Chicago School of Architecture,
and are virtually silent about the developers who commissioned them.

Thousands of speculative structures were erected by these anonymous developers, and they remain the ghosts of urban history. Their buildings are mute monuments to their efforts.

But if we want to fully understand the evolution of skyscrapers and skylines around the world, we need a much greater understanding of what developers demand from their architects. We can see this clearly through the history of brothers Peter and Shepherd Brooks.

Using their eastern-based capital, they hired local architects and engineers to create their buildings. Without them, the Chicago School architects would not have earned their places in the chronicles of American history. Developers hired them as much for their problem-solving skills as for their willingness to supply a beauty they could live with or, rather, that they could sell.

Peter C. Brooks III (1831–1920) and his brother, Shepherd (1837–1922), grew up on a large estate in Medford, Massachusetts, where their ancestors had settled a century and a half earlier. With the early death of their father, Shepherd inherited much of his father's holdings before he graduated from Harvard in 1857 with a degree in architecture. Their grandfather Peter C. Brooks I had earned a fortune in marine insurance and other investments. At the time of his demise, he was believed to be the richest man in New England.

As members of the leisure class, Peter and Shepherd turned to real estate development. After the Great Fire, they made a concerted effort to build in Chicago. To aid the process, they hired an agent in Chicago, Owen Aldis (1853–1926), to represent them. At home they were New England gentry farmers, but in Chicago they were "office building farmers": speculative developers profiting from the land by planting "crops" of brick and iron.

They pushed their architects to provide what they wanted—more space, more light, and lower costs. Their actions and experiences still ring familiar. Though the world has become more complex and interconnected, a skyscraper today is built from scratch as much as it was in

Chicago circa 1890. While the details and methods have changed, the key steps are the same: Find and buy a lot in a central area, plan the ideal building, raise money, erect the structure, fill it with people, and earn profits. Repeat. The Brooks brothers represent an early branch of the skyscraper developer genealogy from which we can draw lines to the twenty-first century.

They did it without fanfare and attention seeking. It was Brooks' vision and cash that built Chicago. Peter Brooks understood this as early as 1881—long before the skyscraper was feasible—when he wrote in a letter to Aldis: "Tall buildings will pay well in Chicago hereafter, and sooner or later a way will be found to erect them." His words are reminiscent of those of Manhattan fur trader turned real estate specu-lator John Jacob Astor, who on his deathbed allegedly quipped, "Could I begin life again, knowing what I now know and had money to invest, I would buy every foot of land on the island of Manhattan."

It was from Aldis and the Brooks brothers that Burnham & Root received their first tall building commission, and from which they learned a costly lesson. Aldis hired Burnham & Root to build the Grannis Block for the Brooks brothers, who leased it to Amos Grannis for 40 years. Completed in 1881, the seven-story building was destroyed by fire in 1885 and nearly ruined Burham and Root's practice, which was housed there. The frantic, overweight Burnham fled the burning structure with as many drawings as he could carry before he lost everything.

Over the years, the brothers commissioned some of the most famous office buildings in Chicago, including the Portland Block (1872), the Montauk Block (1882), the Rookery (1888), and the Monadnock (1893), which Carl Condit says "was unquestionably the Brooks brothers' most profitable investment."

If we are to define a skyscraper based on its towering height, then the construction of the Montauk Block (1882), as real estate historians Earle Shultz and Walter Simmons write, "was nothing less than the building of Chicago's first 'skyscraper.'" The project was commissioned by Peter

Brooks and brought to fruition by Aldis. The two communicated through many revelatory letters. The first letter regarding the Montauk, dated February 5, 1881, from Brooks to Aldis, describes the purchasing of the lot:

> Having thought over a building on the 89 1/2-foot lot on Monroe Street . . . I think, by utilizing all the space on the main floor and by building up eight stories with also a basement—if the earth can support it in the opinion of the architects—that it may be large enough to support an elevator. If you can get this lot for $100,000 cash I am rather inclined to purchase it.

Next, Brooks established exacting demands on the architects Aldis chose, Burnham & Root. We can see how he pushed the birth of not only the skyscraper but also the Chicago School of Architecture. He wrote to Aldis in March 1881:

> I prefer to have a plain structure of face brick, eight stories and also a basement, with flat roof to be as massive as the architect chooses and well braced with iron rods if needed. The building throughout is to be for use and not for ornament. Its beauty will be in its all-adaptation to its use.
>
> Windows as well as doors should be all worked in brick with as little stone and terra cotta to be introduced as possible consistent with not absolute plainness. . . . Indeed all the entries might be of face brick with red or black mortar (if as cheap as plaster) which would convey the idea of "fireproof" to the whole structure—a valuable idea in a building of eight stories. . . .

When Burnham & Root submitted their plans in July 1881, Brooks responded to Aldis:

> The most is certainly made of the lot, to the credit of the architects, but I have no idea if it can be built well for the sum proposed. The building

is a much more extravagant one than my original design although much
on the same plan. The architects are of course indifferent to the future
costs of repair and care, an item worthy of much consideration.

Then echoing the same confusion that many non-Chicagoans have
today, Brooks writes: "Is this Montauk Block—or Montauk Building?
M. Block sounds best but it is not a block. M. Building is more appropriate and this I think it must be."

In the end, the developer and architects were able to work out an
agreeable compromise. Its ten-story height allowed it to lord over the
Loop, setting viewers "agog." The Montauk Block proved correct the
Brook brothers' vision, as it quickly filled with tenants, primarily from
insurance companies and law firms, as well as the offices of *The Economist*, one of Chicago's most important real estate journals. The final
structure had 150 offices, with three hundred occupants.

Ironically, Illinois state law forbade forming a corporation for the
sole purpose of developing real estate, though business corporations
were free to build their own offices. The law was passed in 1872 because
Illinois leaders feared that speculators masking as corporations would
gobble up valuable farmlands. Workarounds were thus needed. One
was the bank vault scheme. Banks and industrial concerns—like that
of Cyrus McCormick—desperately needed vault space to store their
money and documents. But since one can't simply place a vault in the
middle of an empty lot, it had to be covered by a building. Because it
was perfectly legal to start a vault services corporation, some of the earliest skyscrapers were really vault delivery systems. The investors would
pool their money, buy a lot, build a vault, and then enclose it in a tall
building, with the rest rented for offices.

Likely those vaults contained many fire insurance policies, the
demand for which created the fireproof fire insurance company headquarters building. As cities grew and more economic activity was taking
place there, businesses and residents had more to lose by fire, which

had been the scourge of cities ever since humanity settled down. In the early nineteenth century, fire insurance became a vital industry and was a driving force in providing companies the security to get on with their affairs. Fire insurance thus fueled the first generation of skyscrapers.

The history of the Home Insurance Company of New York illustrates this. After witnessing fire after fire—including in New York in 1835 and 1845—a group of noninsurance businessmen formed the Home Insurance Company in 1853 with the goal of providing insurance across the country. The investors felt that the typical behavior of companies insuring only local businesses was not sound; insurers tended to go belly-up when a local conflagration hit.

The directors of The Home—with their initial offices on Wall Street—established from the onset a strategy of risk diversification. They created a network of independent agents throughout the country to sell fire insurance. In their initial year, they instructed their Supervising Agent:

> First, you will direct your early attention to the most important points for introducing The Home . . . say, Albany, Utica, Rochester, Buffalo, Cleveland, Pittsburgh, Wheeling, Cincinnati, Louisville and St. Louis. In returning, you can take the upper route, Chicago, Milwaukee, etc. . . . Second, you will very well understand the importance of securing the right class of men in our service . . . it is of vast importance that our dealings should be with good men.

Their business acumen, their diversification strategy, and their insistence on employing and trusting "good men" were profitable, despite repeated payouts for conflagrations. During the Civil War, the company continued to honor its claims, even in rebel territory.

After the war, the Chicago fire hit them badly, forcing them to pay out more than $2.5 million. Only thirteen months later, much of Boston burned in an eighteen-hour fire, putting The Home on the hook for another $750,000. Then another Chicago fire in 1874 produced additional troubles.

Despite these calamities, they ran a tight ship. Between 1855 and 1903, the company issued dividends of at least 5 percent every six months, except in four instances. If any company was aware of the need to make office buildings safer, it was the Home Insurance Company, whose executives had this on their minds when they commissioned Jenney to build them a Chicago headquarters.

Six hydraulic elevators were installed to carry up the tenants and their visitors. The Home contracted out to the United States Company to provide two thousand incandescent lamps—the latest in lighting technology. The insurer was generous in its provision of a "private toilet room" on every other floor, along with "dressing and toilet rooms for women, many of whom find employment in offices." It was agreed by many that the structure contained "one of the most elaborate and carefully-executed job of plumbing which has been done in the city."

Along with toilets, "[m]ost offices have direct telephonic communication." Jenny hired the contractor C. N. Fay to build large crown moldings with channels to hide all the horizontal wires, while the vertical wires were carried through the elevator shafts.

The Home spared no expense to make their building feel as inviting as possible. As highlighted in the *American Architect and Building News*, the building's

> chief charm . . . is in the interior, which is certainly the most successful of its kind in the city. The vestibule . . . extends through two stories and is finished in polished white marble, with the column supporting the wall and the stairwork, including rails, the posts and the elevator-screens, all in dark bronze. The vaulted roof of the vestibule is of marble slabs, supported on bronze ribs. . . . It seems like an expensive building but when we consider how charming the combinations of marble and bronze and tinted plaster are, it would seem worthwhile to pay more to be in

such a building than to have to put up with the black walls and dreary
corridors of even so good a building as the Opera House.

Among all the architectural kudos heaped on the building, not one
writer mentioned anything about it being the "first skyscraper."

The Home paid about $800,000 for its showcase structure. In 1888,
the *Chicago Tribune* reported: "The Home Insurance Company has
done quite well with its handsome building in this city. It earned about
9 per cent on the capital last year, and its offices are now filled with
tenants of an excellent class." The Home was earning the kind of profit
that produced the Chicago skyline.

THE CAMPAIGN

Despite the transitional nature of the Home Insurance Building's structure, perceptions gradually changed. By the time of Jenney's death in
1907, nearly all his obituaries pronounced him the inventor or the father
of the skyscraper. What happened in this two-decade period? How did
the Home Insurance Building win the prize in the public's mind?

The short answer is through a dogged public relations campaign
by Jenney, his partners, former employees, and friends, including the
dean of Chicago Architecture, Daniel Burnham. The "Jenney Myth"
created by this group was easily believed because there was no way to
contradict the leading Chicago architects. They were the experts who
were on the scene from day one and participated in and created the
Skyscraper Revolution. In addition, no one really knew what the guts
of the structure looked like, as it was hidden in stone.

The story of the Home Insurance legend begins—in public at any
rate—in June 1896, when the president of the Bessemer Steamship
Company, a manufacturer of steamships, sat down and inked an inquiry
to the editor of the *Engineering Record* (ER), one of several trade journals of the day:

Sir: Will you have the kindness to inform me to what architect or engineer the honor is due of discovering and practically working out the idea of lofty steel construction of buildings? -F.T. Gates.

In that issue, the editor responded with a quick note saying that his journal had featured many protoskyscrapers, including the Home Insurance Building (1885), the Drexel Building (1889) in Philadelphia, and the Rookery (1888) in Chicago, though did not state a clear "first." However, the question piqued the interest of the real estate community, who over the next several weeks chimed in with their "votes" in the journal.

The first was from Jenney himself, introducing A. C. Ducat's former business partner, who recalled the meeting between Jenney and the Home Insurance Company building committee described previously. Behind the scenes, Jenney had asked Home Insurance executives to run interference for him. His private letters to them show he was nearly desperate to win the title.

In his letter to the ER, Jenney claims: "The skeleton construction was a radical departure from anything that had heretofore appeared and was exclusively my invention." This is a bald rewriting of history. As discussed earlier, his building was not a radical departure, and he likely knew it, at least at the time of completion.

In other private letters written in the 1890s, Jenney keeps referring to his building as the first steel skeleton. But this is also wrong. Jenney did, in fact, introduce steel beams into the upper floors, but only because the Carnegie-Phipps mills asked him to do it. The addition of steel was a last-minute substitution, and just a small fraction of the structural metalwork was, in fact, steel. To say that his building was a "steel skeleton" is a gross exaggeration.

On July 25, Daniel Burnham weighed in:

This principle of carrying the entire structure on a carefully balanced and braced metal frame, protected from fire, is precisely what Mr.

William L. B. Jenney worked out. No one anticipated him in it, and he deserved the entire credit belonging to the engineering feat which he was the first to accomplish.

This statement is, at best, misleading and, at worst, an outright lie, which Burnham likely knew given his own long history of creating Chicago's early skyscrapers. The comment "No one anticipated him" blatantly ignores that iron framing had a long history, from eighteenth-century iron bridges in England and railroad bridges in the United States in the 1830s to the Crystal Palaces of London and New York in the 1850s.

Burnham's remark that Jenney "deserved the entire credit belonging to the engineering feat which he was the first to accomplish" implies and propagates the "birdcage myth" that says Jenney was smoking a pipe in his living room when he spied a birdcage, which gave him the idea for the skyscraper. This is bunk. Jenney's career was the embodiment of the typical ambitious and smart individual who came of age during the Industrial Revolution and who flocked to Chicago to participate in its economic ebullience. He was one person in a community of figures like him, and Jenney frequently relied on them to help him. The collective genius of American architects and engineers created the skyscraper at the behest of the American developer.

But Jenney's perseverance at PR worked. A report commissioned by the Marshall Field Estate in 1931, when the Home Insurance Building was demolished, continued the obfuscation by telling Chicagoans what they wanted to hear—that the Home was the first skeletal structure.

There were other authorities with fewer vested interests who disagreed with the "Chicago Consensus," most notably the Western Society of Engineers, which issued its own findings. The report was emphatic that the Home was not the first but rather was one of several important transitional structures.

"The Home Insurance Building," the report states, "was erected during the development period of the skeleton type of building and is a notable example of its type; while **it does not fulfill all the requirements of a skeleton type** [*emphasis added*], it was well along in this development and was principally lacking in not having curtain walls, no provision in the framing for wind loads, and not having made full provision for starting the masonry, above the first floor." However, most people were not interested in the arcane details.

Despite the truth, a tourist visiting the Windy City will still hear the claim that it was home to the first skyscraper. And yet, in 1893, just as the city was getting its skyscraper mojo, it gave it all up. In that year, Chicago banned skyscrapers, making it illegal to build anything taller than 130 feet (38 m, 10 floors). The city would keep some form of height limits well into the twentieth century.

But New York City did what Chicago did not. It ran with the skyscraper and continued to innovate. Gotham not only changed with the times but also changed the times. It showed the world not to be afraid of height but rather to embrace it. In the process, New York created a skyline metropolis that was the envy of the world and laid the foundations for the twenty-first-century global quest for skyscrapers and skylines.

CHAPTER 2

New York City

The Height King in the Zone

The Empire State Building in 2023

THE EMPIRE STATE BUILDING

It seems cliché to start a chapter on New York City with the Empire State Building. Rising a quarter mile upward (0.4 km), perhaps no other building is as iconic or famous. It is described in nearly every child's book on the world's amazing wonders, along with the Egyptian Pyramids, the Eiffel Tower, and the Great Wall of China. But why should we still return to it? Hasn't so much been written about it already?

The reason is that the structure has been so shrouded in myth that we can hardly separate fact from fiction. It was the world's tallest building when completed and remained so for four decades. It won a three-way height competition for this title. It was constructed in a record time of eighteen months. And when it was completed, the Great Depression was well underway. The newly dubbed "Empty State Building" was seen as the folly of unbridled ego—of (land) lords playing gods among us mortals, like a chapter in a twentieth-century *Bulfinch's Mythology*.

And yet, the building remains an intensely beloved trophy of a venerable city. As Lady Liberty is the symbol of America's democratic triumphs, the Empire State is the symbol of our economic striving. The truth of its origins, however, is much more mundane. The Empire State Building, while a glorious and proud structure, was born from the underlying economic environment that characterized 1920s Manhattan. It was built with such speed because of three key economic factors. First, office rental market contracts were normally signed as of May 1. If the building was to start on a sound economic footing, it had to be completed on the first May 1 that was reasonably possible. Construction started in the fall of 1929, and the logical completion date was May 1, 1931.

Second, there was nothing new about its technology. Rather, the building resulted from a forty-year learning curve that had improved construction, standardization of parts, and logistics. In essence, the Empire State Building was but a fractal replication of itself. Its lot was large and rectangular, with bedrock not far below the surface, and no engineering contortions were needed to build around smaller buildings whose owners refused to sell.

But just as importantly, this task was accomplishable because the developers—Al Smith, former governor of New York and 1928 Democratic presidential candidate, and John Raskob, former General Motors executive, successful Wall Street investor, and Smith's presidential campaign manager—hired the firm of Starrett Brothers & Eken to erect their building. Paul and William Starrett, along with Andrew J. Eken, had been in the general contracting business for decades. Their collective career experiences were shaped by the skyscrapers and skylines they helped create.

Paul Starrett (1866–1957) and William Aiken Starrett Jr. (1877–1932) were both born in Lawrence, Kansas. Their father, William Aiken Starrett Sr., was a farmer, carpenter, and preacher. When he became ill, their mother moved the family to Chicago. After trying his hand at various jobs, Paul went to work in 1887 as a stenographer in the office of Burnham & Root, but Burnham recognized his talents at leadership and encouraged him to pursue them out in the world.

Follow his destiny, he did. After studying at Wake Forest, Paul went into the construction business. He joined George A. Fuller Company and became its president in 1905. At Fuller, Paul was responsible for the construction of many skyscrapers around the country.

George A. Fuller (1851–1900), born in Worcester, Massachusetts, was trained as an architect. He worked in Boston and New York and moved to Chicago in 1882 to start his general contracting business. Fuller's business innovation was to popularize the so-called cost-plus system. Fuller would construct the building—that is, hire the subcontractors, organize the shipment of materials, and see to its completion—for a fixed fee, usually a percentage of the total costs. However, the developer would pay the construction cost out of pocket.

A developer would choose Fuller because he not only could promise a more professional and efficient operation but also would handle the countless details. In addition, the project could begin even before the architectural plans were complete, in what today is known as fast-track construction. Fuller thus demonstrated how to streamline and "industrialize" the tall building process. Though Fuller died young at the age of forty-nine, his company and legacy would continue well into the twentieth century. It is said that Fuller's company built Chicago's skyline.

William Starrett Jr. also learned how to build from Fuller. As a boy, William showed an aptitude for mathematics, and he attended the University of Michigan but left without graduating to work with his older brother Paul at Fuller. In 1901, he became vice president of the Thompson-Starrett Company, cofounded by his brother Theodore and Henry S. Thompson.

During World War I, William was chairman of the Construction Committee of the War Industries Board, charged with leading the army's war construction program, including building garrisons, hospitals, and army bases in the United States. After the war, in 1922, he joined up again with Paul to start the Starrett Brothers firm.

Andrew J. Eken (1882–1965) grew up in Virginia. Before partnering with the Starretts, he was a vice president at the Fuller Company and president of George A. Fuller Company of Canada. Thus, through the history of Starrett Brothers & Eken, we can see the direct lineage between the entrepreneurial efforts of George A. Fuller to build Chicago's earliest skyscrapers and their culmination in New York.

When Starrett Brothers & Eken was bidding on the Empire State Building job, they were in the process of completing the Bank of Manhattan Building (seventy stories) on Wall Street. It had the dubious honor of holding the world height record for only a few months when it was beaten by Walter Chrysler's building, which topped out in November 1929. The general contractors were able to build the Empire State Building in record time because they had already learned how to perform lightning-speed construction with the Bank of Manhattan Building, which was erected in thirteen months.

Upon command, they called forth an army of workers to erect the Empire State. The contractor, like the maestro of a vast orchestra, waved a baton, the music flowed, and the structure rose. During the construction, for example, instead of wheelbarrows, a narrow-gauge cart system was introduced. Small cars were loaded in the basement, ran onto the hoists, and moved to the desired floor. Each railcar carried four hundred bricks, versus one hundred for a wheelbarrow.

Just as importantly, the Empire State Building was made possible by a smooth-functioning, yet decentralized, supply chain, orchestrated from Midtown Manhattan. When asked about the logistics, Eken revealed, "We ran trucks the way they run trains in and out of Grand Central. If a truck missed its place in the line on Tuesday, it had to wait until Wednesday to get back in."

Legend has it that the building's fifty-seven thousand tons of steel were delivered so quickly—within eighty hours after rolling off the Pittsburgh mills—that the beams arrived still warm to the touch. Between the near-seamless flow of materials and demanding organization of labor by the Starrett brothers, the building went up at a rate of five and a half floors per week.

The design of the electrical system also shows how the builders were able to overcome problems due to the building's massive size. In a smaller skyscraper, the high-voltage power coming from the street mains is reduced to an intermediate voltage in the basement. Risers—the vertical ducts that enclose the wires—carry that voltage upward, and on each floor a transformer in the electrical closets reduces the voltage to the standard used for lighting and office equipment.

In the Empire State Building, such a system would have greatly expanded the size of the risers and the conduits extending from the closets, eating into otherwise valuable rentable space. The mechanical engineers, Meyer Strong & Jones, employed several clever strategies. They first used two risers, placed on opposite ends of the elevator core, to reduce the size of the floor conduits. Next, they directly fed the high-voltage power to transformers on the forty-first and eighty-fourth floors, removing the subbasement transformer. Adding this equipment on the upper floors allowed them to reduce the thickness of the risers. As engineering historian Donald Friedman reports, "The two design decisions taken together effectively turned the building into six small buildings—two side by side, stacked three high." This remains a common practice.

And when times were good and rents were high, a developer with a large lot could hire a construction company, such as Starrett Brothers & Eken, to build them a soaring tower in the clouds and make a tidy sum. This is exactly what the developers of the Empire State Building were facing in the summer and fall of 1929 when they green-lighted the project. In fact, the Empire State Building lot was so big that not building a skyscraper would have been foolish.

However, when it was completed in 1931, the upper half of the building went unrented. The Great Depression, like the COVID pandemic eighty-eight years later, was utterly unforeseeable. To understand if their actions were reasonable or not, we need to look at the economics of the project in mid-1929.

The corner of 34th Street and Fifth Avenue, the site of the Empire State Building, was home to one of New York's most famous hotels—the Waldorf-Astoria. The Waldorf Hotel first opened on the southern half of the lot in 1893, and then merged with the Astoria Hotel, which opened on the northern side in 1897. Over the decades, the hotel's ballrooms hosted lavish parties, and its beds provided solace for Gilded Age elites. By the 1920s, however, the hotel was a relic. The ponderous building was expensive to maintain, and New York's society was increasingly living—and socializing—farther away. In December 1928, the hotel's owners announced they were selling the site and would be looking for a new location.

The winning bidder was Bethlehem Engineering, a company founded and run by Floyd deL. Brown. He was the consummate New York real estate man who knew the field as well as anyone. He was born in New York City in 1885, studied architecture in Paris, and received an engineering degree from Columbia University. In 1918, he organized the Bethlehem Engineering Company to engage in real estate development. He was one of the thousands of builders who made New York what it is today. By 1928, he had a long track record of successful projects, including several tall Manhattan office buildings.

Brown's purchase price for the lot was about $14 million plus fees, which, at about $200 per square foot, was typical for the times. Once he took control of the property, given his knowledge and experience, he decided to build a fifty-story loft, office, and showroom skyscraper, with 2 million square feet (185,806 m²).

Brown's company had negotiated the deal with an initial burst of financing from the Chatham Phenix National Bank. Though for many of their projects Bethlehem Engineering was listed as the architect of record, Brown hired the firm of Shreve and Lamb to design his Waldorf-Astoria Office Building.

This moment was pivotal for New York City's history. A seasoned real estate developer, who normally designed his buildings in-house, Brown turned to architectural specialists for help. And though Brown would lose control of the property six months later, Shreve and Lamb, with partner Arthur L. Harmon, would remain with the lot, so to speak, and go on to transform their original design into the world's tallest building. Part of the reason the Empire State Building was erected was that Brown had already done a lot of the groundwork for Raskob and Smith.

In February 1929, Brown secured a $24 million construction loan from the Metropolitan Life Insurance Company. But the contract with Chatham Phenix had Brown making three payments before the sale was final. Brown made the first two. However, the MetLife loan, as large as it was, was not sufficient to cover the total cost. Brown needed to find another $10–12 million to make it all work. He could not raise the money and failed to make his third payment. Chatham Phenix took over his claim.

Normally, a bank would not want to get involved in real estate development and would quickly get the contract off its books. But in this case, one man decided to take the lead. The pivotal figure was Chatham Phenix National Bank president Louis Kaufman, without whom the Empire State Building would have never gone forward. If he had decided to let the whole thing go, who knows what would have happened to the site, but instead, this one banker was excited to try his hand at Manhattan real estate.

Kaufman was born in Marquette, Michigan, in 1872. After high school, he dabbled in mining out west but returned to Marquette to work in his father's savings bank. He showed an aptitude for the business and, in the following years, became an important member of the Marquette banking community.

At the age of thirty-eight, he took over as president of the Chatham National Bank in New York City. By the mid-1920s, he built it up through mergers and acquisitions into the Chatham Phenix National Bank and Trust Company, with assets valued at $300 million. Just as importantly, he joined the General Motors board of directors in 1910 and remained in that position for the next twenty-two years. As a director, he worked intimately with Raskob.

After Brown's default, Kaufman quickly formed a syndicate of like-minded men who were going to proceed where Brown left off. The syndicate members pooled their equity and bought the lot from the bank. But, two months later, the property flipped hands again. Kaufman and his syndicate would remain involved, but the leadership would be taken over by Smith and Raskob, along with a substantial investment from Raskob's mentor, colleague, and friend, Pierre S. du Pont.

The exact details of how Raskob and Smith took control of the site are somewhat murky. Some say Raskob spearheaded the effort, which is plausible given that he had a long history with Kaufman. Others say Smith knew about the project because he was on the Board of Trustees of MetLife, who gave the owners a mortgage. There is no record, however, of what Floyd Brown thought in 1931 after the Empire State Building rose out of the ashes of his failed deal. He might have believed it was either the big fish that got away or the whale that took down Ahab. Regardless, he does not seem to have been hurt too much thereby. Brown, unlike many other New York developers who failed to make it through the Depression, would continue in the business for another twenty-five years.

In August 1929, Smith headed a press conference where he announced his building was going to be eighty stories and 1,000 feet tall. It would be the tallest building in the world and would surpass Walter Chrysler's by about 50 feet. But some weeks later, after Walter Chrysler topped out his building, Raskob and Smith cooked up the idea of the mooring mast to extrude theirs to 1,250 feet (381 m).

Smith was a politician, Raskob and du Pont were business executives, and Kaufman was a banker. What did these guys know about real estate? Surely, the historiography goes, they were deluding themselves that they knew what they were doing, and the Great Depression slapped them in the face. But if we take a deeper look at the likely profits of the Empire State Building in the fall of 1929, their conception of the project lies within the parameters of "reasonable," if not ideal.

How can we understand the economic prospects of the Empire State Building (ESB)? To do this, we need a benchmark. For this, we turn to the findings of W. C. Clark and J. L. Kingston (CK), economist and architect, respectively, who in 1930 published their book, *The Skyscraper: A Study in the Economic Height of Modern Office Buildings*. In it, they play the role of a hypothetical developer of an office skyscraper in Manhattan, on a large lot directly across from Grand Central Terminal on 42nd Street. In fine-grained detail, they itemize the various costs and revenues from erecting a building with varying heights, to identify the one that maximizes the return on the investment.

Based on their calculations, they found that the profit-maximizing height was sixty-three stories, with a seventy-five-story one a close second. When we start comparing the costs and revenues from their hypothetical sixty-three-story project to the Empire State Building, the differences between the two seem relatively minor. The ESB lot was ninety-one thousand square feet; the CK lot was eighty-one thousand square feet— pretty close. CK estimated $16 per gross square foot for construction costs, and the ESB was nearly the same. CK assumed operating expenses of $1.39 per rentable square foot. ESB came in at $1.31—not that far off.

CK estimated an average per-square-foot rental income of $3.81, while the ESB folks came in at $3.37. This seems reasonable given the pros and cons of the ESB. First, it was farther south, so average rents would be lower. But its footprint was bigger, so it would have more tower space, which would increase average rents.

When one does all the math and assumes that both buildings were totally filled up and devoted only to office space with retail on the ground floor (and no observatories), the estimated return relative to the total cost for CK was 10.24 percent and for the ESB it was about 9.5 percent. Thus, in August 1929, the Empire State Building had a strong economic rationale, even if its height was not profit maximizing.

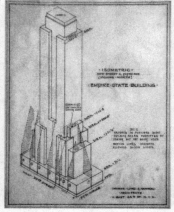

LEFT: Rendering of the Waldorf-Astoria Office Building (1928)
MIDDLE: Early rendering of the Empire State Building ca. 1929
RIGHT: Hypothetical skyscraper rendering from Clark and Kingston (1930)

Ironically, however, in the long run, the final iteration was likely more profitable than the original version by Smith and Raskob would have been. Adding the observation deck has been a boon to both the building owners and the world. The structure's height also made it ideal for long TV and radio antennae, which generate additional income.

For the first crop of owners, things did not go well. During the 1930s, the shareholders were frequently required to pony up more cash, lest they lose their building. Yet persistence turned to profit. In 1951, when the building was sold to a new set of investors, it fetched the highest price ever for a Manhattan skyscraper. The developers' vision did pay off, but it was their heirs who would reap the returns.

The total cost of land and structure in 1931 came to $41 million. Then in 1951, the building was sold for $51 million, for a capital gain of $10 million. In 1990, when Donald Trump was battling to take control of the building (he ultimately failed), the *New York Times* appraised it at about $700 million. In 2013, the market value was about $2 billion. For simplicity, using 1931 and 2013 numbers, we get an inflation-adjusted growth rate in the skyscraper's market value of 5 percent, which reflects its consistently positive net income. Not bad for the "Empty State Building."

IN THE ZONE

One of the iconic features of the Empire State Building is its wedding cake style. Out of the five-story base rises the tower with various setbacks along the way until the eighty-fifth floor, on top of which sits the mooring mast, bringing the structure to 102 stories. Its shape was influenced by the city's zoning regulations, which helped give the Roaring Twenties its Art Deco aesthetic.

Zoning and Art Deco, however, were the result of a four-decade debate regarding the best or proper shape, style, and height for skyscrapers. Soon after New York and Chicago's initial crop in the 1890s, other business districts across America began sprouting their own tall buildings. As a result, residents and government officials formed all sorts of opinions about the merits and demerits of such structures.

In their shadow—literally and figuratively—emerged the questions: What hath we wrought? What do we do about these Towers of Babel in our midst?

To many, they were dangerous. Officials and insurance companies saw them as a safety hazard. Firefighters did not have the ladders to climb above ten floors. Residents, concerned about living in a well-functioning city, feared congestion. To them, tall buildings were like a giant magnet drawing forth throngs of workers, packed into narrow streets that were better suited for old-style walk-ups.

Reformers worried about the darkened streets and the newly carved canyons of capitalism. They saw the tall building as a beggar-thy-neighbor situation. A building would rise, dwarfing the low-rise structures nearby, causing their owners to suffer the indignities of lower property values. Many a hapless landlord, no doubt, looked up at a light-sucking skyscraper, shook his fist in anger, and shouted, "I'm ruined!"

To others, tall buildings were incompatible with a beautiful, low-rise city. Skyscrapers rendered impossible a Paris-on-the-Hudson or Paris-on-the-Prairie. Critics were convinced they were a waste of resources—"freak buildings"—monuments, not moneymakers. The tall building required much from society but gave little in return.

Edward Bassett, one of the most influential planners of the early twentieth century, expressed this sentiment in a 1913 report that led to the birth of skyscraper zoning:

> [V]ery tall buildings demand many things out of proportion to their increased bulk. All piping has to be made disproportionately heavier; special pumps and relays of tanks have to be provided, foundations often call for special construction, wind-bracing assumes an important place, long-run elevators are more costly than short-run elevators, the extra space taken up by the express run of the elevators is an additional cost. Thus in the aggregate the total cost per cubic foot of a very tall

building may be 60 to 75 cents per cubic foot where a low building of the same class would cost only 40 to 50 cents per cubic foot.

Bassett itemizes the ways in which the costs of going tall increase but ignores their benefits (to be described in chapter 8). Ironically, those very same buildings that were cursed at their creation are the ones most eagerly pressed by preservationists to be landmarked because of their beauty, history, and monumentality.

One physician in 1916 even declared skyscrapers were causing indigestion:

> A great many people suffer from gastric troubles. This is due in the first place to the fact that the people are compelled to eat a dry lunch, sandwiches, etc. . . . It is also due to the congestion. It is hardly possible for a great many of the factory employees, especially on the higher floors, to have the time to go down and eat their lunches in a neighboring restaurant and then have time to come back again to their work in the high buildings. They might have time if there were not such congestion.

It was important for the early planners and officials to play down the private financial returns so they could more easily attack the public costs. Once people were convinced that the buildings were harmful both from within and without, then they could be regulated out of existence. In this way, skyscraper regulations were (and are) not value-free—they were not written with a careful weighing of their costs and benefits to society but rather were made by people who could not stomach intense population density and rapid urban change.

Planners created height and building bulk limits that *felt* right, and when they didn't yield the desired outcomes, they tightened the knot a bit more. In New York, however, their wishes were checked by the business community and the public at large, which frequently resisted dramatic government interventions.

The real estate community itself was of mixed minds about sky-scrapers. Some landlords were adamantly opposed to them because they competed directly with their own holdings. To others, skyscraper construction was too prone to booms and bubbles. The ensuing gluts meant that the entire real estate sector would pay for the overoptimism of a handful of developers.

To the social agitator, the tall building was nothing but an altar to Mammon himself and the oppressor of the working class. Skyscrapers were built by the rich, for the rich, and from where the rich could orchestrate their exploitation. The capitalist developer destroyed the workingman's dignity by making him no more important than a hammer in the modern construction process.

If it was glaringly obvious to their detractors that the skyscraper must be banished from the city, however, it was equally as obvious to their builders that they were a force for good. Of course, skyscraper develop-ers, who earned nice profits, were keen to extol their virtues. But those virtues were mostly that white-collar workers paid handsomely to be inside. There was a great demand for offices in the sky because they were more comfortable, made people more productive, and provided a pres-tigious address. Because the tall buildings amply accommodated them, businesses could remain in the clusters that they found so beneficial.

The propertied interests in early twentieth-century America were a strong class and their vote, one might say, counted for more than that of the average person. The real estate men (by and large, they were men) had influence among leaders, who, cynically speaking, were in their pockets or, less cynically, agreed with them. But the propertied interests did not speak in one voice. The outcome of any debate about regulating tall buildings would depend on which group held sway and whether they could form a compromise.

As the twentieth century began, each city had to decide its own skyscraper fate: to embrace, regulate, or reject. The outcome was not as predictable as we might assume. America was the world's first skyscraper

laboratory, and each city was like a lab bench on which a unique experiment could take place.

Chicago had set about its own experimentation. The 1880s growth
spurt served as a catalyst for the (temporary) demise of the Chicago
skyscraper. City officials, who were against the increased density and
shadows, along with fire safety officials and insurance companies still
afraid of conflagrations, made common cause with real estate owners
who wanted to limit supp'y. They joined with the "good city" planners,
and together they worked to outlaw tall buildings. Chicago couldn't quite
stomach what it had created, and starting in 1893, as noted earlier, no
building could rise more than 130 feet (40 m, 10 floors).

Ironically, the full impact of the ban would not be felt for a few
years, since any developer already having a permit could proceed with
the old plans, and there was a rush to build. Several more towers were
completed, the grandest of which was the Masonic Temple, more than
two and a half times greater than the height limit.

But by the late 1890s, the real estate community was having second
thoughts, as economic growth caused the glut to dissipate, and the
profits from building tall reappeared. In an oops kind of moment, Chicago raised the height caps in 1902 to 260 feet (79 m, 20 floors). This
prompted a tongue-in-cheek announcement in the *New York Times*:
"That sky-scraper limit [in Chicago] has now positively been fixed at
260 feet, until someone comes along who wants to build a taller one."

Contrary to that prediction, however, shortage led to glut, and the
maximum height was lowered to 200 feet (61 m) in 1911. Chicago raised
the limit again to 260 feet in 1920 but allowed for ornamental towers that
could rise to 400 feet (122 m). In 1924, Chicago adopted citywide zoning
and changed its building height rules again. This time the maximum
height of the main structure was capped at 264 feet (80 m), but a tower
was allowed if its footprint was less than 25 percent of the lot's area and
its total volume was less than one-sixth the volume of the main structure.
In 1942, the rules changed once again with skyscrapers in downtown

Chicago having maximum volume caps. This phase lasted fifteen years until the modern form of zoning was implemented in 1957. Chicago couldn't make up its mind for decades.

The Windy City's desire to limit height was not an isolated phenomenon. By 1921, at least twenty-three major North American cities had height caps in their central districts. Baltimore, for example, restricted its buildings to 175 feet (53 m), while Boston went in for 125 feet (38 m). Chicago's 264 feet (80 m) at the time was more generous than the rest, with Cleveland coming in second at 250 feet (76 m). Philadelphia didn't have a de jure ban but rather adhered to a "gentleman's agreement" that no building would rise taller than the hat on the head of the statue of William Penn standing atop City Hall, which rises 548 feet (167 m, 40–45 floors), which, in truth, before World War II, was hardly binding. America was not alone in capping heights. Europe was even stricter. London was capped at 80 feet (25 m), while the caps of Paris, Berlin, and Rome were lower than that.

The beauty of height caps was their simplicity. While there was always some way to game regulations, it's that much harder with outright caps. The famous French mansard roof, however, was a way to overcome the limit. Since the building's height was measured up to the cornice line, a builder could add an extra floor under the roof to squeeze in more space.

While height restrictions could create a more pleasing uniform downtown, there was no flexibility. If the real estate market became hot, the caps limited supply, which raised prices, angering those who paid them. And Chicago's draconian actions were New York's gain, which had a more liberal attitude. "New York could and did build office buildings to house the great expansion of business. Some of this business wanted to come to Chicago and would have if it could have been accommodated there," concluded Shultz and Simmons.

New York City took a different path because, ironically, its reformers had a more ambitious agenda. For planners, building height caps were fine and desirable, but they did little to address the urban "diseases" infecting the metropolis. At the turn of the twentieth century, for example, Manhattan's Lower East Side was arguably the densest neighborhood on the planet, overcrowded with "huddled masses yearning to breathe free." After Jacob Riis's 1890 exposé in his book *How the Other Half Lives*, reformers were determined to obliterate the slums.

Just as worrisome, suburban districts had no protection against factories or apartment buildings or possible future "slumifications." Private builders, reformers felt, also had little sense of civic responsibility or desire to create a beautiful city. None of these problems could be solved in isolation or with height caps alone.

In the end, the reformers and propertied interests worked out a deal that was mutually acceptable to all, though few were wholly satisfied. The grand bargain was the creation of American zoning, the process of placing each plot of land into one of several zones, which specified use, height, and bulk. It was implemented in New York in 1916 and spread to the rest of the country in a great wave after World War I.

The height regulations were arguably the most important regarding skyscrapers, as they required setbacks as the building rose taller. This concept, adapted from nineteenth-century German zoning, began with the width of the street facing the lot. Wider avenues, like Broadway or 42nd Street, were allowed to have taller buildings than narrower side streets. Each zone also had a so-called setback multiple, which ranged from 1 to 2.5. Downtown, around Wall Street, had the highest multiple, while residential districts outside the center had the lowest.

The street width and setback multiple created a hypothetical hypotenuse, starting from the street's center. The building had to fit within that hypotenuse or envelope. The narrower the street or the lower the setback multiple, the lower the angle of the envelope, and the stricter the setbacks. One other provision was added to please skyscraper developers—a tower could be built to infinite height if its footprint was less than 25 percent of the lot area. Hence, we get the Empire State Building, with its wedding cake design.

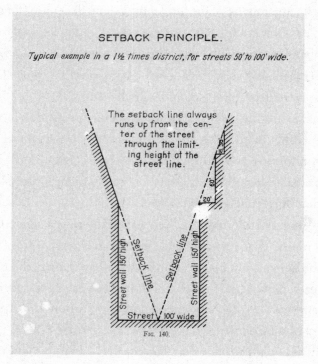

An example of the building envelope regulation
in the 1916 Zoning Resolution

The basic idea for the height regulations was that buildings could
go taller if they got thinner as they went up, not only reducing total
volume but also allowing for sunlight to hit the streets. It was a way to
"tax" away some of the buildings, without directly banning skyscrapers.

Over time, however, people have come to confuse the 1916 Zoning
Resolution with the Art Deco architectural style that formed in parallel.
The 1916 rules encouraged but did not require architects to design the
wedding cake or ziggurat style.

In fact, the rule that a thin tower could rise to infinite height meant
that with a large lot a skyscraper need not have any setbacks. For that
matter, on a small lot a developer could have simply stopped at the
maximum height before setbacks had to kick in. There was nothing

in the law that dictated an architectural style. In fact, some skyscrapers built under the zoning rules were not Art Deco.

The first tall building completed under the new rules in New York was the Heckscher (Crown) Building. With a Beaux Arts style, it has a nine-story base or podium that covers the entire lot and a seventeen-story tower that rises in the center. So, under the rules, the podium-with-tower was one option (and later became popular in Hong Kong and Dubai).

Another approach could be to build a straight-up tower that occupied a fraction of the lot and left the rest open as a plaza, though this strategy was less common because developers were reluctant to "waste" space. Ludwig Mies van der Rohe's 1958 Seagram Building, at Park Avenue and

Two New York City buildings completed under the 1916 Zoning Resolution but with different architectural styles. LEFT: American Radiator Building (1924) RIGHT: Seagram Building (1958)

52nd Street, considered, along with Skidmore, Owings & Merrill's Lever House, as the vanguard of the Modernist—or International Style—buildings, was erected within the 1916 codes. The Seagram Building is a glass box in a plot, while the Lever House is a glass tower on a glass podium.

The Art Deco aesthetic that emerged in New York in the 1920s was the second Modernism movement in the United States following the Chicago School, which tended to be limited to Chicago or buildings that Chicago architects designed. Architects began rejecting many of the classical features of the earlier generation to create something not only new but also futuristic. Cities like Philadelphia, which did not have zoning until 1933, copied New York's architecture before then.

The old European designs, be they classical, Renaissance, or Beaux Arts, were replaced by a hybrid of machine-age styles—such as the stainless-steel spire on the Chrysler Building—and even older traditions like Egyptian or Aztec pyramids or Mesopotamian ziggurats.

If you look at the aspirational or visionary drawings from the early 1900s and compare them to those of the ensuing decades, you see a vast difference in the way skyscrapers and the city were conceived. In the older drawings, such as one printed in 1908 called *King's Dream of New York*, the city is a hyperdense mass of tall "classical" skyscrapers rising fifty stories into the air. Zeppelins zip past the towers, and a vast network of sky bridges carry pedestrians this way and that. Down below, elevated rail lines pump commuters into and out of the metropolis. The visions were future projections of capitalistic overbuilding (and would later be embraced by Hong Kong).

By the 1920s, we see the visionary renderings of architects Hugh Ferriss and Francisco Mujica. The giant Art Deco pyramidal towers shoot up into the heavens, surrounded by open space. They were the ultimate symbols of a polished modern era. For the first time, the skyscraper was seen as a machine for living—a device that could rationalize the irrational city into the perfect form, a Modernist utopia engineered by the scientific, architectural, and industrial spirit of the times.

LEFT: Future skyline vision from 1908 by Moses King
RIGHT: Future skyline vision from 1929 by Hugh Ferriss

Developers embraced the new Deco style because it sold. Like the Chicago architects before them, the 1920s generation worked to please their corporate clients who paid handsome commissions and through whom they could enhance their reputations. In this way, Art Deco was the perfect marriage between the artistic and the corporate zeitgeists. The innovators—Raymond Hood; Shreve, Lamb & Harmon; Charles Severance; and William Van Alen—were providing a vision that worked for the business community.

For architects such as Severance, the designer of the Bank of Manhattan Building, "the real classroom for an architect was to be found in the client's boardroom," writes author Neal Bascomb. "There an architect pitched his services, closed the deal, budgeted the cost of the building, finalized deadlines, and settled on design and floor plans."

The Roaring Twenties, however, proved a disaster for one group: city reformers. The building boom caused them to throw up their hands in despair. They assumed that the zoning codes would push builders to reduce heights and bulks. But, rather, the decade witnessed the ideal real estate conditions: brisk demand for office space, a Wall Street handing out bags of investment cash, and a grand architectural spirit to capture the ebullience of the Jazz Age.

But then the Great Depression came along, and local officials were able to rethink the rules. Within this era, a new concept to regulate building bulk or density emerged — limits on the so-called Floor Area Ratio (FAR). The FAR dictates the amount of allowable building space that can be constructed based on the size of the lot. For example, an FAR of 10 means a builder can create a 10-story building on the whole lot, a 20-story building on half the lot, or a 40-story building on a quarter of the lot. To give a sense of scale, the Empire State Building's FAR is 31 and the Chrysler Building's is 28.

When urban planners realized they could not control bulk through setback rules, they turned to establishing maximum FARs for each property. They measured the extant building densities and then created FAR caps by chopping off a few "FAR points" to lower future densities.

The FAR was appealing because it could be dictated in simple multiples of the lot size, say 0.5 for freestanding housing in the suburbs, 3 for low-rise apartment buildings, and 15 for tall skyscrapers. Planners preferred to limit the number of people per acre, but that was an impossible task. So, the FAR offered the next best thing. It limits total building area per acre and, along with minimum room sizes, nearly sets limits on population density. With one number, officials could better control what got built.

The urban planners who developed the idea of the FAR appreciated not only its simplicity but also that it incentivized open space around each building. The taller the structure the narrower it had to become. It was thus left to the developer to decide on a configuration that was either short and squat or tall and thin.

In 1961, New York City dropped the 1916 regulations and replaced them with a brand-new set of rules and maps, with the FAR limits as the mainstay. Since New York was so important, there has developed a belief that New York's 1961 rules were the first use of the FAR in the world. The truth, however, is a bit different.

New York implemented the FAR in a limited way in 1940 and went full-scale two decades later (which is still used today). Chicago went to an FAR system in 1957. The City of London adopted FAR restrictions in the 1940s (though gave them up in the 1980s). Hong Kong embraced the FAR in the 1960s, and mainland China in the 1980s. But the important point is that what was invented in 1930s New York then spread across the world throughout the rest of the twentieth century.

Presently, the FAR—also called the plot ratio in other countries—is arguably the most important planning tool for skyscrapers across the world. If we look at entire cities, we will find that Paris is basically an

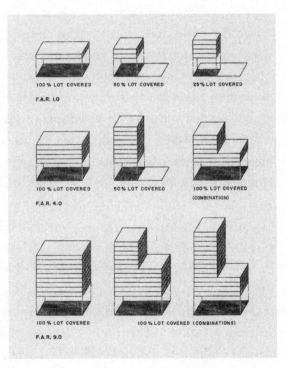

Examples of the Floor Area Ratio (FAR)

FAR 3 town and Manhattan has an overall FAR of 4.5. If you tour city after city in China, you will see high-rise estate after high-rise estate— thirty- or forty-story residential towers all clustered together in one large development. You might be surprised to learn that they were built with an average FAR of less than 3. The reason is that they are thin towers surrounded by open space.

Chicago's 1940s experiment with capping building volumes dictated that no building could have more volume than 144 times the lot area. Assuming each floor had a height of 12 feet, then the rule produced about an FAR of 12. However, volume limits incentivize cramming in more floors to increase rental income. Maximum FARs avoid this problem. However, with today's superslim towers in New York, there's the opposite issue. Developers extrude them with extra-high ceilings to offer more units with views. Some builders have even gone so far as to double or triple the ceiling heights on mechanical floors, which don't count toward the FAR limits. However, this caused pushback by residents, and the government banned "voids" that were higher than twenty-five feet.

Like the 1920s, the 1960s also saw the confluence of zoning reform and architectural styles. The move to FAR-based zoning was compatible with the tenets of Modernism, which advocated for the square glass tower. Developers liked the box-style structure because it was cheaper to build since each floor was identical to the one below it. And tenants loved the huge windows.

But Modernism and the glass box style long predated the use of the FAR. The Swiss-French architect Charles-Édouard Jeanneret (1887– 1965), known as Le Corbusier, one of the pioneers of Modernism, introduced his tower-in-the-park designs in the 1920s. In Chicago, in 1948, developer Herbert Greenwald commissioned Mies van der Rohe (1886–1969) to design the 860-880 Lake Shore Drive Apartments—early glass box residential buildings—a decade before Chicago adopted the FAR. While there was some pushback in the 1980s with the Postmodern movement, the glass box has remained because it is profitable, sleek, and regulated in a way that people could live with.

For skyscrapers, the minimum FAR needed is about 10, and allowable FARs for very tall buildings can run as high as 30. Interestingly, when we look around the world and compare the strictness of central city FARs to the heights of the tallest building and the number of skyscrapers, we see positive correlations, but not strong ones.

Cities that are "pro-skyscraper" have higher FAR caps in their central areas, but FAR caps are not the only component. Hong Kong has more skyscrapers than any other city on the planet, but its maximum FARs are relatively restrictive. For that matter, Singapore has some generous FAR limits but does not, as a rule, build very tall. Dense yes, but not tall.

The reason: a lot depends on the site and the motivations of the developers and local officials. FAR caps can be overcome or negotiated. If land values are very high and FAR caps are too tight, developers will find a way to get extra floor area, through legal or extra-legal means. And if a developer can strategically acquire a large lot, she can go tall with the overall density remaining relatively low.

In New York, a developer can automatically get an FAR bonus for an open plaza. She can also buy unused development (or air) rights (the extra unused allowable floor area) of neighboring properties and, in some cases, can negotiate with planning officials to get more FAR in exchange for paying for other civic benefits, such as an improved subway station or a fixed-up park. Air rights are valuable indeed. In 2018, St. Bartholomew's Church in Midtown sold fifty thousand square feet of air rights to JPMorgan Chase for $20 million, enabling the bank's new headquarters to rise seventy stories.

In many Hong Kong neighborhoods, a retail podium of, say, five floors won't count toward the residential FAR, so it becomes a "free" way to incentivize more building space without making residential high-rises too restrictive.

From the perspective of global urban history, the FAR's simplicity gives planners control over the density and limits the negative externalities — such as shadows, excessive bulk, and congestion — without alienating the real estate community that is relied upon to construct the city.

By the late twentieth century, it was clear that any city with national or international ambitions needed skyscrapers. But hardly anyone would say they should be allowed to exist simply in a laissez-faire, dog-eat-dog world. As a result, the world witnessed the emergence of a global consensus: on net, they were good but required oversight — and the FAR would be the predominant means to regulate their size and bulk.

Born in twentieth-century New York, the FAR helped shape — literally and figuratively — the global quest for skyscrapers in the twenty-first century.

CHAPTER 3

The American Century

Hive Minds in the Sky

Sears (Willis) Tower (1974)

THE SEARS TOWER

Sears, Roebuck and Co. never set out to build the world's tallest building, but rather it just fell into the retailer's lap.

The story of the Sears (today Willis) Tower helps to disprove the idea that the world's record breakers are devoid of economic rationales or are simply self-monuments to an ego-driven developer. So, if the flashing headlines for the world's tallest building are about the quest for preempting would-be rivals by adding unneeded height, then the story in Chicago in the late 1960s is that there is no story. New York's Twin Towers (1972/3) were each 1,368 feet (417 m) and the Sears Tower (1974) was 1,451 feet (442 m), a mere 6 percent taller.

The Sears Tower, nonetheless, presents a fascinating case study. It was the world's tallest building for a quarter century, and with that honor comes all types of superlatives and legend making. The building has 110 stories, with a gross building area of 101 acres (41 hectares), or nearly 77 football fields. It has 104 elevators, and at 77 feet (23 m), its antenna rises higher than most buildings on the planet.

The building's weight is 445,000,000 pounds (201,849,000 kg) or 20,000 city buses. Inside its walls run 15,000 miles (24,140 km) of electrical cable, longer than the distance from New York to Shanghai. Its cubic volume is equal to 4.8 million 12-cubic-foot (0.34 m^3) refrigerators. On a clear day, the view from the observatory spans 50 miles.

To Chicagoans, no doubt, the skyscraper was a source of great pride, and a kind of "see we told you so — we invented the skyscraper and now we are champions again!" The primacy that New York took for granted from 1890 to 1974 was over, as Gotham no longer had the world's tallest building. After the sustained controversy and difficulty of constructing the Twin Towers, the city seemed to lose its appetite for height competition.

But, just as importantly, the Sears Tower represents that rare alignment of forces that allowed Chicago to obtain the world's tallest building. The process began with the corporate need. By the end of the 1960s, Sears was America's leading retailer, with revenues of $8.9 billion and a profit of $441 million (larger than the gross domestic product [GDP] of Iceland at the time). It had more than 355,00 employees, including 31,200 in the Chicago area. Nationally, it operated 826 retail stores, 11 catalog mail-order plants, and more than 2,100 sales offices and independent catalog merchants. It owned subsidiary companies in thirteen countries.

Since 1904, Sears had occupied a giant complex on Chicago's West Side, with the then state-of-the-art mail-order house, warehouse, and fourteen-story office tower. The facility had become outdated, while the West Side had fallen on hard times.

Sears hired a consultant who determined that it would need about 2 million square feet of office space in the short run to centralize its staff and, down the road, in thirty years, it would need to double that (now that's optimism!). Furthermore, to enhance productivity, especially among the staff taking phone orders and dealing with customers, floor plates would need to be around 50,000 square feet (over an acre, or 4,645 m²). The natural conclusion was that Sears needed a skyscraper or even two.

The company then sought a location. "[Sears CEO] Mr. Metcalf particularly was determined to find a site to which transportation to thousands of Sears workers would be simple," reported the *New York Times*. After about a year of searching and some hard-fought negotiations, the company's real estate agents were able to secure a three-acre (1.2-hectare) lot in the Loop along South Wacker Drive for $11 million.

Given the large lot, the company could erect a huge structure and still be within the relatively lenient zoning regulations established in 1957. After World War II, in large part due to the leadership of Mayor Richard J. Daley (1902–1976), Chicago re-embraced its earlier skyscraper roots and developers were freed to go taller. The base FAR in the Loop was a generous 16, but with a system of bonuses for setbacks and public amenities, a shrewd developer could get more than double that.

The site was about 138,000 square feet (12,821 m²), 50 percent bigger than the Empire State Building lot. Given this much land, the Sears Tower could have been 300 stories high, with a total of 13.5 million square feet! If anything, by the ego standard, the constructed structure was too short and too small. The tower's height, however, was limited by Federal Aviation Administration (FAA) restrictions, which capped it at 1,451 feet (442 m).

With a lot secured, the company solicited proposals from five architectural firms, four of them from Chicago. By the end of 1969, it had chosen Skidmore, Owings & Merrill (SOM), which, as Sears Tower historian Jay Pridmore writes, "was considered the leading specialist in cost-efficient and often striking corporate buildings, and the emphasis was on cost efficiency." An important strength, since "Sears wasn't interested in building a monument. . . . They wanted to build something that was economical," recalled one of its real estate consultants.

The earliest plans produced by SOM were two large glass boxes, connected by a sky bridge over Quincy Street, a narrow lane that ran through the plot. The lead architect, Bruce Graham, preferred a larger tower and pushed Sears to acquire the street from the city. Thanks to the efforts of Mayor Daley, Sears was able to purchase the street for "a price that made the store's counting room smile," recounts Pridmore.

Graham and SOM engineer Fazlur Khan went back to the drawing board. According to legend, Khan and Graham were at the Chicago Club one day eating lunch and discussing design ideas for the building. Khan pitched his idea of the bundled tube, where the entire building is erected as nine vertical square "tubes" to make the building more rigid.

But this was not appealing since it meant a very bulky structure. As Pridmore relates, "Graham frowned and looked down at his pack of cigarettes and was about to reach for one when a thought struck him. The architect took out a handful of Camels, held them in his fist, and showed them to Khan. Each cigarette rose to a different height, and Khan understood immediately."

The lower sections would be one large mass, made up of the nine tubes, rising forty-nine stories. Here Sears got its much-wanted fifty-thousand-square-foot floor plans. Then above that, the tower would set back at various heights, giving the building the smaller floor plates that were desirable to would-be renters and providing a dynamic silhouette on the skyline.

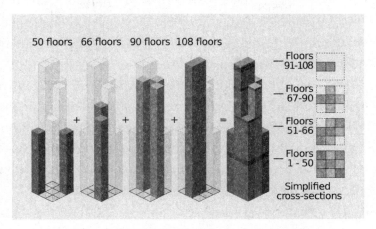

The Sears (Willis) Tower's tube structure design

Initially, Graham and Khan's structure rose to ninety-five stories, but "[t]he architects quickly realized that this was not many stories short of the World Trade Center. . . . The possibility of making Sears Tower the world's tallest building excited the architects and interested Sears Chairman Metcalf nearly as much," writes Pridmore. Thus was born the world's tallest building.

What Sears wanted was iconic but ultimately practical. Unlike the developer of the Burj Khalifa, the current world's tallest building, who in the early 2000s kept the final height a secret until it topped out to drum up more publicity, Sears announced its final height on the day it made public the project. And, as William Dunlap, a member of the architectural team at SOM, said in 1970, "We kept the height, for reasons of proportion, and aesthetics. There was some mention that it would be nice to have the world's tallest building. But the idea of a space race is silly."

Obviously, the executives who ran Sears did not know it, but its thirty-year plan for remaining the world's largest retailer was, to put it mildly, overly optimistic. In the 1980s, Sears got mired in unsuccessful ventures, particularly within the financial sector, such as buying Discover Card and Coldwell Banker. Then Walmart rose to dominance, and online retail was the final blow. As of this writing (September 2023), fewer than a dozen stores are left, and probably when you read this, Sears will have little more than a Wikipedia page to keep its memory alive.

But what about the building? The tower has seen many ups and downs over the years in terms of its market value, but its future seems bright. The glut in office space that swept across America after the 1980s boom took a toll. By the early 1990s, the skyscraper's vacancy rate had topped out at 45 percent. There simply wasn't enough money to pay the bills, and in 1994 Sears forfeited its baby to its creditors.

In 1997, with the tower's occupancy improved, the creditors sold it to a Canadian real estate firm, TrizecHahn, for $110 million. Things didn't pan out, especially when 9/11 struck a blow to the demand for iconic towers, and Trizec forfeited it to MetLife Insurance, the main creditor.

In 2004, MetLife sold out to a group of investors for $835 million. Then in 2009, the owners made a deal with the Willis Group, a London-based insurance broker, which purchased the naming rights, along with renting a large chunk of space. In 2015, in a show of optimism, the Blackstone Group, a private equity firm, purchased the building for $1.5 billion, the highest price ever paid for a Chicago skyscraper. Blackstone put in another $700 million for upgrades.

As a sidenote, $1.5 billion is considered pocket change for a building sale in New York. In fact, Blackstone, in December 2021, bought a 49 percent stake in One Manhattan West, a sixty-seven-story office tower that is part of the larger Hudson Yards project; the price it paid gave the tower a market value of $2.85 billion.

Nonetheless, Blackstone's investment in the Willis Tower reflects confidence in the Chicago market and in the building. Like the Empire State Building, the Willis Tower has three sources of revenue: the antennae, the observation deck, and the offices. Blackstone's massive renovation was designed to "highly amenitize" the building to reflect the tastes of modern workers. It built out a large retail operation, with dining and entertainment on the ground floor; installed a fitness center, lounges, and event spaces; and invested in improved elevators and tech. It upgraded the observatory, the Skydeck, with a glass floor perfect for TikTok or Instagram.

The building still appeals to firms like United Airlines, which rents 700,000 square feet (65,032 m²) for its global operations. At the onset of the COVID pandemic, the building was 95 percent rented. By the summer of 2022, it remained above 85 percent rented.

The observation deck adds about $35 million per year in revenue alone. The building's two steel antennae used for radio, television, and cell phone—provide another $10 million annually. In 2019, the average rents were about $24 per square foot, but with considerable variation based on the location of the building. The law firm Schiff Hardin LLP was paying more than $40 per square foot for its 181,000-square-foot space.

So, taking a long-run view, what we can say about the return to the market price of the Sears Tower? If we begin with the initial cost of $175 million in 1974 and adjust for inflation, that gives a real initial investment of $918 million. Then if we end with $1.5 billion in 2015, adjusted to $1.64 billion in 2020, this gives an estimated annual return in its market price of about 1.3 percent, which, ironically, is much worse than that of the Empire State Building.

Why did the Sears Tower fare so badly? First was that Chicago was particularly hard hit by decentralization and deindustrialization. Unlike New York, it continued to lose its population until 2000 and has been flat since then, as the Windy City has remained a national city more than a global one. Second, the lower floors with their huge floor plans were not appealing to many would-be renters looking for sunlight. Third, Chicago since the 1960s has been pro office development. As a result, its office sector was constantly being upgraded with new buildings, and over the decades its vacancy rates have remained systematically higher than in New York.

Ultimately, however, the times have caught up with the building. It retains its symbolic status. For the right corporations, the floor plans work, and there's an electrical substation in the basement to provide the juice needed by high-tech firms. And lastly there has been a general resurgence of the South Wacker neighborhood. The new construction there has made it a hotspot within Chicago's downtown.

THE SECOND SKYSCRAPER REVOLUTION

The Sears Tower's architecture presents a stark contrast with the old Art Deco towers of the Roaring Twenties. During the post–World War II decades, American downtowns transitioned to Modernist boxes. Along the way, American architectural and engineering firms honed their craft at making the skyscraper part of the modern American landscape.

In Manhattan, for example, between 1947 and 1963, 166 high-rise office buildings were completed. In 1947, the office vacancy rate was a mere 0.2 percent. The demand for new space was fierce and New York answered that call, and by 1963 some 44 million square feet of speculative office space had been constructed. Glass boxes surrounded their Art Deco predecessors as the business districts expanded outward. Even by 1963, office vacancy was still only 4.7 percent, showing that the supply could barely keep up with the demand.

As summarized by one 1967 report:

> The postwar upsurge in demand for floor space in office buildings appears to reflect three main influences. First, there has been a sharp increase in the total volume of office activities. Despite the growing use of electronic computers and other office equipment. Second, there has probably been an increase in the share of total office activities and total office employment that has been accommodated in office buildings rather than in other kinds of facilities. Third, there appears to have been an increase in the average amount of floor space occupied

per worker in office buildings, partly to provide room for more office machines and equipment.

Inside these buildings, whether it was General Motors, International Business Machines, General Electric, or Exxon, the iconic corporate skyscrapers that rose were not just symbols of American business might but were also hives that produced hive minds, where a company would oversee and coordinate its vast global operations and plan its corporate strategy. Large metropolises like New York and Chicago, as a result, became a hive of hives. The grand lesson of the twentieth century was that what happened in the skyscraper had benefits far beyond its glass walls.

And, as the Sears Tower demonstrates, the real secret of skyscraper design is that buildings must be designed from the inside out. The first rule of the Skyscraper Club is "give the tenant what it wants." Once the expected occupants are determined, then the layout follows. Units in apartment buildings, for example, are not normally expected to run more than thirty feet long, since sunlight will not penetrate that far in. Office lease spans will be longer on the lower floors where less valuable activities take place; higher up, the spans will decline to a sweet spot of between thirty and forty feet, again, to allow light into every office. A key to understanding the history of the skyscraper is that it represents the ongoing attempt to blur the boundary between inside and outside — to provide a vista to the outside, while not actually being outside — the quest for the ultimate fishbowl.

After the layout, next comes the height. Choosing the right height is what could be termed a constrained optimization problem — that which best balances the various trade-offs. First is the benefit of going taller — more people inside means more revenue both in total and on a per-square-foot basis (see chapter 8). However, going taller can increase the per-square-foot costs — more elevators, more materials for wind bracing and against gravity, more and/or deeper foundations, and more mechanical, electric, and plumbing (MEP) equipment. Tall buildings are also more costly to operate.

The floor count that best balances the costs and revenues to maximize profits is called the Economic Height. The quest to overcome the roadblocks to increasing the Economic Height led to the Second Skyscraper Revolution—the implementation of new technologies and building methods that allowed skyscrapers to burst through their former limits.

Innovations in structural designs reduced the cost of skyscrapers and represented a kind of "punctuated equilibrium"—a rapid flowering of new concepts in a short time span, due in large part to the invention of the mainframe computer. And thanks to this revolution, Sears got more building for less money. Crunching the numbers reveals that the company's tower cost $39 per square foot ($419 per m²), compared to the average cost of $42 for shorter skyscrapers built in the period.

As yesterday's barriers are broken, they become today's givens and so it will continue. The cycle generally works as follows. Buildings get built within a suite of current technologies—ones that everyone is familiar with and at relatively low cost.

As the economy grows and the limits of the old technologies become apparent, engineers, architects, and developers search for solutions. A new suite of methods and materials starts to percolate upward, and then there emerges a well-financed backer who is willing to test the new technologies to their limits. From this, a technological revolution emerges in earnest, where all the parts of the new system come together to create a structure more efficient than before. Developers are not fools, however. They are only willing to take the risk on the new if they either have seen "prototypes" in earlier buildings or know that the physics has truly been mastered.

Again, it's worth stressing, the skyscraper revolutions that have emerged since the 1880s are not about breaking through engineering barriers per se. The Great Pyramid of Giza was 482 feet (147 m) tall.

European Gothic cathedrals routinely rose 328 feet (100 m) or more. The knowledge to create tall buildings was never really the issue by the end of the nineteenth century. Rather, the real problem was how to get light inside, people easily to the top, and prevent people from feeling the building sway, all within budget.

Until the Great Depression halted construction, most of the skyscraper innovations were incremental. The guts of the Empire State Building were not that much different from the Woolworth Building (1913). The changes were a matter of degree rather than kind. Obviously, there were improvements in engineering and scientific know-how, steel manufacturing, supply chains, and construction logistics, as well as improvements in elevators, electricity, and so on. But the skyscrapers of 1900 and 1930 were riveted steel frames.

With the renewal of the American economy after World War II came the next generation of builders and designers who were interested in building for the new corporate landscape, and who cut their teeth during the New Deal and on the war effort. These firms built America's Modernist skylines and helped give birth to the Skyscraper Industrial Network—the network of engineers, architects, general contractors, consultants, and suppliers who design and build the world's skylines (and who work in skyscrapers themselves).

Arguably the most important firm of the era was SOM, which opened for business in Chicago in 1936, by the brothers-in-law Louis Skidmore (1897–1962) and Nathaniel Owings (1903–1984). They established a practice that would cater to the growing needs of both corporations and governments. They provided not only architectural services but also master planning. In addition, they brought engineers in-house to contribute to its one-stop-shopping approach.

After the war, SOM hired the top Modernist architects, most notably Gordon Bunshaft and Bruce Graham. Bunshaft (1909–1990), who worked out of the New York City office, was the dominant designer at SOM for forty-two years. Born into a Russian immigrant family, he grew up in Buffalo, New York, and graduated from MIT. Bunshaft was one of the leading International Style architects of his age, with the Lever House being his most famous structure. During the 1950s, SOM gained a reputation among architects as a "Miesian" firm by hiring the students of Mies van der Rohe.

Bruce Graham (1925–2010) worked in the Chicago office. Born in La Cumbre, Colombia, he attended college in Puerto Rico and then studied engineering in Ohio. He obtained a degree in architecture from the University of Pennsylvania in 1948. From there, he joined SOM and remained for forty years. Graham, like Bunshaft, can be called a Corporate Modernist. As architectural historian Nicholas Adams writes:

> When it came to talking about their architecture, designers like Gordon Bunshaft and Bruce Graham subscribed completely to the logic of functional process. Phrases such as "that's the way the building had to be," or "the building was a product of the spaces we needed," or "we simply looked at the needs of the client and made the building accordingly," are invented, but their equivalent can be found in the many interviews with Bunshaft and Graham.

Graham's approach to Modernism helped usher in the second Chicago School of Architecture. To bring his Modernist ideas to life, as in the case of the Sears Tower, he collaborated with engineering genius Fazlur Khan (1929–1982). Khan was born in Pakistan, where he studied civil engineering at the University of Dhaka. In 1952, he moved to the United States to further his studies and received a Ph.D. in structural engineering at the University of Illinois Urbana-Champaign. After working for a few years in his home country, he returned to the United States to join SOM, where he stayed until his untimely death from a heart attack.

Khan's success in promoting new types of skyscrapers lay not only in his devising new structural strategies but also in selling them to architects and clients alike. Khan also had a "hidden" partner who perhaps was the real hero of the story and was the lynchpin of the Second Revolution. For the first time in human history, the computer was extensively used to work out and test the physics of new designs. It, literally and figuratively, opened new doors. As retired SOM partner and lead engineer on Dubai's Burj Khalifa William F. Baker writes:

> This cloudburst of new systems was made possible by the advent of computers and engineering pioneers such as Fazlur Khan, Hal Iyengar, William LeMessurier, Leslie Robertson and others. Although the conceptual foundations of these systems were straightforward, earlier computational methods were not adequate for use in design. At last, the viability of these systems could be demonstrated by utilizing the mainframe computer. In addition to validating the systems, important parametric studies were done to establish the applicable height range for the various systems.

Baker further elaborates how Khan's ideas were enabled and tested on the newfangled computing machines:

> Part of it is not so much [Khan's] designs as much as it was the environment that the office had—that was his legacy. He did a lot of his innovations down at IIT, Illinois Institute of Technology, in the College of Architecture. He and [SOM architect] Myron Goldsmith taught down there for years, and together they would work with a student doing their master's thesis. In this case, it would have been someone who already had a five-year degree in architecture and wanted to do a thesis; and they would spend a couple of years doing one problem. And they would use that as a research field to try to develop new ideas and new systems. The John Hancock was originally a master's thesis. It wasn't tapered but it was a straight up and down braced tower. They were able to resolve the technical issues there and when the

opportunity came up, they knew that they could propose an idea with confidence. . . . After Faz Khan passed away, I started going down to IIT and that's how I helped develop my ideas through this process, this tradition that he created.

The August 1973 issue of IBM's corporate magazine, *Think*, could hardly contain its glee about the company's role in the Sears Tower:

> When Chicago's 110-story Sears Tower topped out last May at 1,454 feet—the world's highest skyscraper—it became yet another record-breaker for the architectural firm of Skidmore, Owings & Merrill, an IBM customer.
>
> It is also the biggest piece of evidence to date of the growing bond between architect and computer. "But for the computer," say Dr. Fazlur Khan . . . "Sears Tower would not have been built at all. It would have cost too much."

Khan's innovations were motivated by what he called the "premium for height," which is the extra cost that a developer must pay for more and thicker steel as a tower rises higher using conventional framing methods. As a building gets taller, the wind forces rise exponentially. For a ten-story structure, the wind is not such a big deal. At twenty stories, you need to worry. At one hundred stories, you had better do something or else you will have a giant pendulum on your hands. So, more steel is needed to keep the building stiff. If builders only needed to worry about gravity, for example, they could get a seventy-story building using steel that weighed 20 pounds per square foot. But to counteract the wind loads they would need almost 40 pounds per square foot.

Older skyscrapers like the Empire State Building had the benefit of extra masonry. Its cladding was predominantly limestone, and the elevator core was enclosed by brick. Though engineers at the time calculated a building's stiffness based on the amount of steel, they unwittingly got extra help from the masonry. As a result, buildings were frequently too stiff for the purpose of keeping the occupants comfortable.

But masonry buildings lost favor after the war. As a result, skyscrapers became lighter and more easily subject to wind forces, which then required more steel, jacking up the costs. From SOM's perspective, a structure with less steel also meant cheaper buildings and more commissions.

Arguably, the first and most important idea, widely attributed to Khan (though there is a debate, discussed later), was the invention of the framed tube. The steel skeleton, also called a moment-resisting frame, had columns and beams distributed throughout the building to resist gravity forces. Then, usually in the core, were additional horizontal or diagonal beams to stiffen the building against wind forces. The core was a perfect location for these beams because they were hidden away and surrounded the elevators, stairwells, and ducts.

As mentioned with the Sears (Willis) Tower, Khan's idea was to create a skyscraper where closely spaced columns were placed around the exterior and joined together by horizontal beams or spandrels. This array of external columns was similar to a supertall rectangular tube placed vertically, which could resist both gravity and wind.

The tube added more strength with fewer materials—nearly a "free lunch." While the Empire State Building's steel weighed in at 50 pounds per square foot, the Sears Tower, both bigger and taller, had its steel weigh in at 33 pounds per square foot. Plus fewer internal load-bearing columns were needed, creating open floor plans, something corporate America craved.

Legend holds—though no proof exists—that Khan's idea for the tube emerged from the bamboo huts seen in his home city of Dhaka. As a sidenote, bamboo holds a certain fascination in the skyscraper world. William Le Baron Jenney's partner William Bryce Mundie also claimed bamboo huts inspired the Home Insurance Building. And today there's a handful of Asian supertalls that supposedly look like bamboo (discussed in chapter 6).

Another possibility was that Khan got the idea from his own residence, designed by world-famous architect I. M. Pei. "I wouldn't call
them tube structures, more like proto-tubes," architectural historian
Tom Leslie told me. "Their innovation was just enlarging the typical
mullions until they became structural, but they definitely don't have the
megastructural properties that Khan's tube structures do. Khan and his
family lived in the University Apartments that Pei designed in the late
1950s, so there's no doubt that he understood the principle."

Dewitt Chestnut Apartments (1966), Chicago
(Chicago History Museum, Hedrich-Blessing Collection, HB-28864-F)

To add additional stiffness, the core could also be designed as a tube to
create a tube-in-tube structure. Tubes could be "bundled" by creating several
tubes and attaching them together, as was the case with the Sears Tower.

The first completed tube building was that of the Dewitt Chestnut Apartments in Chicago, designed by the SOM team of Graham and Khan in 1962 and opened in 1966. The forty-two-story apartment building is tall to be sure, but not super- or megatall. Rectangular in shape, it contained 407 apartments. The tube consists of closely spaced exterior concrete columns, which gives the aesthetic of an exoskeleton.

The building was a product of Herbert S. Greenwald (1915–1959), whose real estate company Metropolitan Structures embraced Modernist high-rises. Greenwald, in his relatively short career—he died at forty-three in a plane crash—partnered with Mies to develop other apartment buildings in Chicago. As Tom Leslie recounts:

> Metropolitan Structures is the great tragedy of Chicago—Herb Greenwald was a real visionary, and the force behind all of Mies van der Rohe's residential towers in the city.
>
> The story that Graham and others tell about Dewitt Chestnut Apartments is that they didn't want to crowd 860-880 Lake Shore Drive, which is literally next door, so they took two planned towers and stacked them on top of each other, making a very tall, very slender building that couldn't be braced adequately with conventional systems—that seems to have inspired Khan to soup up the paired tube structure/core shear wall system he was working on simultaneously for the Brunswick downtown.

As William Baker recalls about the structure:

> This simple, elegant tower–now dwarfed by its neighbors–was a major development in modern architecture. The integration of the tubular system and Miesian architecture was complete and seamless. Architecture and structure were one and the same, inseparable. The computer was able to verify that this concrete building could be viewed as one continuous structure rather than merely a collection of columns and beams. Designers could now verify that the building behaved as a

three-dimensional system much like a solid tube, only partially softened by the openings for the windows.

The next step in the advancement of the tube was the John Hancock Center (1968; 1,128 feet, 344 m) in Chicago, again designed by SOM's Graham and Khan. At one hundred stories, it was the first *completed* steel tube structure in the world. It also had the added innovation of external diagonal beams connected to the columns to provide more stiffness.

As one engineering historian has recorded:

> The architectural problem posed by the Hancock Center was to provide 1 million square feet of office space and an equal amount of apartment space, plus about 800,000 square feet for commercial use and parking. Since the Center was to be an investment property, the cost of the building was of prime concern. A typical architectural solution would have been to design two buildings, so there would be no premium for height, which the investors did not wish to pay. But two buildings on the site would have crowded the complex at street level, which the architects did not like. Hence a structurally efficient single tall building was looked to, and Khan proposed an "optimum column-diagonal truss tube," as he then called the structure that has become so familiar a part of the Chicago skyline.

SOM is unusual in that its architects and engineers collaborate from within the same firm. However, the standard is that the architect designs the building and then recommends to the developer a structural engineering firm. That was the case with the Twin Towers.

In 1962, when the Port of New York Authority (PA) was charged with building the World Trade Center, it decided to go with Minoru Yamasaki as the chief architect. Yamasaki was instrumental in getting the engineer Leslie E. Robertson selected to turn Yamasaki's ideas into reality. Yamasaki, who was afraid of heights, wanted his building to have

The Twin Towers under construction in 1970

a sense of enclosure to calm occupants like himself, so he designed the Twin Towers to have exterior columns about two feet apart.

To realize not only Yamasaki's vision but also the PA's quest to have the world's tallest twin towers, Robertson spearheaded many innovations that have since become the norm. And his experience as lead engineer shows how he fought "the battle of the trade-offs."

Robertson (1928–2021) was born in Los Angeles. At age sixteen, he dropped out of school and lied about his age to join the navy. After World War II, he obtained a degree in engineering from the University of California, Berkeley, eventually joining the Seattle office of Worthington and Skilling in 1958. From there, at the tender age of thirty-five, he found himself charged with engineering the world's tallest buildings. In the process, he helped revolutionize the industry.

When asked to devise a structure that would conform to Yamasaki's architectural wishes, Robertson obliged, as he writes:

The structural concept for the World Trade Center was that of a "tube,"
where the perimeter walls resisted all of the lateral forces of wind and earthquake while carrying all the vertical loads tributary to the perimeter wall. . . .
The tubular framing system also precluded the need for the customary
30-foot column spacing in interior areas, resulting in column-free rentable
space, a circumstance that pleased both the architect and rental agents.

What's incredibly gutsy is that while the tube idea was known in the
profession, there were only two cases in Chicago to date where it was
in the process of being employed. That he would propose such a novel
concept with nearly nothing under his belt except good math skills and a
computer to back him up (and the imprimatur of his engineering mentor
and boss, John Skilling) is all the more incredible. But he convinced
both Yamasaki and the PA that it would work and he was right (despite
the collapse on 9/11, which can no way be pinned on him).

But going with a lighter tube design still required additional wind-
bracing strategies. For this, he pioneered the use of wind tunnel testing. A
model of the building was placed in a wind tunnel, then measurements
of its performance were taken, and structural adjustments followed.

Robertson and his colleagues, however, had no idea how much
swaying occupants could actually handle without getting sick. For this,
he created a "sway box" and "tricked" unsuspecting study participants
into the box and simulated different amounts of sway to see if they got
sick. As reported in the *New York Times*:

> To answer that question, Robertson turned to an expert in human percep-
> tion in Eugene, Ore.—a spot as far removed from the New York press as he
> could find. Paul Hoffman, a psychologist, agreed to perform a secret series
> of experiments to find out just how much swaying motion was too much.
> Hoffman purchased a small office building in downtown Eugene and in
> the summer of 1965 put an ad in the local paper offering free eye check-
> ups at a "vision research center." But it was actually an elaborate ruse: the

optometrist who conducted the eye exams was one of Hoffman's employees, Paul R. Eskildsen. And as each patient stared at triangles projected on the wall, a hidden technician would trigger a giant set of hydraulics underneath the room that heaved it back and forth like a big saltshaker. . . .

Patient after patient reacted the same way—becoming dizzy and confused soon after the eye exam began. Humans, Hoffman discovered, were much more sensitive to motion than anyone had realized. A few inches of sway over 5 or 10 seconds set off psychophysical alarm bells.

Out of the test results emerged two additional design features. First was "a viscoelastic damping system," that is, a large pendulum-like damper that would help slow down the sway. And to add more rigidity, Robertson installed "outrigger trusses." Outriggers are thick beams that emanate from the core to the perimeter to add more stiffness. A belt of steel trusses connected to the outriggers also firmed up the tower. As I will discuss in more detail in chapter 6, outriggers, wind tunnel testing, and dampers are all the norm in skyscraper design today.

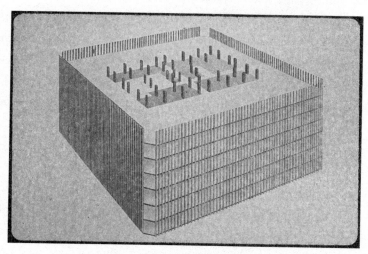

The structural tube system of the Twin Towers
(Archives of Michigan, Michigan History Center, Manuscript
Collection: MS 2010-5, AOM/Negative: 6211_WTC_1105)

Given his investigations, Robertson was able to figure out the calculations for acceptable sway in normal conditions. However, no building can be perfectly rigid. During hurricanes, the top floors of the Twin Towers could move some 13 feet (4 m) out of their plumb position. But, over the years, before 9/11, the building was popular, and evidently, there was little motion sickness that would affect occupancy rates or office rents. For what it's worth, around 2000 my wife and I had a drink at Windows on the World, the restaurant on the 106th floor and neither of us noticed rattling ice cubes in our cocktails. But I do remember that the name Windows on the World was a misnomer, as the view was negatively impacted by the columns being so close.

A debate, reminiscent of which building was the "first" skyscraper, has circulated about who invented the tube — was it Khan or Robertson? While both sides seem willing to concede the "in the air" hypothesis, Khan's victory in the public's eye is likely because he wrote academic journal articles and conference proceedings about the physics (and implicitly the economics) of different designs. In this way, Khan had a more academic side that allowed his voice to spread widely outside the small community of structural engineers designing supertall buildings. Robertson was also writing about his buildings, but Khan was more active in the publishing and public relations sphere.

Khan's daughter, Yasmin Sabina Khan, wrote a book in 2004 about her father's career. Like many before her, she tipped the balance to her father but was willing to concede that the answer is still unclear. She writes:

> The coincident development of a tubular system for the World Trade Center and the Chestnut-DeWitt Apartments has led to the speculation over the years about which tube concept was the "first." According to structural engineer Leslie Robertson in 1972, his firm developed the Vierendeel tube structure for the New York project in 1962. "Later, in 1963," Robertson reported, SOM designed a framed tube for

Chestnut-DeWitt Apartments (Robertson, "Theme Report," 405). My review of SOM's files, however, confirms that SOM was designing the structure for Chestnut-DeWitt Apartments in 1962; in January 1964, when the scheme for the World Trade Center's 110-story towers was announced, Chestnut-DeWitt construction was already underway. Although my father did not take up the question of initial development of the structural type, he did make it clear in his papers and lectures that he had developed the framed tube system that he utilized for the design of the Chestnut-DeWitt Apartments.

Word of the tubular idea may have spread from one engineering office to the other in the 1962–63 period (but I have found no evidence pointing to this possibility); in either case, progressive thought in the architecture and engineering fields was moving in this direction at the time.

Robertson chimed in with his perspective in his 2017 book:

Much has been written as to who first created and used the tubular framing system. Almost surely, it was either the incredibly creative Fazlur Rahman Khan (of Skidmore, Owings & Merrill) or our team (Skilling, Helle, Christiansen, Robertson)—one or the other, or both at about the same time. It seems to me that it was an idea in need of realization, making it likely that several engineers, more or less simultaneously, came up with the same concept. In any event, I neither lay claim to nor disavow authorship, believing instead that ideas are creatures of their time, not of an individual or a team.

Today tubular designs remain in use, though not as popular as other forms. The main problem is the narrow spans between the perimeter columns. They are acceptable for apartment buildings, but less so for offices, where businesses like the expansive views. Then there's the aesthetic dimension. Narrow columns suggest a particular style, and if an architect has a different design in mind then other structural solutions are preferred.

Nonetheless, the Second Skyscraper Revolution planted the technological seeds for the skyscraper's global future. During the postwar period, the quest for taller, cheaper, and more user-friendly structures created a highly skilled interconnected web of architects, engineers, consultants, and suppliers. Their skills became in great demand as non-Western countries began to build skyscrapers. In the twenty-first century, the skyscraper moved like a wave across the rest of the world.

PART II

EURASIA

CHAPTER 4

London

From No to Yes

LEFT: The Shard (2013); RIGHT: The Tower Bridge (1894)

THE SHARD

In June 2019, I was in London to attend an economics conference. This was my first time there, and I was ready to be ensnared by all the tourist traps. After my strolls along the Strand and to Westminster Abbey, I walked east and then over the Thames via London Bridge. On the south bank, amidst the brick industrial buildings, buoyantly rises the seventy-three-story, twenty-first-century crystal palace — the Shard.

I entered the lobby to go up to the viewing deck. After I bought my ticket, I went past the photo station and hopped into the elevator. At the top, I saw a 360-degree view of low-rise Victorian London pierced by a new crop of skyscrapers sprouting here and there, especially in the City. Just across the river, you can see the Tower of London, where kings and political rivals were sent to die. If you look straight up, you can see the "shards of glass" spiking the air and giving the building its trademark spire.

As a tourist destination goes, it was pleasant enough—a great way to see London's skyline, though not as dramatic or awe-inspiring as New York, Chicago, Dubai, or Shanghai. The blingyness of the tourist experience, however, smacked of fake elegance. For an hour or so tourists can simulate a jet-setting billionaire lifestyle. It didn't work for me, but a young couple who purchased the "VIP package" was walking around with champagne flutes and smiles, so I guess emulations of the leisure class work for some.

The Shard is nothing if not the embodiment of twenty-first-century wealth—crystal is the new gold. But for many years, the developer, Irvine Sellar (1934–2017), labored to make it so, and despite having hit numerous obstacles and crises, unlike the alchemists before him he made something from nothing. It was, in the end, a successful (ad)venture.

The Shard's story is interesting for many reasons. The first is that it is now Western Europe's tallest building. At 1,004 feet (306 m), it's not as tall as the Empire State Building (1,250 feet, 381 m) and is positively diminutive compared to the Shanghai Tower (2,073 feet, 632 m), but it demonstrates that Western Europe can also play the tall building game.

Just as importantly, the Shard embodies the evolution of London's thinking about tall buildings and the recent emergence of a "meeting of the minds." Irvine Sellar was what one might call a disrupter—one who seeks, in the name of profit and self-satisfaction, to undertake large-scale projects. Disrupters were aplenty in British history. When it came to manufacturing, they reformed an agricultural-based society into one based on wage labor and mass production. On the high seas, they colonized or conquered in the name of Empire. The American colonies were so filled with disruptors that they turned on their motherland.

And yet they were notably absent in London in the 1890s when the skyscraper was a possibility. For nearly a century, London rejected skyscrapers. And in the twenty-first century, the Shard is London's skyscraper debutante ball. But completing it took a long, long time and is emblematic of London's remaining ambivalence.

Sellar first conceived the project in 1999, and the Shard finally opened in 2013, nearly fourteen years after the lightbulb went off in his head. In contrast, the Empire State Building offers itself up as a counterpoint to New York's earlier ability to move quickly. In December 1928 the Waldorf-Astoria Hotel sold the property, and by May 1, 1931, the Empire State Building was open, despite that the property flipped hands three times. For that matter, the developer of the Burj Khalifa, the world's tallest building, took a little more than half as long as the Shard from conception to completion.

London's slow going is due in large part to the battle between two coalitions—the preservationists and the pro-growthists—who jockey for control over London's image. The preservationists seek to keep London's focus on its past; while the real estate community argues it needs a modern skyline to make it more future oriented. In the end, the two factions have reluctantly compromised—or rather, compromise has been foisted on them by the power brokers: London's city planners, who act as the gatekeepers.

On one side are groups like London Heritage and the Commission for Architecture and the Built Environment (CABE). Their aim is to preserve, preserve, and preserve—to not only keep London's buildings the way they are but to "freeze" London as an icon of its Londonness, arguably in the way central Paris is frozen as a remnant of the mid-nineteenth-century city. To the preservationists, it is a matter of pride and beauty and the desire to keep alive London's heritage. The philosophy is, in effect, "We know who we are from our buildings and to destroy them is to destroy a part of ourselves." The groups are also the guardians of the sight lines to St. Paul's Cathedral and the Tower of London. Keeping the sight lines clear of skyscrapers is nothing short of an obsession. As a New Yorker, I find the notion of sight lines strange. In the United States, skyscrapers *are* the sight lines.

Alongside the preservationists are the anti-skyscraperists, who feel tall buildings are not consistent with good design and planning and are antithetical to the teachings of urbanists such as Jane Jacobs and Jan Gehl, who argue that low-rise cities are the best. This group of Londoners claims that tall buildings are out of scale, block light and views, spew carbon dioxide, and add to income inequality. They house the superrich and harm the working classes who find themselves priced out of their gentrifying neighborhoods (we will return to the merits or demerits of these arguments in chapter 9).

On the pro side is the real estate community, who see rising prices and argue that office and housing space is becoming too expensive without new buildings. London needs to build to satisfy the demand and remain competitive. Alongside them are the financial and business services factions. London sits atop the global financial pyramid and faces competition from Frankfurt, as well as Hong Kong, Shanghai, and Singapore, farther afield. If London wants to remain king of the hill, it must build upward.

Then there are the local and national "growth machine" officials who believe in pro-growth policies. Encouraging real estate development will provide more jobs and improve the economic health of London. This group sees cities and nations in a competitive battle for valuable capital, high-skilled labor, and tourism. The skyscraper is a ship that will lift London's tide.

The planners stand in the middle and arbitrate among the warring factions. Planning officials must give their blessing before any tall building can be constructed. While planners suggest guidelines in their urban plans, no decisions are made until a developer first submits a proposal to the respective local planning office, which then initiates a review and negotiations.

To balance the demands of the various factions, the planners have hit upon an idea: each skyscraper must be iconic, novel architecture. Each must not only make up for the perceived architectural mistakes of the past but also provide the great architecture that the former-imperial-now-global city deserves. The planners say, "If we are going to destroy the old, we must get something 'good' in return." And that is the way London does skyscrapers in the twenty-first century.

So how did the Shard rise amidst the history of London's reluctance to go tall? The short answer to this question is "through the unrelating quest of Irvine Sellar." Sellar was born into a Jewish family in 1934 and grew up in Southgate, a North London suburb. His father owned a gloves shop in the East End. At sixteen, Sellar quit school and, with little formal education but with large ambition, he went to work in the garment trade.

He was something of a fashion hustler, opening boutiques on Carnaby Street that sold hip clothing to 1960s youth. In the process, he helped to make Carnaby Street into Carnaby Street—from edgy and vanguard to tourist mall. His key innovation was Mates, a chain of clothing stores that sold to both men and women. Women could shop on the ground floor, while the men browsed in the basement.

By 1981, he owned Britain's second-biggest clothing store chain, which he sold to South African investors, who proceeded to flush the business down the drain. This did not financially affect Sellar, who by then had decided to focus on real estate. Retail and real estate, he learned, are two sides of the same coin, since good retail is having the right location and good real estate is location, location, and location.

He then cofounded Ford Sellar Morris, a property company listed on the London Stock Exchange. The 1980s were heady days for real estate in both the United States and Britain, and Sellar rode the wave.

But easy money and good times morphed into irrational exuberance, and, when the bubble burst, there was a bitter hangover. By 1992, Sellar filed for bankruptcy. Ever tenacious, he regrouped and founded the Sellar Property Group.

In 1998, he acquired the Southwark Towers in the London Bridge neighborhood. The structure was a twenty-five-story (100 m) Modernist box completed in 1976 and the London headquarters of the accounting firm PricewaterhouseCoopers (PwC). Sellar bought the property as an income-producing investment. "As dry as you can get," he said about the deal. But then, in early 1999, the government published a white paper meant to encourage high-density development around transportation hubs. Southwark Towers sits atop London Bridge Station.

As a result, Sellar found himself in possession of a speculator's dream. All he had to do—it seemed—was convince officials to allow him to knock down the old building and construct something larger and taller in its place. His project would also help spruce up the neighborhood, which would lead to more ventures down the line. From Sellar's point of view, the city hit the switch from No to Yes, and he was ready to cater to the demand. Little did he know what lay ahead.

After working with some local architects, Sellar was warned by Fred Manson, the head of planning for Southwark Borough, that unless his building had an outstanding design it was going to be vetoed. Even then, however, he would have no free pass. Sellar managed to secure a meeting with architect Renzo Piano, the 1998 winner of the Pritzker Prize, considered the "Nobel Prize for architecture."

Piano was born in Genoa, Italy, in 1937. He studied architecture in Florence and Milan and taught for a few years at the Polytechnic University of Milan while also pursuing an architectural career. In 1970, he received his first international commission, the Pavilion of Italian Industry for Expo 70 in Osaka, Japan. This led to his teaming up with the British architect Lord Richard Rogers, with whom he had a joint practice from 1971 to 1977.

The two rocketed into international fame in 1971 when they won the competition to design the Pompidou Center in Paris, which includes a national public library and a museum of modern art. Their novel design became famous because it literally turned architecture inside out, with the structural frame and the heating and air-conditioning ducts on the exterior painted in bright colors. The escalator, in a transparent tube, crosses the façade diagonally.

Two architectural phenomena emerged as a result. It popularized the concept of making structural elements part of the architecture. And it started the modern concept of exotic architecture to renew and "brand" a place. Frank Gehry took this to the next level with his design for the Guggenheim in Bilboa, which opened in 1997.

In March 2000, Sellar flew to Berlin to meet with Piano. At their dinner, Sellar showed him the initial designs; Piano was unimpressed. He then flipped over a napkin and started sketching a structure — something that looks a lot like the Shard today. The dinner led to a handshake agreement and the process moved one inch closer. But as exuberant as Sellar must have felt that night, the Shard's future was still highly uncertain.

One year later, the building plans were submitted to Southwark Borough. A full year after that, the Borough finally gave permission. But that was not the end. Protests by preservation groups and the Greater London Authority (GLA) planning committee prompted the United Kingdom's deputy prime minister, John Prescott, to initiate a public inquiry. In essence, the Shard was to be put on trial. If Prescott believed the building was not in the public interest, he could veto it.

The hearing began in April 2003. On the pro side were, of course, Sellar and Piano, who argued that the building would make a positive contribution to London. Studies were performed to make sure that it did not block sight lines to St. Paul's Cathedral and money was going to be spent on upgrades to the local infrastructure. Piano's design offered a crystalline structure that added to the skyline without overpowering it. Sellar also had the backing of London's mayor, Ken Livingstone.

Those arrayed against the project included English Heritage, Historic Royal Palaces, and CABE. English Heritage and Historic Royal Palaces argued that the building would destroy the sight lines to St. Paul's. English Heritage went as far as to pronounce that, if constructed, the building would be a "shard of glass through the heart of historic London." Ironically, this vivid metaphor—used against itself—gave the skyscraper its trademarked name.

CABE even polled the beefeaters of the Tower of London, who give its tours and are the de facto guardians of its history. One CABE commissioner offered, "We spoke to a senior beefeater who could not see what all the fuss was about. We regarded the beefeater as a significant stakeholder."

As Sellar later recalled:

Virtually any city in the world would have been an easier place to develop a project of this scale, although few would be as rewarding. . . . We knew we were in for the long haul. In total we had more than 300 meetings with the public. . . . We produced 150 CGI renderings from every conceivable angle, and met with all the stakeholders. . . . Ultimately, we reduced the height of the planned tower, but were still able to fit 30 acres of property onto a one-acre site.

After weeks of testimony and rebuttals and arguing back and forth about the merits and demerits of the building, Prescott finally gave approval in November 2003, with the caveat that construction begin by 2008. That seemed reasonable enough until the Financial Crisis hit in 2007 and Sellar lost his financing. As far as the press was concerned, the Shard was no more since Sellar needed money to pay the interest on a £196 million interim loan. As one chronicler recalled:

He found a solution for all his woes—the lack of funding, the need to begin construction and the need to pay back the loan—in a single masterstroke. . . . In insecure times, you need a secure partner. With the effects of the credit crunch looking increasingly long term, there was almost nobody in the world more secure than the Qataris.

Qatar was awash in oil money and seeking to invest the proceeds abroad. London is a draw for both consumption and investment by superrich Arabs, and the Shard offered the promise of both. By the end of 2008, the financing was secure, and construction proceeded apace.

The Qatari investment, however, fuels the perception that super-luxury skyscrapers in the West are funded largely by Arabian sovereign wealth funds (SWFs), but this is not quite true. SWFs are reluctant to jump directly into development because of the risks involved in investing in cities with different cultures and laws. Rather, SWFs tend to build real estate closer to home, where it's easier to manage their projects.

The Qatari investment in the Shard is an example that shows that international backers tend to invest after a local developer has done much of the groundwork. Given how large the pool of global capital is, local developers are constantly courting investors from the world over. And with planning permission in hand and glossy renderings, these local developers can entice foreign investors to get a piece of the action.

SWFs, along with investors from nations with large trade surpluses, however, prefer purchasing "trophy assets" in global cities because of the cache. The mid-2000s saw an investment wave by Middle Easterners, pouring their petrodollars into commercial real estate. As reported in 2005 in the *New York Times*:

> One of the [Dubai] royal family's companies, Istithmar, closed this week on the $705 million purchase of 230 Park, known variously as the Helmsley Building and the New York Central Building. A separate Dubai company closed in September on the $440 million acquisition of the Essex House, home to Alain Ducasse, the restaurant which recently won a coveted three-star rating in the Michelin guide to New York City.

In May 2008, a consortium of U.S., Kuwaiti, and Qatari investors purchased the General Motors Building and three other Midtown towers for $3.95 billion. Arab investors were also gung-ho for London properties. In 2008, a Kuwaiti fund bought the twenty-six-story Norman Foster–designed Willis Building, on Lime Street in the City of London.

While in July 2008 the business press was abuzz with the news: The Chrysler Building was purchased by an SWF from Abu Dhabi for $800 million. The land, however, would remain with its original owner, Cooper Union, which had leased the lot to Walter Chrysler back in 1928.

Over time, however, Arab investors would find that owning real estate in a foreign land is not so easy. In March 2019, the Abu Dhabi fund sold the Chrysler Building for a huge loss. In 2012, Strategic Hotels & Resorts reacquired the Essex House from the Dubai Investment Group for $50 million less than the fund paid for the property six years earlier. Istithmar, however, was more prudent. It sold 230 Park after three years for a hearty $300 million profit.

Nonetheless, the Shard shows how perseverance can pay off, and Sellar's fourteen-year, £2 billion dream morphed into a moneymaking machine. London has some of the most expensive office space in the world and its attraction as a tourist destination means its hotels and restaurants buzz with visitors. The Shard's Shangri-La Hotel has also become a romantic go-to for marriage proposals. All the office space was rented before the building was completed. The Shard appears in the backdrop of TV shows and James Bond movies. And what's more, the Southwark neighborhood is now popping with new investments.

Before Sellar passed away in 2017 at the age of eighty-two, he was given a chance to look back at all the naysayers. He was asked if, given all he went through, would he do it all again. His answer: "Yes, I would. Why? Because it's profitable."

THE IRONY: FROM YES TO NO

The Shard's difficulty in getting built reflects London's unusual planning process. Perhaps no other country has such a strange relationship with tall buildings. Across the world, we generally see three planning models: ban them, allow them as demanded, and set them apart in special zones.

Cities in northern Europe for the most part make them illegal, so they don't get built. Dublin is the most extreme, without any buildings greater than 262 feet (80 m). Its Capital Dock Tower, completed in 2018, at twenty-three stories seems misnamed. A skyscraper in Dublin to be sure, but a stump in most cities.

North American cities allow tall buildings by first setting the ground rules. Developers can normally build skyscrapers "as of right" without any planning review if they conform to the local zoning and building regulations. In downtowns, the regulations are generous enough that if a builder wants to go tall, then she can simply proceed (though there's still a lot of paperwork and interactions with officials). The Empire State Building and the Sears (Willis) Tower are examples of as-of-right supertalls.

The other model is master planning. Local officials designate areas where they want tall buildings to go and then work with developers to see them built. Shanghai's Pudong, Paris's La Défense, and Frankfurt's Financial District are cases in point.

But Britain's take on the skyscraper is a weird mishmash of developer-initiated projects with long-drawn-out battles with government officials and local organizations. Economists tend to view the system as, at best, inefficient and, at worst, dysfunctional.

But, ironically, no other city has had a greater impact on skylines around the world than London. It has been the seed of North American, Hong Kong, and Singaporean skylines. Its real estate influence extends to the United Arab Emirates, which were client states of the British Empire, and even to China, where Treaty Ports like Shanghai were home to British merchants for decades, and whose history has contributed to the rebirth of Shanghai in the twenty-first century. In nearly every city outside Europe that has a skyline today you can see a residual trace of a British presence. .

Yet when it came to its own capital city, Great Britain said no. This is even more ironic given the nature of the United Kingdom's effect on world history. The United Kingdom ignited the industrial and commercial revolutions that launched civilization on its trajectory toward capitalism. No other country was more influential in changing how we produce our goods and how we organize and finance our economic activity.

Alongside, and perhaps because of its embrace of the market system, factory production, and coal-based energy, stood Britain's imperial ambition to conquer lands and create colonies to feed its voracious appetite for luxuries, commodities, and wealth. The British Empire rose to its glory based on the creed "If you won't trade with us, we will force you to do so." By 1850, London was the center of a new world order and was the driver of an economic revolution that was as revolutionary as the Neolithic Revolution. And yet when it came to the real estate arm of capitalism—the skyscraper—London took a pass.

The question is why? A look at the facts would suggest that the Imperial City had more to lose than gain by limiting its building heights. If the Yankee spirit in New York showed anything, it was that great cities went to great heights. London circa 1880 was larger, wealthier, and busier than Gotham, and if any place should have been on the vanguard of skyscraper construction, it should have been London.

Comparing the two cities reveals striking similarities. Both had bustling central business districts with a tight core of finance and insurance companies providing money to thousands of businesses regionally and globally. Both were investing heavily in rapid transit. London started building its rail system in the 1840s, and by 1880 its trains were moving thousands of people into and out of the central city each workday. New

York had elevated railways from the 1870s and the subway beginning in 1904.

By the end of the nineteenth century, London was the world's most populous city with over 6 million people, representing one out of five English residents. In 1898, the City of Greater New York, newly formed by the merger of the five boroughs into one metropolis, contained about half that population. In addition, London was a capital city in a way that New York was not—housing the nation's governmental operations, both domestic and imperial, as well as its financial and business concerns.

Then there was the supply side. The United Kingdom pioneered the use of iron framing in the early nineteenth century and had expertise in both iron and steel construction. Though the United Kingdom started to lose its competitive position to the United States in terms of steel manufacturing it was not far behind.

True, London had a much longer and deep-seated history of architectural conservatism. The fight for the design of the new Parliament building after it burned in 1834 and other buildings like the Foreign Services Offices building (1868) illustrate that the division among the architectural community was between Gothic and "classical" (e.g., Renaissance) and that any building worth its salt was one or the other. The idea of building in a new form like that of the Chicago School— where simplicity of design ruled the day—was unthinkable.

But even New York builders before the 1920s were relatively conservative in their architectural outlook. The city's skyscrapers tended to be classical in proportion, with base, shaft, and capitol modeled after ancient Greek or Roman columns. The earliest skyscrapers were basically historical buildings but larger and taller. The 1870 Equitable Life Assurance Society Building was French Renaissance style. The 1913 Woolworth Building was a Gothic "cathedral of commerce." The 1908 Singer Tower was a French Second Empire building with a goose-necked Second Empire tower shooting out of the mansard roof. The 1909 MetLife Tower was an expanded version of St. Mark's Campanile in Venice. So even if London was architecturally conservative, surely it could have applied that conservatism when going tall. An enterprising developer could have built an office version of the Big Ben clock tower, itself over 300 feet (94 m) high.

In short, everything was in place for a London Skyscraper Revolution. The British were more than capable of building in steel and iron. Landlords and tenants had already embraced elevators and electrification. Businesses wanted their buildings as statements to signal and advertise their seriousness and trustworthiness. The city had rail lines funneling into the center thousands upon thousands of new office workers, putting tremendous pressure on land values. The middling classes had nosed their way past aristocratic society to take control of the nation's economic engine. The victory of the capitalists should have also meant the victory of the skyscraper. And yet the London Skyscraper Revolution fizzled before it even started. On the surface, it makes no sense.

But the bottom line is the bottom line. If there was an economic demand, London would have had no shortage of "disrupters" to push their way into the real estate crowd. They never felt compelled to do so because the demand for tall buildings was never quite there in the way it was in New York or Chicago. London didn't get skyscrapers because it did not need them more than it didn't want them. The architectural purists were able to hold sway because the counterforces were simply not as numerous or burning with such great urgency. London's policy created hurdles by capping building heights, but the forces to topple those vertical "ceilings" were never so great as to muster a willing army of skyscraper revolutionaries.

QUEEN ANNE'S MANSIONS

London folklore has it that the proverbial straw (or brick?) that broke the camel's back and led to height restrictions was Queen Anne's Mansions, a complex of tall apartment buildings erected from 1873 to 1890. These buildings show that a skyscraper "disrupter" appeared relatively early in London's history and around the same time as New York developers were erecting their first apartment buildings.

The Victorian period saw the rise of so-called mansion flats. Most were five or six stories and formed semicontinuous street frontages. They were full-service apartment buildings catering to the middle and upper classes who wanted to live near the action. But then one building rose much higher than the rest and did not "play nice"—Queen Anne's Mansions, which became a lightning rod for all the fears about tall buildings. The first stage of the project was a ten-story, 116-foot high-rise situated between Victoria Street and St. James's Park in Westminster, completed in 1875.

The developer Henry Hankey was a merchant and City banker, who worked the loopholes and did what he could to circumvent the law and operate in the gray areas. Under the 1855 Building Act, new buildings exceeding one hundred feet required consent from the Metropolitan Board of Works (MBW), but this was merely to confirm adherence to safety regulations. Hankey's application does not show up in the files of the MBW until November 1875, by which time, geography professor Richard Dennis says, "the first part of the building was almost finished: so it appears that Hankey did not seek (and receive) the Board's approval until his building was already 100 feet high."

Once completed, the venture was profitable, and in February 1877 Hankey applied to the MBW for a south wing extension along York Street (now Petty France). Similarly, he started this section before submitting his application because he argued that it was referred to in the first application, as the new wing was merely "an additional exit in case of fire."

The fear of fire was ever present. The Brook's Wharf fire at Queenhithe Dock along the Thames River in the City of London in June 1876 demonstrated that the highest the fire department could take their ladders was five stories, and if Queen Anne's Mansions could not be protected, the extension should not be built. As Dennis recounts, "Three times Hankey submitted his plans, and three times the MBW rejected them." Each iteration attempted to get more fireproof measures. Eventually, after a hearing in Westminster Magistrates' Court, Hankey was allowed to continue with his twelve-story tower. To guard against fire, New York–style water tanks were placed on the roof.

The fight to build another extension was perhaps more ferocious than what preceded it. A newly formed Queen Anne and Garden Company Limited applied to the MBW for a new building that would rise 160 feet (49 m) and thirteen stories. But the neighbors were not happy. James Knowles, a renowned architect and journal editor, who lived next door to the mansions, complained to the MBW:

> This vast mass or cliff . . . would totally shut out sun and air from my own house and from the whole south side of the Guards' Chapel adjoining. It would convert York Street into a mere narrow cleft or gloomy chasm. . . . [T]he awfulness of the fate of hundreds who might be caught by a conflagration in such a totally inacceptible [sic] tower of Babel as is now proposed, to say nothing of the serious risks to the whole neighborhood which such a Babel, if on fire, would produce.

Eventually, the case was fought in court, and after negotiations with neighbors and chicanery on the part of the builder, the extension was completed. In the end, the MBW and London officials decided that the best they could do was lose the battle in hopes of winning the war. The successor government to the MBW, the London County Council, in 1890 applied to the national government for legislation restricting new buildings to ninety feet, plus roof space. This was further reduced to eighty feet (plus two attic stories) when the law was passed in 1894.

It's worth noting that part of the reason the battle between the two sides was so fierce is that it became a fight between the "insiders" and the "outsiders." Hankey and the subsequent owners represented those

potential renters who paid handsomely to be inside against officials and
neighbors who were concerned about the negative spillovers. If there
was no demand, there would have been no battle.

Despite the disdain, the units were popular. Records from 1901
indicate that renters included seven members of Parliament, a count-
ess, five "Sirs," one "Lady," one bishop, two reverends, a general, two
majors, three colonels, and one lieutenant. The Irish writer Isabella
Augusta, Lady Gregory, along with the composer Sir Edward Elgar and
the explorer Sir Harry Johnson also rented space in the complex. Other
developers constructing their own versions went so far as to advertise their
mansion flats were like those "successfully carried out by Mr Hankey
at Queen Anne's gate."

Hackey developed his residences near Buckingham Palace, but one
would have expected to see tall office buildings rise in the City of London at the same time. Yet none appeared. Again, this is odd given the
similarities between the district and Lower Manhattan. Both were about
one square mile, both were the center of finance, both were transportation hubs, and both had access to elevator technology, plumbing, steel,
and, eventually, electricity.

Since at least the Norman invasion in 1066, the City of London had
the privilege of raising its own taxes and administering its own laws. The
City Corporation is almost a state-within-a-state, with a unique status
that makes it more like the Vatican than Southwark. But "[t]he role of
London's own Vatican, however, is not to serve God," declares geographer Maria Kaika, but rather to serve the needs of the international
financial and business communities.

By the end of the seventeenth century, the City was the commercial heart of Great Britain. The formation of the Bank of England,
the Stock Exchange, and Lloyd's underwriters helped it develop as an
international financial center. The constant wars of the Crown were

a big source of business, along with the overseas trade that emerged out of these wars. The great banking families of London, such as the Rothschilds and the Barclays, began their ascent in the eighteenth and early nineteenth centuries.

Between 1760 and 1800, the number of commercial banks in the City nearly doubled from forty to close to eighty. London was rising to overtake Amsterdam as the world's leading financial entrepôt. After the Napoleonic Wars, the City's fortunes skyrocketed. By 1873, total deposits in London banks were three times higher than in New York and nearly ten times higher than in Paris. By 1913, the London Stock Exchange accounted for half the world's overseas investment and handled a third of all the world's quoted securities. The decades before World War I were truly the City's Golden Age.

When we look at the history of the City, three facts reveal themselves. First, as banking, finance, and insurance became vital, and then later the joint stock company, these firms increasingly built offices for their needs. The demand for office space gave rise to real estate firms, which built on spec, constructing offices to let. Second, architecture was a tool for banks and corporations to convey valuable information. While architecture looked to the past for inspiration, there was still a strong desire for companies to signal their trustworthiness and profitability. Third, there was, every so often, the rise of a disrupter who would overturn the conventional ways of doing things. The disrupter was not afraid to try something new and embraced it for the pleasure and pride of recognizing an untapped need.

And the City's real estate market showed all the signs of operating according to the laws of supply and demand. As office vacancy rates fell, a building boom would follow, which then increased vacancy. As the new space was absorbed and vacancies fell, office construction would renew itself. This constant renewal for office space gave rise to five building cycles between 1866 and 1914. An initial burst peaked in 1875, followed by a cooling off and then renewed building, with a peak in 1886.

Other peaks occurred in 1895, 1901, and 1908. These construction waves were given a technological boost from electricity—the electrification of the underground railways and trolleys as well as electric lighting and electric-powered elevators. The 1901 peak was particularly high, and if at any time the demand to go tall was present, it would certainly have been at the turn of the twentieth century when America was already a decade into constructing skyscrapers.

As urban economist Richard Barras writes, "Overall, it has been estimated that the cumulative impact of successive waves of Victorian and Edwardian building between 1855 and 1905 was the demolition and reconstruction of as much as 80% of the building stock in the City, increasing its floorspace area by at least 50%."

The location of City office buildings by period shows a clear clustering pattern. There was a concentration of traditional banking and insurance buildings in the core of the City, close to the Bank of England. A second cluster was in the southwest corner in the Temple neighborhood where the legal profession had located in the Inns of Court since medieval days. The average building size of the City office building increased each cycle, to 18,000 square feet in the late nineteenth century and then to 30,500 after the turn of the twentieth century. If New York's experience provided any lesson, it was that successful companies would engage in height competition for the advertising effect.

So all these facts make one wonder, why no skyscrapers?

When you ask a London historian, you'll get the typical answer: The gentleman bankers of the day would not deign to build like upstart Yankees. Rather, London was an imperial city and looked to Paris or Vienna as its architectural comparators. Fair enough. European cities were European cities with their millennial-long histories and cultures.

But when we compare the City to Lower Manhattan, we can see some stark differences that show London did not face the same economic pressures as New York. In short, London had something that New York did not: land and space. London's geography, north of the Thames, is nearly a broad featureless plane, which is conducive to economic expansion from the center outward.

The Square Mile—the nickname for the City—really was a full square mile and could grow beyond its borders into Westminster, Holborn, and other adjacent boroughs. Government offices were concentrated in their own zone of Westminster. Port activity, which traditionally took place along the Thames on docks in the City, left for the Isle of Dogs after the turn of the nineteenth century, and the City lost its warehouses that ate into otherwise valuable real estate.

In parallel to the growth in economic activity was the concomitant fall in the resident population. In 1851, the City's population was 133,000. Then came the railroads and the population left in droves, so that by 1881, the population was down to 59,000. All those who left created thousands of square feet of available space for the growing office sector.

Manhattan's situation, on the other hand, was the opposite. While Lower Manhattan south of City Hall is about one square mile, it's a peninsula, with its business district like an island, hemmed by water and other activities. Thus, the land that was competitive for business and finance was only about half of that. Corporations could not expand north because of the dense tenements and factories there, while the port remained in Lower Manhattan until after World War II and thus shipping concerns competed for space. Similarly, municipal offices did not have their own quarter but were also part of the landscape. The rise of Midtown after the turn of the twentieth century shows that Downtown was too small.

To get evidence for London's lack of demand, we can look at the patterns of construction and office rents. Data on London's office market before World War I shows something very interesting. Developers were able to construct new buildings as rents rose and vacancies fell in a way that did not require them to build tall. In essence, London did not get skyscrapers because there was no economic urgency to build them.

In the forty-five-year period, from 1870 to 1914, the time when America developed its taste—or need—for tall buildings, the City added nearly 3.8 million square feet of space (353,032 m²). This was just new construction and excluded additional space that was added from the conversion of other buildings to commercial use or was built before 1870. In fact, from at least 1875 onward, many city office buildings added hydraulic elevators to take people to the third, fourth, or fifth floors, which were previously underutilized due to the reluctance of people to climb stairs.

Research by two economists, Professor Steven Devaney and the now-deceased Professor Ralph Turvey, have studied office rents during this period. Devaney's inflation-adjusted index shows that rents from the period between 1867 and 1914 grew at an average annual rate of 0.6 percent.

Turvey's estimate shows the demand for office space grew at around 3.4–4 percent per year, while Barras's estimates also show that office stock grew at about 4 percent per year. When you put the statistics together, we can see that the London office construction was able to keep up with demand, so much so that over the forty-five-year period inflation-adjusted office rents barely budged. Had demand been unable to keep up with supply, the pressures to go tall would have been like a juggernaut.

IN A PICKLE

For the rest of the twentieth century, the City of London would remain a low-rise quarter, with a few high-rises scattered here and there. After World War II, there was little pressure on land values and office rents thanks to the Blitz bombings and deindustrialization. There was a tall building boomlet from 1960 to 1980, but compared to New York, it was positively timid.

London's love of its historical buildings, combined with its mistakes with public housing, and the perceived failed experiments with

Modernism and Brutalism, left Londoners cold on the idea of sky-scrapers. Even today, the term "skyscraper" remains a dirty word. As one London developer told me, his firm markets their projects as "towers" instead.

But then, in 2003, the City of London completed its first skyscraper after a thirty-year hiatus—the Swiss Re Building (30 St. Mary Axe), more famously known by its nickname, the Gherkin. By the end of the twentieth century, two things began to change. First was the rise of the modern finance-based economy, which started to take off in the 1980s, as computer technology and globalization spread. In 1983, Prime Minister Margaret Thatcher pushed the deregulation of London's financial markets, which, because of its sudden and sweeping changes, is called the Big Bang. The older forces that drew manufacturers to cities were replaced by those that drew financial concerns. London rebounded, and demand for skyscrapers increased.

One megaproject helped change perceptions: Canary Wharf. In 1985, bankers proposed building a financial services center near the former West India Company Docks, about three miles east of the City. The Big Bang increased the demand for large trading floors and modern office space. The Canadian real estate firm Olympia and York was chosen to develop Canary Wharf along a similar model to that of New York's Battery Park City, which was built on landfill adjacent to the Twin Towers site.

Though it took a while—after a collapse in the office market and a long wait for a new subway line—Canary Wharf eventually became a successful hub for financial firms. The centerpiece is One Canada Square, formerly the United Kingdom's tallest skyscraper at 771 feet (235 m). The project was expanded to include residential high-rises, which today fetch tidy sums.

But Canary Wharf was a single, albeit large, project that could not fully satisfy the high-rise demand. By the mid-1990s, with rising land values, housing costs, and office rents, along with an outdated building stock and the international demand to work, live, and play in London, political officials started hearing a Greek chorus chanting "Build! Build! Build!"

The changing nature of the local and global economy altered the real estate dynamics in London, as it would in other cities such as New York and Hong Kong. Globalization meant a more mobile population, more mobile flows of huge amounts of capital, and larger and more sophisticated international firms that had to be managed from office headquarters.

The reality was that London in the twenty-first century, like its sister city New York, was fueled by brains, fun, and finance—a fact that leaders could no longer ignore. Ironically, thanks to the tourists who come to see the ancient Tower of London, the British Museum, Westminster Abbey, and St. Paul's Cathedral, London would need modern towers, like the Shard, to house them. But it would take a "civil war" to decide London's skyscraper future.

In 1986, Margaret Thatcher, as part of her anti-government, free-market program, abolished what was formerly a centralized government for London, the Greater London Council (GLC), and local government operations were devolved to the thirty-three boroughs. But, in the late 1990s, under Labour prime minister Tony Blair, the government started issuing white papers on planning, sustainability, and governmental reform. Among them, one proposed a new form of governance, the Greater London Authority (GLA), which came into existence in 2000.

For the first time, London residents directly elected a mayor, who, under the law, is required to produce a Spatial Development Strategy (SDS), which then becomes part of the London Plan, the strategic road map that sets out the economic, environmental, transport, and social framework for development. The initial plan was released in 2004 and has been updated several times since. The mayor is also responsible for ensuring that each of the thirty-three boroughs' Unitary Development

Plans (UDPs)—the boroughs' urban plans—are revised to conform to the SDS. And just as importantly, the mayor must be consulted on planning applications of "genuine strategic importance," i.e., big or tall buildings.

As it happened, London got a socialist-turned-skyscraperist as its first mayor when Ken Livingstone was elected in May 2000. Formerly known as "Red Ken" for his leftist orientation, he would become the lightning rod for the transformation of the London skyline. During his campaign, people assumed he would continue with his leftist politics. Yet once in office, he embraced the skyscraper.

Why did Red Ken convert to the skyscraper cause? The times had changed. To keep up, he felt London had to build up. As Livingston testified to a parliamentary Select Committee in 2002:

> What has happened, and this is where globalisation has transformed London, is that over the last 15 years New York and London and Tokyo emerged as the three great financial centres and my fear would be, if, say, you had a Mayor who was going to have a blanket ban on rejecting all of these buildings, they will eventually locate somewhere else in Europe. Clearly, in this third of the world, London, in this band of time zones, is the financial centre but Frankfurt, Paris and perhaps Berlin would all be quite happy to take that off us with devastating consequences—not just for London but for the whole national economy.

Livingstone was a career politician, and he knew from whence his bread was buttered. To get things done, he had to build coalitions. From early in his mayoralty, he prioritized the financial and business service sectors in his planning strategies. In turn, London's business community would work with him.

The man to create the City's new skyline was Peter Wynne Rees. He was hired in 1985 as chief planner and was instrumental in helping the district to reorient itself. As Rees told me:

There was a big change in the perception of tall buildings in London. They were not [previously] seen as particularly attractive or appropriate. Certainly, when I arrived in the mid-eighties, there was nothing you would call a "skyscraper" by U.S. standards. The changes happened . . . following the deregulation of the financial sector in 1986. U.S. banks, German banks, Chinese banks could all come into the City and trade, which hadn't been permitted previously.

The City being one square mile . . . couldn't spread outward because the surrounding municipalities were largely residential and therefore resistant to large-scale commercial development. If the City were to accommodate the large number of overseas firms and provide the square footage for their offices within the Square Mile . . . the only answer was to go upward.

In the late 1990s, I came up with a strategy of having a tight cluster of high-rise office towers in the eastern part of the Square Mile as far as possible from the protected vistas of St. Paul's Cathedral, where the prominence of the dome on the skyline was probably the most important height feature in the City.

With Livingstone now in charge, the City's skyline could rise. Livingstone convinced Londoners more broadly in no small part because of how he framed the issue. Skyscrapers were only going to be approved if they were iconic and had artistic merit. By stressing aesthetics, the debate was no longer about whether London needed tall buildings, but rather how they were going to appear. Londoners were convinced.

To solidify the role of architecture in his development agenda, Livingstone set up an Architecture and Urbanism Unit in April 2001, appointing the internationally acclaimed architect Lord Richard Rogers as his chief advisor. Getting citizens on board also required reversing the negative perceptions about mid-century tall buildings. "The problem is that architects who want to build skyward are paying for the sins of their fathers," argued Renzo Piano. "The generation of architects and builders who spent the postwar years filling the craters left by the Luftwaffe bequeathed London a dispiriting pile of ugly concrete high-rise boxes."

Livingstone's first skyscraper battle was over the new headquarters for Swiss Re, which claimed that unless its tower was approved, it would move back to the Continent, taking its jobs and investments with it. In July 2000, just two months after taking office, Livingstone urged in a letter to Deputy Prime Minister John Prescott that the building's construction should not undergo public inquiry, as it would generate delay and antagonize Swiss Re. Livingstone faced sharp criticism mostly from English Heritage, which, he claimed, was the "biggest threat to London's future since the Luftwaffe." When Prescott rejected the inquiry, Livingstone felt vindicated.

The bullet shape and diagonal gray and green glass panels make the Gherkin, designed by star architect, or starchitect, Lord Norman Foster, one of the world's most unusual skyscrapers—like a giant Fabergé egg. But it's a success story and has emboldened London's method of going tall. Even renowned British journalist Simon Jenkins, a harsh critic of the tall building mania, acknowledged its impact when he wrote:

> It won the 2004 Stirling prize [the highest award of the Royal Institute of British Architects]. It scores as most visited on London's Open House list [buildings normally closed to the public that are opened for the weekend], and was acclaimed by Condé Nast Traveler as one of the "seven wonders of the modern world." It has been on the cover of *Newsweek*, the Olympic bid and *Time Out*'s London guide. The Gherkin features in *Match Point*, *Bridget Jones* and *Basic Instinct II*, supplanting the Post Office tower in London's visual image.

From an economic perspective, it also created great value. The total land and construction costs, adjusted for inflation, were £233 million. In 2007, it was sold for £600 million, making it the world's most expensive pickle.

FROM LEFT: The Cheesegrater (2010),
the Gherkin (2003), the Walkie-Talkie (2014)

THE UNINTENDED CONSEQUENCES

But iconic architecture can generate unintended impacts, both good and bad. Like the Gherkin, most London skyscrapers get their own nicknames, be it the Shard, the Cheesegrater, or the Razor. Part of this stems from Britain's cheeky culture — every kid in the playground must get a nickname as a form of social play. But just as important is the branding. Nicknaming started by the press to demonize tall buildings but morphed into a golden marketing opportunity.

Since all tall buildings must first get planning permission, a common strategy is for developers to submit plans that are completely over-the-top. They know there will be negotiations, so the "opening bid" is always too big. Then the planners retort, "Shrink it!" And the back-and-forth continues until both sides come to an agreement.

In the case of the Gherkin, the previous building on the site, the Baltic Exchange, a large Victorian structure, had been destroyed by a terrorist bombing in 1992. The landlord, the Norwegian developer Kvaerner, commissioned Norman Foster to design a supertall called the Millennium Tower, to be as tall as the Empire State Building. But Kvaerner lost interest in the project and sold out to Swiss Re in 1998.

Foster was kept on, in part, because of his status. Swiss Re was going to need all the help it could muster to get planning permission with "extended negotiations with the City of London Corporation and English Heritage, not to mention many other bodies, including the Royal Fine Arts Commission (RFAC) and the Commission for Architecture and the Built Environment (CABE)," documents author Ken Powell.

Over the course of negotiations, Foster eventually produced a flat and squat structure. One day, one of his associates brought a model to Peter Rees, who thought it looked too much like a pumpkin, and as he recalled to me, "I looked at it and said, 'Don't you think it might look better if it was thinner and taller?' So you might say it was Foster who designed The Gherkin and it was Rees who squeezed it."

But I asked Rees how it got its nickname. "The British press," he told me, "is always very negative against anything new." They kept reporting stories about how the project was going to be a failure. And when it seemed clear that it was going forward, Rees recalled, "[t]he very last attempt by the press was to be rude about it. And some people were asking, 'Where do you put the batteries in it?' And other people were saying, 'Oh, it's an erotic gherkin.' This attempt to criticize it had the opposite effect intended because the public was starting to fall in love with its unusual shape." The shortened, less-bawdy moniker was now its new unofficial name.

The next nickname came when Lord Rogers, now deceased, was designing the Leadenhall Building. It had a sloped southern façade to prevent the blocking of the sight lines to St. Paul's and is reminiscent of Keanu Reeves in *The Matrix* ducking backward to dodge a bullet. As Rees recalled, "When I saw the first small model of this project, the triangular shape reminded me of Lord Rogers's wife, who was a chef at a fine restaurant called the River Café in London, and I could imagine her using something like that to grate the Parmesan on the pasta. So I said, it looks just like a cheesegrater. Well, it stuck."

Taking a helicopter view, Rees concludes, "Fosters, Rogers, and the all the others hated the nicknames. They thought it was making fun of their buildings. But, of course, the public loved it. And it gave identity to buildings which had a distinct character to them in their form. And it went on from there."

However cute nicknames may be, iconic buildings can have dangerous side effects. When Rafael Viñoly's thirty-eight-story "Walkie-Talkie" building opened in the City in 2013, its concave glass façade produced a "death ray" that was "wreaking havoc on London," according to one outlet. In particular, the façade was focusing the sun's rays downward. The owner of a parked Jaguar returned one afternoon to find his car melted. On sunny days, local shopkeepers stood by as their carpets went up in flames. Fortunately, no one died before the building's owners installed sun-blocking screens.

Viñoly cast the blame elsewhere, complaining to one reporter:

> One of the problems that happens in [. . . London] is the superabundance of consultants and sub consultants that dilute the responsibility of the designers until you don't know where you are. . . . Architects aren't architects anymore. You need consultants for everything. In this country there's a specialist to tell you if something reflects. It's the fault of the architectural discipline which has cast itself into a completely secondary thing.

The Walkie-Talkie is also hated by the architectural community and the press. In 2015, it was awarded the "Carbuncle Cup" by *Building Design* magazine as the worst building of the year. As hyperbolically reported in *The Guardian*:

Responsible for a catalogue of catastrophes, it is hard to imagine a build-ing causing more damage if it tried. It stands at 20 Fenchurch Street, way outside the city's planned "cluster" of high-rise towers, on a site never intended for a tall building. It looms thuggishly over its low-rise neighbors like a broad-shouldered banker in a cheap pinstriped suit. And it gets fatter as it rises, to make bigger floors at the more lucrative upper levels, forming a literal diagram of greed.

And "forcing" icons on the public has political and economic conse-quences. When star or "trophy" architects, such as Viñoly, Gehry, and Piano, are hired by private developers in New York City or Chicago, it's done because they add value to the building itself—for the internal occupants—and to a lesser degree to provide something for the civic realm. Of course, developers can use their buildings to enhance their reputations, but it's their own prerogative. In the United States starchitects are a form of charity, but in London they are tithes.

Or rather, as two London School of Economics (LSE) economists, Paul C. Cheshire and Gerard H. Dericks, see it, the hiring of starchitects is a form of rent seeking—the making of a payment or the expenditure of resources solely to get access to a valuable "prize." In fact, they found that in Chicago only 3 percent of offices were designed by trophy architects. In Brussels, none were. But in London, the share is about one-quarter.

Since planners are the gatekeepers, they restrict office supply, helping to promote excessively high office rents in London, which are nearly the highest in the world. Developers know that *if* they can enter the market with a new office building, they can earn substantial profits. The way to do this is to pay to play. As Cheshire and Dericks argue:

> Because in London every proposed new office block requires a political decision, getting permission is transformed into a game: an expensive game. Would-be developers can use all their wiles to persuade local and national politicians that their project is desirable. . . . The scarcity of

quality office space creates incentives to take risks and throw resources
at finding ways to secure permission for buildings that would ordinarily
be turned down.

Despite the extra costs and fees associated with these "signature"
buildings—often as high as an additional 15 percent—they are worth it.
Cheshire and Dericks conclude that, on average, a starchitect's "reputation gets an extra 14 floors on a given site. So even factoring in the extra
visible costs, a [starchitect] boosts the value of a typical site in central
London by 152%, apparently capturing 'economic rents' of £148 million."
And in that way, London's expensive and iconic skyscraper minuet
continues apace, with death rays and erotic gherkins as just part of the
normal course of business.

CHAPTER 5

Hong Kong

From Barren Rock to World's Densest City

The Pearl Tower featured in the 2018 movie *Skyscraper*.

THE PEARL

In 2018, Hong Kong celebrated the opening of its newest skyscraper, The Pearl. At 240 stories (3,500 feet, 1.07 km), it is the world's tallest building, beating the former record holder, the Burj Khalifa, by 755 feet (230 m), and is triple the height of the Empire State Building.

We typically assume that those with outsized egos extrude their skyscrapers to go taller and taller; this building does not refute that theory. A new-money tech titan/"visionary entrepreneur" Zhao Long Ji channeled his resources into architecture for his own glory and as a monument to his home city. At a total cost of $6.5 billion—it's the ultimate tree of money and power. As one BBC reporter stressed on opening day, "Mankind has been consumed by one singular desire—to touch the sky." The Pearl casts a shadow on Heaven's door.

No such structure, of course, would be complete without a complement of symbols. At the very top is the world's largest pearl—a ten-story orb as observation deck—being held aloft by "fingers" of steel. High-res cameras on the inside and out allow the walls and floors to disappear virtually, producing the feeling that you are an eagle flying over modern Hong Kong.

Rising on reclaimed land on the southern tip of Kowloon Peninsula in Tsim Sha Tsui, directly across from Central, the skyscraper demonstrates Asia's "crazy richness." Not content to produce a stolid glass box, Zhao hired a starchitect to give it a twisting form, like an old oak tree in an ancient forest.

The building is a showcase of seemingly impossible futuristic technology. The elevators run on magnetic levitation and require no cables. The structure has a negative CO_2 footprint. The outer skin is made of solar panels, and from floors 200 to 230 giant wind turbines generate enough energy to power the entire structure.

Inside are all the luxuries of a modern skyscraper: world-class shopping and dining in its six-story mall, a three-star Michelin-rated restaurant with rotating views of Hong Kong, an Olympic-sized swimming pool, three gyms with basketball courts, a driving range, a movie theater, and a hotel. In the middle is a spacious botanical garden.

Though the construction proceeded relatively smoothly, The Pearl's official opening was mired in chaos. Once completed, the bottom half was humming with life. However, the top part—the residential zone— remained unoccupied. Zhao's insurance company, Hawthorne/Stone, refused to insure the apartments without a full review of the building's fire and safety features. As a result, Zhao hired an American building security expert, Will Sawyer, to provide an unbiased analysis.

As Sawyer was ready to finalize his report, however, the building went up in flames. All of Hong Kong was agape as images flashed across LED screens throughout the city. Later, when the dust settled, news reports indicated that members of an international crime syndicate lit The Pearl on fire because Zhao stole money from them. It was further revealed that he, in fact, stole back the "protection money" that they extracted from him. To punish Zhao, the syndicate turned The Pearl into a monstrous candle.

Unbeknownst to the gangsters, however, Will Sawyer's wife and two children were trapped inside. Sawyer, a former FBI hostage rescue agent, climbed a fifty-story crane and jumped into the building in an astonishing rescue attempt, while helicopter camera crews recorded it. Using the best military training the FBI could provide, Will, along with Zhao, defeated the criminals and saved the building and his family. And Hong Kong lived happily ever after.

This astounding tale about the world's tallest building, however, never happened. It is a Hollywood fiction—an action movie called *Skyscraper*, starring Dwayne "The Rock" Johnson. When released in 2018, *Skyscraper* had a worldwide box office gross of $305 million against its production budget of $125 million, a hearty return on investment, which was likely 4 percent of the cost of an actual Pearl skyscraper.

A popular criticism is that the movie was a reboot of the 1974 film *The Towering Inferno* (with a twist of *Die Hard* thrown in for good measure). That Hollywood blockbuster was chockablock with A-listers for the era. The movie features Paul Newman playing the free-spirited, but honest, architect, Doug Roberts, who designed the world's tallest building in San Francisco for a tycoon, named Jim Duncan, played by the aging William Holden. This skyscraper—called the Glass Tower—was 138 stories (515 m) (pretty shrimpy nowadays) and taller than the Sears Tower by 236 feet (73 m), though it seems to have a striking similarity.

Roberts has wanderlust and goes off on far-flung travels while the building is being erected. When he returns, he realizes that Duncan's son-in-law, overseeing the construction, cut corners on the wiring to keep under budget. On opening night, during a gala reception on the top-floor restaurant for San Francisco's most prominent residents, the building ignites and must be evacuated.

The film then morphs into *The Poseidon Adventure* in the sky, though, in this case, fire marshal Michael O'Halloran (played by Steve McQueen) leads the rescue effort (along with a firefighter played by O. J. Simpson). One by one, the occupants risk their lives to escape. Some die horrible deaths—they fall a hundred stories or get fried in an explosion. Others get lucky and rescue themselves by their derring-do. Finally, the fire is put out and we are left to wonder why any developer would be so crazy to build such a tower.

Although the Glass Tower was in San Francisco, the writer of *Skyscraper*, Rawson Marshall Thurber, intended for The Pearl to be in Shanghai, to represent the rise of China's wealth. But the Chinese government objected because of the film's gun-toting mobsters. Officially, at any rate, in Communist China, organized crime does not exist in twenty-first-century Shanghai. Gangsters not only suggest that China is violent but are also a remnant of Western imperialism.

The crew then searched for a new location and was ready to decide on Macao, but, for all its libertine and laissez-faire history, the island is not known for its skyscrapers. Thurber made a site visit expecting to see the Chinese Las Vegas but was disappointed in what to him was "more like the Reno of China."

In the end, Hong Kong, now a Special Administrative Region of the People's Republic of China, with its background in freebooting and criminal gangs, was justifiable. Ironically, flying the cast and crew there would have busted the budget; as a result, most of the film was shot in Vancouver or Hongcouver as it's sometimes called, given its large Chinese expat population.

Both *Inferno* and *Skyscraper* succeed by playing to our fear of heights and our belief that we should not tempt fate—the hubris of building "too tall" and the deserved punishment. The films also feed into the perception that the superrich are inherently corrupt and hurt society by their greed. The developer's spoiled son-in-law cuts corners so as not to be ripped off by the contractors. Zhao pays a syndicate extortion money, so criminals don't shut down his worksite. He then turns the tables on them by keeping block-chain "bread crumbs" on the trail of their laundered money so he can steal it back.

Hollywood exaggerates, of course, for the purpose of storytelling. The moviemakers take our hidden anxieties and put them out on display. Yet, when one starts to "deconstruct" The Pearl, it's rife with fictions that say more about our beliefs than reality.

Take Zhao himself. His skyscraper is his toy. But when you look at Hong Kong, the tallest buildings are built mostly by "big land," an oligopoly of real estate companies that dominate local construction. The city's first generation of developers rose to great wealth in the 1970s, building Hong Kong into a laissez-faire metropolis. And by their nature, they are a conservative bunch, who put profit before ego. They are long gamers, not risk-takers.

Hong Kong's current richest man is Li Ka-shing. He was born in Guangdong Province in 1928, and his family fled to Hong Kong in 1940 as refugees from the Sino-Japanese War. In 1950, Li founded a plastic flower factory with personal savings and funds borrowed from relatives. He eventually became the largest supplier of plastic flowers in Asia.

As his business grew, he began dabbling in real estate when he purchased a site for his factory. From there, he increased his landholdings. In 1972 his real estate development company, Cheung Kong Limited, was listed on the Hong Kong Stock Exchange.

Over the decades, through sharp investment and skilled business acumen, he rose to be Hong Kong's wealthiest citizen. His path is more that of Warren Buffett than Mark Zuckerberg, and he is typical of the skyscraper builders of Hong Kong, not Zhao Long Ji.

Next is the technology on display. Despite the movie's wishful, futuristic thinking, we are not quite there yet for the suite of technologies shown in The Pearl. We are still in a world where elevators are moved up and down by cables. In 2019, I had a chance to chat with Michael Cesarz, the then-CEO of MULTI, the group at TK (formerly ThyssenKrupp) Elevator charged with creating the world's first cableless elevator, which will run by magnetic levitation. According to Cesarz, the problem was not with the maglev technology, which is well known, given the trains that operate throughout East Asia.

Rather, the remaining issue was how to switch the direction of the cabs to move them horizontally. The plan is to have several cabs run in the same shaft to improve efficiency. But if, say, one cab is going up and the other down, one will need to move horizontally to let the other pass. When the elevator cars can seamlessly change directions, they will circulate like blood cells in arteries. Eventually, the maglev elevator will be a reality, but not yet.

As for green energy, no building can generate more than a small fraction from carbonless means. Given that tall buildings are surrounded by wind, one would think they could cheaply harvest it. This idea has motivated a handful of developers to embed turbines directly into their skyscrapers. Completed in 2010, the Strata SE1, aka the Razor, a forty-three-story residential skyscraper in London, has three turbines on the roof, making the building look like an electric razor. The turbines were expected to generate 8 percent of the building's total energy consumption.

The Bahrain World Trade Center, opened in 2008, has three turbines in between its twin towers, which were shaped to better funnel the wind. They were designed to add 3 percent to the construction cost but generate 11 to 15 percent of the towers' energy consumption.

In Guangzhou, China, the 2011 Pearl River Tower is a seventy-one-story skyscraper with turbines placed at about one-third and two-thirds up on mechanical floors. Initial studies predicted that the façade openings would accelerate the wind speed by 2.5 times, resulting in more than 8 times the power generation of a turbine located in an open field. In Houston, Texas, the Hess (Discovery) Tower, a twenty-nine-story high-rise, completed in 2010, included ten vertical-axis turbines on the roof.

But none has proved a panacea. The problem is that buildings split the wind, which generates eddies and turbulence as opposed to ideal conditions of high-speed but steady flows. And for the wind to generate sufficiently large quantities of energy to produce a satisfactory return on investment, the blades need to be quite long—much longer than anything that can be put in or on a building without destroying its economic feasibility.

At London's Strata SE1, the turbines have been turned off because the tenants complained of the humming noise emanating from the rotating blades. They never went into operation on the Hess (Discovery) Tower, after one blade fell off the roof and landed in a pickup truck. And there is little reporting on the energy production from the Bahrain towers or the Pearl River Tower, suggesting little to boast about.

Then there is the usage of the fictional Pearl, which is one-third shopping mall, one-third "playground" and hotel, and the rest apartments. This is unlike any mixed-used structure today. Shopping usually takes up five to ten floors, while above that are twenty to sixty floors of offices, and above that is reserved for hotels and luxury apartments. Many super-talls have observatories—so the pearl in The Pearl is a variation on that. Mixed uses often have better economics because they help diversify the income streams as well as maximize income by floor based on whether businesses or residents pay more at various vertical locations. Having apartments on the top floors also reduces the plant and equipment, as well as elevator space, because fewer people will be up there.

The Pearl also contains a helicopter pad at 3,000 feet (914 m), which is absurd, as there is no way a helicopter can safely operate with such unpredictable winds. Similarly, the dramatic roof scenes between the good and bad guys take place with nary a gentle breeze.

But the world's tallest fictional building raises another question—why doesn't Hong Kong have or ever had the world's tallest building? If any place was the essence of free-market capitalism it was Hong Kong. Constructing the world's tallest building—even fictional—seems reasonable given its wholehearted embrace of skyscrapers.

This absence is even more incredible when you think about the history of the world's tallest skyscrapers. In the first half of the twentieth century, the Empire State and Chrysler Buildings were products of economics peppered with ego. In the 1980s, just as Hong Kong was taking off as a global financial and business capital, it constructed two very iconic structures that might have been the world's tallest in other parts of the globe. In 1985, HSBC opened its new headquarters (44 stories) and was interested in producing an icon, hiring the young Norman Foster to make it so. But because of aviation height restrictions due to the airport, it was limited to 44 stories, though it was arguably the most expensive building in the world.

HSBC Building (1985) with V-shaped trusses on the left and
Bank of China Tower (1990) with X-shaped cross bracing on the right

The Bank of China headquarters followed five years later (1990; 72 floors, 1,205 feet). The bank was eager to express the power of rising China and hired starchitect I. M. Pei, whose father had been a director in the 1920s. Though not limited by flight-path restrictions, the bank "settled" for the tallest building in Hong Kong and the second tallest in Asia due to engineering challenges from its unusual "origami-like" shape, and restrictive FAR caps imposed by the government.

The Bank of China Tower also demonstrates that if you plan to go supertall, you'd better consider the local culture. The "battle" between these two skyscrapers unexpectedly created a feng shui controversy. Foster, eager to have his structure embraced by the Hong Kongese, hired a geomancer who gave it a thumbs-up. However, things did not go smoothly for Pei. The tower's sharp corners were seen by the feng shui masters as akin to a knife pointing at the neighboring buildings. The most severe criticism, however, was lodged at the tower's X-shaped façade. In traditional Chinese culture, an X was used to cross out the name of a person marked for execution. The building's design was seen as placing a curse on the city.

But stepping back to take a global view, we can see how other cities used record-breaking buildings to renew, advertise, and instill confidence. The Twin Towers started the process in the 1960s to revitalize an aging Lower Manhattan. Then at the dawn of the twenty-first century, Asian cities embraced the ethos: If you create a record breaker you will draw forth the magic of global recognition, foreign direct investment, and tourism.

The Petronas Towers (88 floors, 1,483 feet, 452 m), completed in 1998, sought to arc the world's gaze to Kuala Lumpur. The project was promoted and abetted by Malaysian prime minister Mahathir bin Mohamad, who viewed megaprojects as a way to not only build up the country but also demonstrate its economic success. "But supporters say the symbolism itself is worth the cost of construction," reported the *New York Times*. "The twin towers are a symbol of Asia's dynamism and growth," said Abdul Razak Baginda, executive director of the Malay-sian Strategic Research Centre. "The towers will do wonders for Asia's self-esteem and confidence, which I think is very important, and which I think at this moment are at the point of takeoff."

LEFT: Petronas Towers (1998); RIGHT: Taipei 101 (2004)

The structures were also designed to lure high-tech firms. "The Petro-nas towers have also been designated a distant spur of the Multimedia Super Corridor, Malaysia's answer to Silicon Valley," the *Times* wrote in a follow-up article. "Not surprisingly, the list of tenants in Tower 2 includes some of the biggest names in technology. . . . Microsoft occupies two floors, the 29th and 30th. . . . The towers' biggest draw, however, is not fiber optics, tax incentives or discount cappuccino." And as one tenant confided, "The best thing about working here is status. People look at you differently."

Next was Taipei 101, which opened in 2004 at 101 stories (1,667 feet, 508 m) and resulted from economics, urban boosterism, and patriotism.

The structure was promoted by Chen Shui-bian, the mayor of Taipei in the 1990s. He was eager to have a skyscraper built in a newly planned neighborhood close to City Hall. He worked with one of Taiwan's wealthiest developers to make it so. The first plans had the building only 66 stories, but then the election of Chen to the presidency drove them to increase the height. "As with other very tall buildings in Asia, the construction of this one is as much about politics and pride as commerce," the *Times* wrote. President Chen Shui-bian told the newspaper, "As the world's highest building, Taipei 101 will attract attention to Taiwan's excellence, and carve 'Taiwan first' in the minds of people around the globe."

Finally, rose the Burj Khalifa (discussed in chapter 7), which opened in 2010 at 2,717 feet (828 m) high. By constructing the world's tallest building, the Dubai government was seeking to promote its strategy of economic diversification and to move away from its dependence on oil revenue.

In this regard, where does Hong Kong fit in? It would not be a crazy venture to build the world's tallest building. Hong Kong is the densest city in the world, with astronomical land values and office rents. The city regularly creates large lots through land reclamation and has made a habit of turning the megaproject into the mundane. It has more tall buildings than any other city on planet Earth, and if there's one key fact it's that more means taller.

There's a very tight correlation between the number of skyscrapers a city has and the height of its tallest building, which also strongly suggests that cities' tallest buildings typically are economically rational, since counts and heights are two sides of the same coin. We can, in fact, predict how high a city's tallest building "should be" from its skyscraper count. If we compare two cities, one with 10 percent more skyscrapers than the other, we'd expect its tallest building to be 1.6 percent higher.

But since the correlation is not perfect, we can see which cities deviate from the trend to measure which cities have the "too tallest" buildings given their total skyscraper counts. In first place is Mecca, with its Makkah Royal Clock Tower (2012; 1,972 feet, 601 m). Next is St. Petersburg in Russia with its Lakhta Center tower (2019; 1,516 feet, 462 m), and in third—not first—place is Dubai with its Burj Khalifa. Other high-ranked cities include lower-tier Chinese cities, such as Jiang-yin, Zhenjiang, and Yinchuan. We will return to China in the next chapter, but suffice it to say that local officials there use tall buildings to draw attention to themselves and their cities.

Considering how many skyscrapers Hong Kong has, it would be "justified," from a statistical point of view, in having or having had the world's tallest building. Yet it does not. Hong Kong is dense, but not excessively tall. We can see the city's restraint with its most recent supertall, the International Commerce Centre (ICC). At 1,588 feet (484 m, 108 stories, 2,950,000 ft²), the ICC is almost half as tall as the Burj Khalifa (3,331,140 ft²) and well below the 530-meter mark that would put it into the top ten (the ICC is on the far right of The Pearl rendering on page 113). The story of the ICC shows how even in the supertall realm, zoning and practical considerations dominate.

The structure was designed by the New York–based firm Kohn Ped-erson Fox (KPF) for Sun Hung Kai (SHK) Properties, one of Hong Kong's big four real estate developers, with the ambition of making it a "vertical Wall Street" and producing an additional business hub across from Central. It contains 2.5 million square feet (232, 258 m²) of office space, mostly for banks and financial firms. On floor 100 is the observatory and above that is a Ritz-Carlton hotel.

In 1989, the Hong Kong government decided to shut down the old and congested Kai Tak Airport in East Kowloon, where jets flew so close to apartment buildings that residents could watch them land from their kitchen windows. In its place, the City built a new one in Chek Lap Kok on Lantau Island. With the airport—and height restrictions—out of the way, the government created 99 acres (40 hectares) of new land through reclamation on the western edge of Kowloon. The mixed-used master-planned neighborhood includes a transportation hub and the West Kowloon cultural quarter with museums and performing arts spaces.

The ICC site is owned by Hong Kong's transit company, Mass Transit Railway Corporation Limited (MTRCL), which auctioned it off to the winning bidder, SHK Properties, to create the skyscraper above the rail hub. In Hong Kong, skyscrapers and rail transit are two sides of the same coin. This is, in part, because the government cheaply sells the land along the subway lines to the MTRCL, which uses its real estate profits to fund the rail system.

The ICC is a ten-minute walk to Kowloon's Tsim Sha Tsui neighborhood, a five-minute subway ride to Central, a twenty-minute subway ride to Hong Kong International Airport, and a thirty-minute ride to Shenzhen on the Express Rail Link. All the lines feeding into the station make it a "super transport node."

And why didn't the ICC become the world's tallest building? It would have made perfect sense: a huge lot, a massive transportation hub, and a great location. But when the master plan for the Union Square neighborhood within the West Kowloon site was approved by the government, it had fixed FARs and limits on total floor area. Officials had no interest in abetting the quest for record breakers—they laid out something that would function well within Hong Kong's economic and social objectives.

The original skyscraper rendering issued by the MTRCL to showcase its vision for the neighborhood had a building coming in at 1,919 feet (585 m) and with a long spire, which would have placed it as the fifth tallest in the world. However, SHK decided to use its maximum allowable floor area to widen its floor plates rather than go taller, and it eliminated the spire. Though the ICC is still the tallest building in Hong Kong, SHK chose a more practical and profit-maximizing tower that neither was a record breaker nor had funky architecture. "You can do any shape, but it has to be a square," the developer told KPF.

But why did Hong Kong develop such an attitude? For this, we need to go back to the beginning.

FROM GETTING HIGH TO GOING HIGH

On January 25, 1841, a wooden navy vessel pulls in at what is today Victoria Harbour, a calm stretch of sea between the island of Hong Kong and the Chinese mainland. The crew disembarks and wanders around the shores.

They find little to fear—some fishermen here and a sleepy hamlet over there—and the next day, the naval commander of the British expeditionary force, Gordon Bremer, plants the Union Jack. The Island of Hong Kong is now the official property of Her Royal Majesty, Victoria, Queen of the United Kingdom of Great Britain and Ireland.

When the monarch ascended the throne in 1837, Great Britain was in the process of becoming the largest empire—in terms of land and population—the world had ever seen. Able to command technology never available to Alexander the Great, Caesar Augustus, or Genghis Khan, the queen was the figurehead atop a vast trading network protected by an efficient and ruthless navy.

Starting in the mid-1600s, British ships arrived in China and shouted to anyone who could hear, "Tallyho! We are the British and we've come to trade!" The Chinese leaders, while not pleased, tolerated their presence, as long as the barbarians operated under the arrangements they created, known as the Canton (or Cohong) System.

International trade was handled through a group of authorized Chinese merchant houses (*cohongs*). Western merchants could operate in Canton (Guangzhou), but only from October to March, and they were confined to manufactories rented from the Chinese merchants or hongs. While traders complained of the inconvenience, they could reap substantial profits from silk, porcelain, and tea exports back to the motherland.

From the start, however, there were fundamental clashes between Western and Eastern civilizations. The Chinese thought they were superior, and this notion was justified by millennia of imperial rule. Though dynasties came and went and the occasional civil war disrupted the peace, the story of China was one of nearly two thousand years as a nation-state.

For decades, the balance of trade favored China, as the British had little to offer. But as the British Empire grew bigger, richer, and more technologically sophisticated, it began making demands for territory and mercantile autonomy. And the British finally found a product that could swing the balance in their favor: opium. Poppies grew well in the Indian subcontinent, where they were processed into the drug for export.

The rapid rise in addictions caused Chinese officials to declare opium contraband. Though the British government and East India Company were reluctant to escalate the situation, the Canton traders did what they could to agitate for loosening the trade yokes. They pushed for the United Kingdom to take Hong Kong, which provided a deep-water harbor sheltered from typhoons and was easily accessible from both China and the open sea, and from where they could conduct their business without restraint.

The First Opium War (1839–1842) broke out between the two nations in the autumn of 1839. "Although he would go down in history for later dismissing Hong Kong as little more than 'a barren island with hardly a house upon it,'" historian John M. Carroll writes, "Foreign Secretary Lord Palmerston declared his intention to seize Hong Kong."

When the British took possession, there was a debate about what to do with it. Until matters were finally formalized by the Treaty of Nanking (Nanjing) in 1842, the island's status was unclear. Some back home thought it should be developed for commercial purposes, while others thought it should simply be a military base.

Nonetheless, the island was now the property of the British government, and, like that, it had a valuable resource. Traders engaged in fierce competition to buy the choicest lots. But uncertainty about the colony's future made officials think twice about selling off land to the highest bidder. Officially, from April 1843 onward, the governor of Hong Kong was going to sell land *leases*, rather than freehold land. For a fee, the lease owner had the right to occupy and use the land for a specified period, generally seventy-five or ninety-nine years. And in one decision, Hong Kong and world history were—unwittingly—changed forever.

Over time, the leasehold system turned Hong Kong into Hong Kong—an unusual mix of laissez-faire capitalism and tight government controls over land and housing. To this day, about 20 to 30 percent of the Hong Kong government's revenues comes from land-lease sales or fees. This stream allows it to keep other taxes proportionately lower and helps maintain Hong Kong's competitiveness. "Land for the government is like oil for Saudi Arabia," remarked one Hong Kong resident I spoke with.

Land leasing in England was an old practice. The Crown Estates, the corporation that oversees the monarch's properties, dates to the time of George III and still generates hundreds of millions of pounds sterling for the government. Much of London's West End, for example, was developed through land leasing by aristocrats. They would first create squares on their holdings and then issue ground leases surrounding them to developers who would build town houses for the well-to-do. In this way, wealthy landlords could control the development next to their city mansions. Grosvenor Square, created in the early eighteenth century by the Duke of Westminster, is a case in point.

In New York City, during its colonial days, the Crown deeded large lots to Trinity Church. Unlike their landlord counterparts in London, Trinity Church sold ground leases to developers of all stripes, many of whom proceeded to build low-quality tenements. In the nineteenth century, Trinity Church developed a reputation as a slumlord, earning ground rents off their impoverished Irish tenants.

Despite a concern back in England that Hong Kong would never amount to much, the harbor city eventually found its way.

Industrialization, investments in global infrastructure, such as the Suez
Canal (1869) and the Panama Canal (1904), and the laying of seabed
cables after 1865, put Hong Kong in a favorable position. The colony
grew into an entrepôt, with the mainland as a key source of trade. By
1900, about 40 percent of Hong Kong's imports and exports were with
China.

Light industry began to emerge at the end of the nineteenth century,
but the outbreak of war between China and Japan in 1937 was a big
boost. Mainland enterprises fled to Hong Kong, bringing large infusions
of financial, physical, and human capital. Between 1936 and 1941, the
volume of Hong Kong's industrial activity grew from 3 to 12 percent of
total exports. In December 1941, Japan, however, invaded the colony,
and its economy ground to a halt.

With the defeat of Japan and the return of British control after the
war, economic growth renewed itself. Crucial was the decision for the
United Kingdom to officially recognize the People's Republic of China
(PRC), which allowed for continued trade. During the 1950s, Hong
Kong's industrial sector took off as more capital and workers flowed into
the colony, which specialized in feeding the world's growing appetite for
consumer products, such as textiles and clothing, plastics, electronics,
and toys. But the rise of the other Asian Tigers and China's reforms
starting in 1978 eroded the colony's manufacturing prowess.

Hong Kong's relatively laissez-faire business climate, however,
allowed it to adapt to a changing global economy. Like London and
New York, it began to diversify into the growing "tertiary" sector of
financial services and global headquarters. The number of registered
businesses rose from 16,507 in 1970 to 45,025 in 1980, with employment
rising from 549,000 to 907,000. Unlike New York and London in the
1970s, Hong Kong never lost its population as it managed to restructure
without widescale unemployment.

And yet, despite its success as a global commercial hub, Hong Kong
doesn't boast or brag about its skyscrapers. After World War II, the city's

planners methodically embraced density and tall buildings with nary a peep. We can call Hong Kong the Mushroom City, with its mycelial network of skyscrapers bursting up from the ground and a "root system" of mass transit, pedestrian walkways, escalators, and sky bridges.

British planners imported "Town Planning" concepts from the United Kingdom, which favored greenbelts and decentralization, and they adopted FAR caps from New York City. However, British planning philosophy, which saw density as an unmitigated evil, clashed head-on with realities on the ground. Planners could not, and would not, lead with the kind of visionary thinking or dogmatic approaches that had swept across the Western world after World War II. But officials could use their land-lease power to establish a detailed planning framework, along with strict FAR limits and other zoning regulations to control and organize the colony.

Since Hong Kong was an economic venture—with little funding from Parliament—planners focused their energies on one thing and one thing alone: making Hong Kong work for the profit-seeking business community, and they would not abet crazy pie-in-the-sky real estate ventures. The resultant urbanism was a blend like nothing ever seen before. Such a thing was "accidental" in that no one set out to design it from scratch, yet in the twenty-first century its formula is being replicated (or simulated) the world over.

As it happened, the skyscraper in Hong Kong was housing led—skyscrapers for everyone, not just the rich. And perhaps this made all the difference. Unlike other skyscraper cities, currently, 90 percent of its tall buildings are residential. Hong Kong planners learned after World War II that apartment living could work for the masses and that they needed to provide public housing, social services, and a vast transit network to make sure the colony had a ready workforce.

While Hong Kong public housing has generated some unintended problems (discussed in chapter 9) it has proved an enduring success. Residents gladly accepted such housing because it was built at the right time, in the right location, and for the right price. Hong Kong's experience is opposite that of the United States. There reformers wanted to clear the slums and provide open space and low-density buildings instead, while politicians wanted high-density housing only for the very poor (so as not to upset middle-class voters who believed cheap housing for other middle-class citizens was unfair). In the end, the comprise created new slums, unhappy residents, and a fear of building heights.

In 1961, Jane Jacobs in her classic book, *The Death and Life of Great American Cities*, showed how Americans got the whole thing in reverse. Instead of fearing naturally occurring density and trying to surgically remove it, she argued, density should be embraced. Cities work not despite density but because of it. And city planners should not try to engineer perfection because the quest for utopia transformed American cities into dystopia.

A 1961 report of Hong Kong found that some neighborhoods had densities that would have made the typical Modernist American planner retch with disgust but were otherwise sound and healthy. It certainly negated the idea that density, in and of itself, was the ruin of the lower classes. Current density statistics are equally astounding. Across neighborhoods, 400 people per acre (1,000 people per hectare) is ordinary, while on some blocks 1,619 per acre (4,000 per hectare) is obtained.

But of course, Hong Kong is unique. Most people in the world—particularly in the United States—want freedom from their neighbors. They want a little space of their own where they can grill beef in their backyards, luxuriate in privacy to walk around in their pajamas, and have separate zones for each element of their domestic lives—a *living* room, a *dining* room, a *bed*room, a *car* room (aka a garage). Not to mention the green monocultured lawns that are so prized in American society. So, part of the story of Hong Kong is that its residents have very different perceptions of, and relationships with, dense living and urban space more broadly.

Despite its international nature, the overwhelming majority of residents were from the mainland, and this meant the residents were going to have similar beliefs, experiences, and perceptions to their kinfolk back home. There dense agricultural village life had been the norm for thousands of years. China had long embraced a Confucian culture that imparted a deep respect for leaders, who if they ruled benignly and with the public interest in mind were to be left alone to make the decisions. This is not to say that citizens were uninterested in democracy, only that Chinese culture had produced an implicit political contract: If you rule well, you can keep doing it. This allowed the British to confront challenges head-on.

However, the problem was always land. While Hong Kong Island— shaped like a kidney—is similar in size to Manhattan, most of it is steep. To make an analogy, imagine that Manhattan was 90 percent Central Park with the rest available for development.

Aerial photograph of Hong Kong Island,
much of which was too steep for development.

As things took off, British officials were faced with the possibility of running out of land. In response, they adopted two strategies: acquisition and reclamation. In 1898, the Conventions for the Extension of Hong Kong Territory (the Second Convention of Peking) allowed Britain to lease from China for ninety-nine years the rural areas between the Kowloon Peninsula and the Shenzhen River, along with 230 outlying islands (producing land leases from leased land). At around 365 square miles (945 km²), the acquisition was a nearly tenfold increase in the colony's landmass.

Even so, the colony still had land shortages given its rugged terrain and rural communal ownership. From time immemorial any settlement along marshy waters or where the sea floor (and beyond) revealed itself during low tide was ripe for infill. The Dutch did this in the Netherlands, where 65 percent of the country would otherwise be underwater at high tide if not for the dikes, dunes, and pumps. They repeated the process in Lower Manhattan in the seventeenth century, and the British kept going during their colonial rule. About one-third of Manhattan south of City Hall is made land. Today 6 percent of Hong Kong's land is human-made, but more telling, however, is that 35 percent of its developed territory is landfill.

The land issue, however, would fester to crisis proportions after World War II when the mainland Civil War caused major dislocations in the Pearl River Delta. With its housing stock in bad shape after the war, Hong Kong was ill prepared for the population tsunami that followed, when migrants began pouring in at a rate of 100,000 per month.

By 1950, 300,000 squatters—one-quarter of the resident population—packed into shantytowns, which "spread like an unsightly rash around the permanent buildings of Victoria and Kowloon, filling the valley floors and mounting the steep hillsides," recounts architectural historian Charlie Xue. Nearly 60,000 people were living on rooftops in makeshift shelters.

The shanties were also firetraps. On Christmas Eve of 1953, a fire broke out in the squatter area of Shek Kip Mei, in the foothills of the Kowloon Peninsula. Fifty-three thousand people lost their homes. "The government felt that the resettlement of the squatters was not possible until specific areas within the urban boundaries were freed for intensive development to accommodate the original inhabitants at a higher density, while providing roads, services and open space in the same areas," Xue describes.

When officials decided to build public housing, they did not simply demolish the slums and let the people fend for themselves; rather, as one group of Hong Kong scholars writes:

> The government's actions were cautious, mostly reacting to pressures rather than anticipating and innovating with foresight. First, it built within the existing built-up area and perpetuated the familiar cubicle-like spaces. Then it reluctantly allowed, and even facilitated, the shopping and industrial activities to occupy the places to which these naturally gravitated, and allowed the schools onto the vacant highest levels. . . . Yet, in conceding pragmatically to the pressures of the day, it created a radical new form of urbanism.

As the colony witnessed the success of its public housing, it took off. "From 1964 to 1970, the public sector on housing completed and delivered more than 25,000 housing units each year, which was 60% more than the private sector during the same period," Xue reveals. "In the 1964–65 fiscal year only, the total number of completed housing units from both public and private sectors reached 61,600. . . . This number is much higher than the annual housing production of Hong Kong in the 21st century."

Just under half of the population currently lives in some form of subsidized housing. Thirty percent of the population live in public rental housing and another 16 percent in limited-profit owned apartments. The rest are free-market units.

Hong Kong as a postwar British-Chinese global skyscraper city was fully built up around the harbor and in New Towns to the north in the four decades from 1960 to 2000. In 1970, Hong Kong had four buildings that reached 328 feet (100 m); by 1990, it had over 900, and at the turn of the millennium it had over 2,000.

When you compare Hong Kong's construction to New York's, its pace is equally astounding. New York got its first 328-foot structure in 1895, while Hong Kong's first one was in 1962. Yet by 1985 Hong Kong had more skyscrapers than New York, and now New York only has a quarter as many. And when you look at the usage, the difference is stark. Both cities have about the same number of office skyscrapers, slightly more than three hundred each. Yet for Hong Kong that is only 8 percent of all its skyscrapers, while for New York it's more than one-third.

SHENZHEN AND HONG KONG: PASSIVE-AGGRESSIVE CODEPENDENTS

On March 28, 2017, Shenzhen's tallest tower, the Ping An Finance Centre, was officially completed in the city's central business district, Futian. Like the ICC, it was designed by KPF. At 1,965 feet (599 m) and 115 floors, it rises like a stainless-steel and black glass rocket ship. Ironically, the founder and chairman of Ping An Insurance, Ma Mingzhe, wanted his icon to look like the Empire State Building. But such a symbol is that of the past; KPF gave the company something for the future.

The original design was 2,165 feet (660 m), making it taller than the Shanghai Tower, but its top was lopped off due to aviation restrictions. Ping An had to settle for having the second-tallest building in China and the fourth tallest in the world. It was the last of the Chinese supertalls (for the time being), since the central government in 2021 banned the construction of skyscrapers above 500 meters (discussed in chapter 6).

In October 2016, I was lucky enough to be part of a tour given by the building's chief engineer, Dennis C. K. Poon, of Thornton Tomasetti, while it was still being completed. It was a great feeling to go to the top for a semiprivate showing. The view, unfortunately, was poor, as it was rainy. But you could see through the gray clouds the hills of northern Hong Kong.

The Ping An Finance Centre as a showpiece for its home city also embodies the new Shenzhen–Hong Kong duality. In a figurative—and

Ping An Finance Centre (2017)

nearly literal—sense, the tower puts Hong Kong in the shade. It can
even be seen in some places on Lantau Island and in parts of the New
Territories.

In a classic example of globalization, I recently began advising a
graduate student at Rutgers who's from China. I was asking him about
himself, and he told me he had just moved from Shenzhen, where he
worked in the Ping An tower for the past three years in real estate finance.
His experience in the building, however, was less positive than mine.
"It was not so special because I feel like it was just the office, stuck in
there for like eight hours or ten hours or twelve hours or so," he told
me. Plus, during his tenure, management removed the desk partitions
to create more open floor plans. I asked him if that made him more or
less productive. "I would say more productive, but I need some time to
be alone, you know. To just be myself," he replied.

Nonetheless, the tower represents the success of Ping An Insurance,
which was born on March 21, 1988, making it the first non-state-owned
joint-stock company in China since Chairman Mao Zedong's rule.

Besides insurance, the company is engaged in banking, asset management, and financial services. From the get-go, Ping An embraced Western-style business practices, which for China was a post-Revolution revolution.

No longer just home to the migratory *lumpenproletariat* living in labor barracks assembling electronics, Shenzhen is now a modern finance and business service hub, though it doesn't get as much press coverage or awareness as Shanghai or Beijing. Shenzhen only appears in the U.S. news when there are scandals. An exposé of Apple's iPhone manufacturer, the Taiwanese-owned Foxconn, for example, revealed horrible working conditions at its plant, which at its peak a decade ago employed 450,000 people.

As documented in *The Guardian*, "In 2010, Longhua [in Shenzhen] assembly-line workers began killing themselves. Worker after worker threw themselves off the towering dorm buildings, sometimes in broad daylight, in tragic displays of desperation—and in protest at the work conditions inside. There were 18 reported suicide attempts that year alone and 14 confirmed deaths. Twenty more workers were talked down by Foxconn officials."

Despite its labor problems, in the history of cities, Shenzhen is arguably the fastest-growing city that ever existed and is on the verge of entering the pantheon of global cities. In 1980 it had a population of around 330,000 residents; today 17.5 million call it home.

During my visit to the city, I was walking one evening through a central shopping area and felt like I was in a scene from the 1976 sci-fi movie *Logan's Run*, where no one was allowed to live past the age of thirty. The Shenzhen streets were filled with young people, who, like my graduate student, arrived to achieve their ambitions.

Shenzhen's rise is so incredible because it was willed to be so by the Communist Party. It was literally created from scratch as a grand experiment in market reforms. Its local leaders were given free rein to attract manufacturing and to make it a global port. As it grows, its rival and next-door neighbor, Hong Kong, becomes diminished as a result. But this is all part of the plan from Beijing.

The story of Shenzhen begins when Deng Xiaoping took the reins of the Communist Party and set about retooling China's failed planned economy. In 1979, the central government formally created the municipality of Shenzhen and, following that, its Special Economic Zone (SEZ). "Shenzhen originated from attempts of post-Mao leadership to undo the economic paralysis of China's economy during the Cultural Revolution of 1966–76," political scientist Jonathan Bach writes. "A major challenge lay in acquiring badly needed foreign capital and technology from the class enemy without appearing to betray socialist principles."

The Asian Tigers—Singapore, Hong Kong, South Korea, and Taiwan—owed their meteoric rise to export-led growth. This was not lost on China's Communists. The model for Shenzhen began in the 1960s when Taiwan created its first export zone at Kao-hsiung, a city on its southwest coast. South Korea soon followed in the harbor city of Mansan. The developed world was eager to offshore its manufacturing to countries with much lower production costs. As a result, the United States would witness a massive reconfiguration of its workforce. From its peak of 19.5 million manufacturing jobs in 1979, it was down to 5.7 million by 2007. During the same time, East Asia gained about 42 million manufacturing jobs, while shipping containerization allowed for the simultaneous plummeting of transportation costs.

Shenzhen was designed to be China's "window to the world," and Deng wanted the SEZ to become a testbed where local officials could experiment with policies to figure out what could work. As a result, Shenzhen became a city of capitalist firsts. The first to have a stock exchange, the first to privatize state-owned companies, the first reforms in banking and financial transactions, the first to provide free-market housing, the first sale of industrial land, the first labor contracts to pay wages, and the first to produce a professional class of entrepreneurs.

For ambitious party officials, Shenzhen offered the promise of party stardom. "Local officials trying to make their way up the hierarchy went to Shenzhen to develop modern buildings, modern businesses, and to enjoy greater freedom and better style of life than in other parts of China," writes sociology professor Ezra Vogel.

The result was to make Shenzhen a culturally dynamic city. "But whereas Hong Kong was dominated by Cantonese people, Cantonese language, and Cantonese culture, Shenzhen was dominated by northerners and Mandarin. It became a melting pot—a cosmopolitan modern society where new ideas from abroad, as adapted by northerners and local Cantonese, could be tried out before they were spread elsewhere in China," Vogel reports.

The municipality would build out the infrastructure, and then within the SEZ, tax incentives and a business-friendly environment would lure international companies. But as is typical for developing cities around the world, as the manufacturing sector grows, it lays the seeds for its own demise.

As Shenzhen became a manufacturing hub, firms invested more in labor-saving technology, and they leaned more on banks and financial firms. As a result, business and financial services arose to support Shenzhen's industrial base. And its skills in making high-tech parts for Dell, Hewlett-Packard (HP), and Apple allowed it to expand into other high-tech manufacturing, including solar panels, wind turbines, and biomedicine.

Hong Kong's earlier growth was fueled by mainland turmoil. Fleeing Shanghainese brought capital and entrepreneurship, while workers arrived from Guangdong Province. Hong Kong absorbed what it could, built up to the sky to accommodate the population, and turned its labor and capital into wealth. And in this way, Hong Kong grew on a meal of Chinese "food."

However, China reversed the flow, starting with its economic reforms and then picking up momentum after Hong Kong was returned to China in 1997. As part of the program, Hong Kong has been used against itself, though the citizens have been willing partners in this (at least on the economic, if not political, side). China needed Hong Kong for financing, expertise, knowledge, and interfacing with the West. Since Hong Kongers were naturally pragmatic and a bit patriotic, they helped the new China emerge and, in this way, contributed to the rise of Shenzhen, which might yet someday come to dominate Hong Kong.

The most radical reforms occurred under pressure from Hong Kongers. One of the most important, especially as it relates to China's quest to go tall, was its land reforms. After 1949, all private property was abolished. In 1986, Shenzhen leaders were seeking a way forward. The government invited real estate experts from Hong Kong to share their thoughts. As Chinese legal scholars Yun-chien Chang and Wei Shen document:

> [A]t a seminar organized by the Shenzhen government, Professor Wu-Chang Zhang, dean of the Economics Department at Hong Kong University, pointed out that land leasing fees made up about one-quarter of the annual revenue of the government of Hong Kong, and in some years it was over 40 percent. . . . Professor Chang's words silenced the room.

Later that year, a small group led by Shenzhen's deputy mayor went to Hong Kong for a ten-day study tour. They visited the government agencies that oversaw land management. By the end of December, the group issued a report arguing for the Hong Kong–style method of land leases. And like that, what was an accident in Hong Kong's history became the central policy of Communist China.

In 1988, the Chinese Constitution was amended to permit municipalities to sell land leases, which has led in no small part to the rise of China's skylines. Before that, no free market for land had existed since after the Revolution. The government or state-owned enterprises

controlled urban parcels, but with no price system in place, there was
no way to reallocate lots if their original use became obsolete. But such
a free-market idea as land leases auctioned to the highest bidder had
to be rationalized within a Communist framework. As two Chinese
scholars write:

> After carefully studying the Crown land leases in Hong Kong, the
> Shenzhen government realized the revenue-generating power of land
> markets. It wanted to sell land, and it created a slogan in response to
> the CCP's [Chinese Communist Party's] call to build a "commercial
> economy with planning." Its slogan was: "No land market, no complete
> commercial economy." Shenzhen's desired reform faced an ideolog-
> ical challenge from Marxism: how could a socialist country that had
> abolished private property sell land? In response to this challenge, the
> reformers separate LURs (land use rights) from land ownership. A local
> reformer searched the classics of Marx and Engels page by page and
> found support for the latter. . . . Thus, selling LURs would not challenge
> state land ownership in China, but would allow the state to utilize
> land rents.

But Hong Kong did not just give China ideas for restructuring. It
invested heavily in the mainland, though the rewards were bittersweet.
While the Hong Kongese lost its manufacturing to north of the Shenzhen River, they got something in return—the financing of Shenzhen's
growth. Between 1986 and 1994, 78 percent of the $1.45 billion in FDI
that poured into the Shenzhen SEZ came from Hong Kong investors
and, along the way, helped produce the Bank of China Tower and
HSBC Building. Shenzhen and Hong Kong were partners and rivals
at the same time.

And Hong Kong didn't just invest in mainland manufacturing. It
invested in building up China's skylines. By 1992, Hong Kong had
gained the rights to as much as 200 million square feet of mainland

property and was investing HK$12–20 billion ($US1.5–2.5 billion) in real estate development annually. Mainlanders have returned the favor by investing in Hong Kong's real estate and helping to keep its housing prices sky-high.

Economic exchanges are fine for Hong Kongers, but the relationship that worries them the most is the political one. The Sino-British Joint Declaration of 1984 promised "one country, two systems" until 2047. But recent attempts by Beijing to strong-arm more control are leading many to believe Hong Kong is on its way to becoming "just another mainland city."

In 2020, the central government pushed Hong Kong to enact a national security law, which creates harsher and less democratic punishments for "[c]rimes of secession, subversion, terrorism and collusion with foreign forces." The law is viewed as an attempt to crack down on free speech and dissent, and when passed it led to massive protests in the streets and by the press, which were followed by arrests. The sense is that expats and companies are also leaving.

An important newspaper, *Apple Daily*, critical of the Chinese leadership, was shut down. "The arrests worsened the feeling of fear prevalent among journalists since the enactment of the national security law," Chris Yeung, a veteran journalist and former chairman of the Hong Kong Journalists Association, told the BBC. "The national security law has caused far more damaging impacts on freedoms and way of life than many people had envisaged one year ago."

In 2021, Beijing also curbed residents' already-restricted voting rights by overhauling the electoral system to make it easier for pro-Beijing candidates to be appointed as chief executive. In 2022, only one candidate, John Lee, a hard-line former deputy chief of the city's police force, was allowed to run.

So, what is the future of Hong Kong? People are not sure, but they are not hopeful. Hong Kong's success, however, is due to its grafting of Western commercial and legal institutions on an Asian society, and

Hong Kongers highly prize this uniqueness. The mainland owes much of its growth and development to those institutions and its business climate, and if Beijing cuts them down, it can, as the saying goes, cut off its nose to spite its face.

And yet if millennia of urban history have taught us anything, it's that it's very hard to keep a great city down.

CHAPTER 6

China

Skyscraper Fever

The Three Brothers. FROM LEFT: Shanghai Tower (2015),
Jin Mao Tower (1999), Shanghai World Financial Center (2008)

THE SHANGHAI TOWER

If you stand on the walkway along the Huangpu River in the Bund, you see toward the east a soaring, massive skyscraper. The glass façade swirls around, appearing almost like a tornado. The tower evokes a tinge of fear that if it could somehow become unmoored, it would unleash powerful destruction like Godzilla. Its gigantism echoes the fictional Pearl Tower in Hong Kong.

You see before you, in all its glory, the Shanghai Tower, a symbol of the rebirth of one of the world's great commercial hubs. Rising in the Lujiazui Financial District, it was initiated by government officials in 2003 and was finally completed in 2015. At 2,073 feet (632 m) tall and with 104 acres (0.42 km²) of internal space, it serves to announce that the "Wall Street of the East" is, indeed, open for business. Capitalism is ascendant as Chairman Mao rolls over in his grave.

Critics have claimed that the Shanghai Tower is the "skyscraper that failed," given the bevy of problems that delayed its completion (discussed later). But viewing it from the Bund makes these problems seem beside the point. It will remain a durable beacon for decades, if not centuries. Sure, it is economically too tall. But that's the point of an icon. It is a bridge between our internal identities and the external world in which we exist. It anchors us and gives us pleasure.

The Shanghai Tower is China's tallest building and currently the world's third tallest. It contains the world's fastest elevators to take tourists to the country's highest viewing deck. The building is built like a glass Tootsie Roll. The internal structure—the candy—is surrounded by a second exterior glass façade, comprised of twenty thousand panes, acting as a wrapper, whose form creates the illusion of movement. To the architectural firm that designed the building, Gensler, the spiraling form is meant to telegraph "the dynamic emergence of modern China."

To make the skyscraper more economically viable, it is a mixed-use "vertical city." The first five stories contain a retail mall. Above that, office space runs to the eightieth floor. A hotel occupies floors 86 to 98, with a restaurant on floor 121. The swimming pool, on floor 84, however, is not the world's highest. That honor goes to the one on the 118th floor of the Hong Kong Ritz-Carlton in the International Commerce Centre. The floors above the hotel are boutique offices, and the uppermost floors are for the observatory and mechanical equipment. Spaces for cultural events are peppered throughout.

The double skin has another function. Floors are extended into the open areas between the two façades, creating atria for people to congregate. Gensler has created a story about these spaces: they were inspired by traditional lane houses found in Beijing's *hutongs* and Shanghai's *shikumen*, where families live in close-knit dwellings organized around a communal open space.

And if you are going to build the world's second tallest building and field complaints from those who say it's too tall and a waste of resources, it does not hurt to do some virtue signaling. The tower was designed to advertise the very twenty-first-century notion of "sustainability."

As one admiring reporter described the structure:

See, the triangular and round double-skin is a deliberate and calculated design choice. While it sacrifices a degree of office space, it's necessary for some of the building's unique innovations. For example, thermodynamics. The extra layer makes the tower a super-sized Thermos bottle. As a result, Shanghai Tower uses 50-percent LESS energy than average to maintain its optimum temperature. In January, when outdoor temperatures drop to around 7-degrees Celsius, the air inside can reach 14-degrees even without central heating turned on. Second, the twisting shape reduces the wind-load by 24-percent. That's important if you're going to build something this high in a typhoon-prone area.

The Shanghai Tower, however, does not stand alone, as does One World Trade Center in New York or the Burj Khalifa in Dubai, but instead is one of three supertalls conceived by the Shanghai government. The story of these three buildings — informally referred to as the Three Brothers — is the story of how China thinks about skyscrapers. The nation uses the tall building not only as part of its mythmaking and storytelling process but also to signal its rising economic power.

Each is in close walking distance and, surprisingly, each has its own observation deck, despite likely cannibalizing revenues from the others. Together they form an equilateral triangle to create a history and harmony. They are the Jin Mao Tower, the Shanghai World Financial Center, and the Shanghai Tower. The idea of the trio is based on Taoist philosophy. For Lao-tzu teaches that three is a very good number:

> Dao begets One (nothingness; or reason of being); One begets Two (yin and yang); Two begets Three (Heaven, Earth, and Man); Three begets all things. All things carry the female and embrace the male. And by breathing together, they live in harmony.

The number three thus indicates the start of everything, and Shanghai is the start of twenty-first-century China. The Jin Mao was completed in 1999. At eighty-eight stories (1,380 feet, 420.5 m), its height was chosen because eighty-eight is a lucky number, associated with abundance, prosperity, and good fortune. Its proportions also revolve around the number eight. The eighty-eight floors are divided into twelve segments, each of which is one-eighth shorter than the sixteen-story base. The architect Adrian Smith, then at SOM, sculpted the building like a rocket-ship-shaped pagoda. It's a nod to China's past.

The next building is the Shanghai World Financial Center, which opened in 2008 and rises 1,614 feet (492 m) with 101 floors. At the time of completion, it was the second-tallest building in the world and the tallest in China. Designed by KPF, the architectural style mimics a bamboo sprout. And the square opening at the top, which inadvertently makes it look like a bottlecap opener, was placed there to reduce wind loads. The original design called for a circular hole, as a reference to Chinese moon gates, traditional garden entranceways. But local officials complained that the opening looked too much like the rising sun on the Japanese flag, and the circle was squared.

The tower was started in 1997 but was halted after the Asian Financial Crisis. Construction resumed in 2003, and during the interval officials pressed for more height to compete with those going up in Taipei and

An early rendering of the Shanghai World Financial Center

Hong Kong. As a result, the developer increased it by 85 feet (26 m), sur-
passing the Petronas Towers (1998) in Kuala Lumpur, Two International
Finance Centre (2003) in Hong Kong, and the top floor of Taipei 101
(2004). The aim was to have the skyscraper recognized by the Council
on Tall Buildings and Urban Habitat (CTBUH) as the world's tallest in
two of its four categories—the "Highest Occupied Floor" and "Top of
Roof." The Shanghai World Financial Center is a nod to China's present.

The Shanghai Tower is a gaze to China's future. Despite that, the
desire for harmony among the three buildings prevented local officials
from making it the world's tallest building. According to one glowing
account in the Chinese journal *Architectural Practice* (translated from
Mandarin):

By comparison, the Shanghai Tower is set at 632m, which is 140m higher than the Global Financial Center, and the Global Financial Center is larger than Jin Mao. The height of the building is 71.5m, and the height difference of the former is about twice that of the latter. In the sky, a three-dimensional rising space arc is formed, which together constitutes a beautiful skyline. This height also has a good echo to the Oriental Pearl in the distance, so that the overall skyline of the core area of Lujiazui in Pudong forms two peaks at two iconic landscapes.

Shanghai's rebirth as a skyscraper city is emblematic of the Communist Party's wider agenda. Exploiting the historical brand of Shanghai, Inc., and as the Paris of the East, it became the logical choice for substantial investment and promotion by both the local and central governments. Shanghai would become the new financial hub, just as Shenzhen would be China's manufacturing center, in order to beat the West at its own game.

In the 1980s, Shanghai officials identified Pudong—which translates to "the East Bank of the Huangpu River"—to jump-start the city's fortunes. The process formally began in 1990 when the State Council green-lighted a plan designating the Pudong New Area as an SEZ, which Deng Xiaoping described as the "Head of the Dragon," the face—and teeth—of the new economy. Local officials, led by Mayor Zhu Rongji, were eager to take business away from Hong Kong—that "frustratingly free city."

The Pudong strategy had three elements. The first was to pour massive quantities of yuan into the construction of new infrastructure, from subways and trains to bridges and roads, to airports, to water and sewage systems. The second was to lure international corporations with generous subsidies and provide access to virtually limitless market opportunities. After all, 1.4 billion people have 2.8 billion legs and feet that can be covered in Levi's and Nikes. Third, the Shanghai government would promote real estate growth by using its power over land leases to dictate development. Skyscrapers were key to bringing Shanghai back to the world stage.

Coming in for a landing at Pudong International Airport, however, you see Shanghai's dueling real estate "stages." On the west side of the Huangpu River is the Bund, where European merchants once controlled the city's trade.

LEFT: Hongkong and Shanghai Bank (HSBC) (1923)
RIGHT: Customs House (1927)

The old merchant houses and banks stand erect like soldiers in one continuous street wall. One of the most notable is the eight-story Customs House, completed in 1927, during Shanghai's Roaring Twenties. The architecture combines the Art Deco forms of the 1920s with more classical elements. The façade references ancient Greek architecture with its base, shaft, and capital. But the limestone piers are thick and rectangular, with narrow window bays that serve to accentuate the structure's verticality. The building could have been constructed in almost any Western port city. In hindsight, the Customs House reflects a transitional era, when the age of globalization based on the ancient notion of Empire was entering its twilight. Then in 1937, the city's economy came to an abrupt halt when the Japanese invaded, and the Communist takeover in 1949 meant that Shanghai's glory days were over.

The legacy of the Bund and the Foreign Concessions remains mixed, however. On the one hand, it created Shanghai as an internationally recognized historical city. One that is nostalgically glorified in television and movies, such as the scene in *Indiana Jones and the Temple of Doom* (1984), where Jones attempts to purchase a large diamond in a Shanghai nightclub. The transaction goes awry, and the club descends into brawling chaos. The orchestra and dancing girls continue their performance, as if nothing is wrong, though a hint of fear is observable on their faces.

Yet to the officials eager to make China the world's largest economy, the Bund is a scar from European imperialism and one that must remain in the shadows. Ironically, the young Shanghainese see the Bund differently. It is part of their international history. As they come to the United States and Europe for leisure and study—bankrolled by their grandparents, for whom there are four for each youth, given China's one-child policy—they imbibe the Western lifestyle and attitudes, and when they return to Shanghai, the Bund makes them feel connected to the world, with its hints of Paris and London.

In stark contrast, Pudong has the new glass skyscrapers. Viewing its skyline from the Bund is like viewing Lower Manhattan from a ferry. They both appear to emerge from a body of water as an island of floating towers, telegraphing financial and economic might. The Pudong skyscrapers are also toys for the amusement of evening strollers. At night, the dancing and splashing of LED lights run up and down the façades, providing a kind of fireworks display, delighting our baby brains in bursts of shapes and colors.

And while Rome might not have been built in a day, Pudong nearly was. As late as 1990 it was little more than an expanse of small farms and villages, and now it is one of the world's top skyscraper hubs. To give you a sense of the scale, Pudong's GDP—the value of the goods and services it produces each year—is $238 billion. If Pudong were its own nation, it

TOP: Pudong; BOTTOM: Lower Manhattan

would rank above Romania and Peru. However, it is still a far cry from matching Manhattan's economic power, whose GDP is $830 billion.

The Lujiazui Financial District contains 31 million square feet (2.9 million m²) of prime office space, which is nearly the same as Manhattan's Wall Street area. The neighborhood houses almost eight hundred finance-related businesses, and the Shanghai Stock Exchange is one of the top trading houses in the world. Though Shanghai has not yet dislodged London and New York in the power of its financial sector, it's racing to get there.

But the attempt to make Shanghai the "Wall Street of the East" has made this grand experiment rife with both successes and failures. No one can doubt that Pudong is on the map and is a global financial hub. But ironically, the Shanghai Tower has developed a reputation as the "skyscraper that failed."

To literally be a failure would mean that the building collapsed or that no one would enter it. Yes, the tower failed to live up to its lofty expectations. Over time, however, the building will no doubt become like the Empire State Building or the Sears (Willis) Tower—not the most sought-after address, but one that holds its own because of its iconic status.

The structure topped out in August 2013 and was supposed to be formally launched in 2015. But by the end of 2017, the developers decided to proceed by "quietly opening." The tower's spokesperson said, "We'd like to keep a low profile. . . . We don't plan to have a grand opening celebration even if all things are ready because we've been exposed too much to the public."

Why has it gotten such a bad rap? First were the long construction delays due to its novel design. To Marshall Strabala, the architect at Gensler who designed it, the double skin was meant to be the triumph of architecture. But building officials were worried about whether the space would act like a chimney drawing up flames should there be a fire (which sounds like a script for a Hollywood movie).

The owners had difficulty finding tenants when the tower was being evaluated as a possible death trap. When the building was finally receiving tenants, the companies that were supposed to fill it were few and far between, as 2015 was a soft time in the Pudong office market. But just as importantly, the double skin and circular design reduced the building's functionality. Tenants did not like their views being blocked by another layer of glass, and the layout was not efficient for large corporations. Then there was the hotel—J Hotel, the world's highest—which took its time moving in. Some five years after the building opened, the hotel was finally ready for guests, while the COVID pandemic was in full swing.

So, why did the process go so awry? The problem stemmed from the combined inexperience of the developer and the architect. The state-owned developer, a unit of Shanghai Municipal Investment Group, a Shanghai Municipal Government SWF, was charged with building China's tallest building. And with a great tower comes great responsibility. But the developers had little expertise.

And the architectural team at Gensler, unfortunately, got ahead of itself. In 2008, Gensler won the design contest against three other firms but also had little tall building experience, unlike SOM or KPF. At the time, its tallest building was the L.A. Live Tower & Residences in Downtown Los Angeles, only one-third as tall as the Shanghai Tower.

The Jin Mao Tower was designed and engineered by SOM. The WFC was designed by KPF and engineered by Arup and Leslie Robertson and Associates. These companies were building supertalls for decades and knew how to provide relatively low-risk icons.

In addition, the double skin had no precedent on the mainland. "There was a constant sort of push-pull during the project where we would design something for which there was no code, so we would need to write a code, and this went back and forth for nearly seven years," said Dan Winey, chief operating officer of Gensler.

There's no doubt in my mind, however, that the Shanghai Tower will find its way. First is its design. Looking at it from the Bund, you can't help but be awed. Second, the Shanghai Tower is a symbol of rising China and will remain a beacon of its ambitions. And it will make money.

Observatories are an easy source of cash. The hotel does not seem to be wanting for guests. A search on its reservation website revealed that a 660-square-foot (56 m²) room in June 2022 with a king-sized bed would cost $735 per night (breakfast was included). The 1,000-square-foot (93 m²) suite would cost $1,700 per night. The mall at its base draws China's eager shoppers, who crave American and European brands. And the offices in the middle will get their companies—maybe not the big guns from abroad but smaller and medium-sized companies that want to say, "My office is in the Shanghai Tower."

As reported in the *South China Morning Post* in 2018:

> The developer would not provide a detailed list of the tenants, but mainland businesses rather than multinational companies appear to dominate, according to an incomplete list and an on-site check by the Post. Exceptions to the rule include Lloyd's and Fitch Ratings.
>
> Allbright Law Offices is one of several domestic law firms that occupy a portion of the skyscraper's 220,000 sq metres of office space. Others include Dentons and Joint-Win Partners.
>
> "The office plays a role in enhancing the image of the law firms and the lawyers," said Maggie Wang, a partner with Allbright. "A landmark building and world-class architectural designs at Lujiazui help impress upon the clients that this is a reputable law firm worthy of their trust."

Recent reports indicate that the building is slowly filling up. By the end of 2020, the tower was 80 percent rented, with 41 percent leased by foreign companies, such as JP Morgan, Allianz, and BNP Paribas.

SKYSCRAPER FEVER

The Shanghai Tower is just one manifestation of a larger movement that has swept across the mainland. There's no way else to put it except to say that China has Skyscraper Fever. A brief swim in the pool of statistics will reveal staggering facts. Nearly every year since 1990, China has built more skyscrapers than any other country. Nearly half of the world's tallest 100 buildings are in the mainland, including the world's third tallest. China has skyscrapers in cities big, medium, and small.

The United States has 2,949 buildings 328 feet (100 m) or taller. By comparison, China has more than 13,540. Even on a per capita basis,

China has 9,681 skyscrapers per billion whereas the United States has 8,936 per billion. This fact is even more remarkable since China had virtually no skyscrapers until 1980, while the United States had a century head start.

Why is this and how did China come to love the tall building? The short answer is due to a combination of economic forces and aggressive actions by government officials. And there's also something rooted in China's perceptions about its place in the world. Capitalist China loves the tall building bling, and skyscrapers are a form of national conspicuous consumption. Or as one news outlet put it, "Skyscrapers, with all their associations with height and prestige as well as service-oriented industries, are still viewed by Chinese cadres as status symbols of their cities, towering icons of a city's wealth and economic triumph."

China's rising skylines are one part of a larger belief-defying transformation. Its economic reforms have unleashed the largest internal migration in human history. In 1978, 82 percent of China's 0.9 billion people were living in rural areas. By 2020, 61 percent of its 1.4 billion people were living in cities. China's cities—old and new—are growing to accommodate the ongoing influx.

And, of course, urbanization in China means a very different thing than in the West. A "small" city in China will house 4 million people. The conurbation along the Pearl River Delta holds 78 million residents, as compared to 20 million for the New York metro area.

Central government officials pore over maps and strategically erect new cities. As one example, the Communist Party is currently producing the infrastructure for a new metropolis outside Beijing, called the Xiong'an New Area, which is expected to hold 2.5 million people to house an SEZ to specialize in high-tech and green industries. To connect its cities into one seamless network, China has undertaken the world's largest high-speed rail project, which by 2035 is expected to extend 43,500 miles (70,000 km), the equivalent of 1.75 times the circumference of Earth.

The country's rapid urbanization has required a vast building spree as residents flock to cities for jobs. In this sense, skyscrapers are like "nets" catching the residents as they arrive. As demonstrated in Hong Kong and Singapore, dense living, and, by extension, living in the clouds, is a natural way of life for East Asian residents as it is part of their cultural DNA. When modern mainland cities spring up like mushrooms, their citizens are more than willing to move up with their buildings.

And if you look across China's cities you see a handful of facts that are similar to those of cities around the world. First, there is a strong correlation between a city's population and the number of tall buildings it has. While China has a "small city" problem when it comes to overbuilding (discussed later), the average small city has fewer skyscrapers than the average large city. China's tallest buildings are also in its largest, more global-oriented cities. And so, part of the reason China's skyscraper growth appears excessive to Western eyes is that China's cities are much larger and more numerous.

China's massive army of urban workers is also a source of cheap labor. Building skyscrapers in China comes with a 30 percent discount as compared to the United States. But even so, take two cities, one in China and one outside with the same population and construction costs, China will likely have more skyscrapers because of its unique institutional, cultural, and planning systems.

Vital is the land-lease system. Local officials auction off large lots of land to developers who then construct housing and commercial buildings. Land leases for apartment buildings normally run for seventy years, while the leases for office, retail, and industrial buildings run for forty to fifty years, though leaseholders can resell the leases if they wish. Apartment building developers can sell the apartments to households. However, since homeowners own their units on leased land, there is a certain fear and uncertainty about what will happen to their investments when the ground leases expire several decades from now. Central government leaders have signaled their intent to allow automatic lease renewals, but a formal policy has yet to be set.

The money that local governments earn from the land leases is used to build local infrastructure. In this way, Chinese officials have a vested interest in promoting density, since more density means more valuable land and more money for infrastructure. When officials announce a land-lease auction or tender, they often require the developer to build a supertall building as a condition of the lease.

Developers go along because they first calculate the profits from the development and then decide how much to bid. As a result, while the project may be risky, a wise developer will only put forth the maximum that it is worth. If the city asks for "too much" in the specifications, developers will bid relatively lower.

These requirements also come with the opportunity to build profitable middle-class housing, so the developer can make up the profit there, even if the supertall is built at a loss or small return. And to the degree that supertalls add monuments and a sense of status, apartments facing them will sell at a premium.

Officials in cities big and small all play the skyscraper game. As reported in the *Asian Times*:

> The trend to pierce the skies is now not limited to Shanghai, Beijing, Guangzhou and Shenzhen. More second-tier cities like Wuhan, Tianjin, Nanjing, Changsha, Suzhou and others are flocking to launch their lofty plans to up the ante in the skyscraper contest to reach new heights.
>
> In fact, many municipal governments offer deep discounts in land prices as well as tax rebates to attract realty developers to build towers, and some even mandate local state-owned enterprises and banks to pool money for such projects, usually bearing the name International Financial Centre or World Trade Center.

The skyscraper-building process is compounded by the single-party system. The Communist Party rewards and promotes municipal officials based on their competence and output. Each year, city officials must produce evidence of urban growth and efficiency. Skyscrapers are a visible way for local officials to show off "their chops."

In China, there is a well-known urban ranking system. Tier 1 cities include Beijing, Shanghai, and Shenzhen. Below that are cities that are a bit smaller and less important, such as Chengdu, Changchun, and Foshan. The lowest-ranked cities are put in Tier 4. Leaders and planning officials are compared to their peers within their respective tiers. Given the narrowing opportunities as one moves up the hierarchy, one mayor "wins" at the expense of another, pitting local leaders in a kind of urban cockfight, which drives them to build even taller than their rivals. Officials in small cities have been particularly prone to build tall skyscrapers pleading, "Don't forget about us!"

Making matters even more extreme is that the central government has a mandated retirement age of sixty. Since officials are worried about a job promotion, they need to act fast. As a result, cities with younger mayors and planning chiefs build taller buildings than otherwise. If all these elements weren't enough, then there's the bevy of state-owned enterprises (SEOs) up and down the real estate chain. Developers and the banks that fund them are frequently fully or partially state owned, so they have less pressure against risk-taking because, in principle, the government will bail them out if necessary.

Finally, there's corruption. Local officials with power over land leases can sell favors or give better deals to developers in exchange for money or perks. Some leaders find that promoting skyscrapers is a good way to line their pockets. In my own research with my graduate student Jingshu Luo, now a professor at the University of Mississippi, we found that an increase in one corruption case brought to light by the press in a city was associated with about 4 percent more tall buildings. We also found that each corruption case was associated with the addition of about 13 feet (3 m), on average, to the city's tallest completed building each year.

Two "weird" Chinese skyscrapers
LEFT: CCTV Headquarters (2012), Beijing; RIGHT: L'Avenue (2012), Shanghai

Along the way, however, the central government realized something. It unleashed a skyscraper dragon of epic proportions. Out west were the so-called Ghost Cities, where local officials sold off land leases to developers without any short-term justification since few people lived there. Ironically, some of these ventures were profitable because middle- and upper-class residents from the east coast were snapping them up as investment properties.

One unusual ghost town is that of Tianducheng, a few hours' drive from Shanghai. It was built as a replica of Paris. An Eiffel Tower sits in the town center along with a re-creation of the fountain from the Luxemburg Gardens. Surrounding them are Second Empire apartment buildings. Original plans had an expected capacity of ten thousand residents, but only 10 percent of the units are occupied.

Senior leaders did not like to see the rampant skyscraper competition, which has come across as wasteful. Compounding China's woes, developers frequently requested bizarre forms that seemed slick on paper but had a very different impact when all was said and done.

The Shanghai Tower, with its double skin and sleek design, was supposed to be a modern high-tech icon. But from the point of view of the central government, the building was a headache. It drew attention to China in a negative way that was never intended. Its reputation as "the building that failed" only served to advertise the riskiness of erecting supertall buildings.

Just as infamous is the CCTV Headquarters in Beijing (2012, fifty-one stories), which was designed by starchitect Rem Koolhaas, as two buildings that each appear to be leaning and are connected at the top by an L-shaped sky bridge. The effect is to make it look like a pair of pants. Or as one Chinese student revealed, the nickname among her friends, translated from Mandarin, is "boy who takes a dump."

But Koolhaas defended himself in 2014 by saying, "I don't have the slightest difficulty in saying, or showing, or demonstrating, that CCTV is a very serious building." He was responding to China's President Xi Jinping's comment that there should be "no more weird architecture." "We're in a stage where people are too impetuous and anxious to produce something that can actually go down in history," Zhang Shangwu, deputy head of Tongji University's College of Architecture and Urban Planning, told the *South China Morning Post*. "Every building aims to be a landmark, and the developers and city planners try to achieve this goal by going extreme in novelty and strangeness."

In the last few years, real estate companies have also revealed themselves to be over-leveraged. In August 2020, Beijing introduced policies aimed at reducing excessive borrowing by big developers. All seemed to be going according to plan, but then the spread of the Omicron variant of the coronavirus in early 2022 drove the central government to implement a "zero-COVID" policy. The lockdown froze the real estate market. Developers struggled to pay their debts, while also abandoning large housing projects that were only half-finished. Homeowners who prepaid for their units lost their money.

Beijing abandoned the strict COVID controls in December, but the eagerly awaited economic boom never materialized. Consumers have lost faith and are holding off on big purchases. China now stands on the edge of an economic precipice—facing the threat of a 2007-2008-style financial crisis—as the erosion of confidence fuels a downward spiral. As of this writing (September 2023), the world is holding its breath to see if China can save itself.

Then there's a concern for the environmental impact. Skyscrapers are seen as energy hogs, both in terms of the embodied carbon that comes from steel and cement production and how, because of their size, they consume a lot of energy (discussed in chapter 10). So, the running of the skyscraper bulls, so to speak, does not signal that Red China is green.

To top it all off, in July 2021, a skyscraper in Shenzhen, out of the blue, started swaying, forcing its evacuation. A study concluded that it was a freak event, and the owners were able to fix the problem (discussed later), but the schadenfreude-laced publicity about a randomly swaying skyscraper didn't help.

As a result of the combined fears of overbuilding, corruption, weird architecture, and a green "black eye," the Communist Party has become more active in restraining the market. Following President Xi Jinping's rise to power in 2012, the government has implemented a large-scale anti-corruption campaign, including a significant jump in local mayors and party secretaries who were prosecuted. The most visible anti-corruption measure is to require public land auctions. Another is to boot corrupt officials from office and scare into cooperation those who replace them.

Then in July 2021 came a height cap. As reported in the *South China Morning Post*:

The mainland, home to almost half of the world's 100 tallest buildings, has sounded the death knell on new **super skyscrapers**, as concerns of an oversupply of commercial offices combine with fears that the blind pursuit of altitudes for decades may have compromised construction safety.

New buildings taller than 500 metres will no longer be approved, according to an order issued on Tuesday by the National Development and Reform Commission (NDRC), the country's top planning agency.

Towers exceeding 250 metres must be strictly limited, and those taller than 100 metres must strictly match the scale and the fire rescue capacity of their locations.

For the time being, the Shanghai Tower's place as China's tallest building is secure. But if there's one thing that history shows: booms lead to busts, and busts lead back to booms. It might take a while, especially given the COVID pandemic and its aftereffects, but one day in the not-so-distant future China will once again get back its Skyscraper Fever.

THE THIRD SKYSCRAPER REVOLUTION

At the end of the twentieth century, not just China but other Asian countries were eager to build up their skylines. As their economies grew and residents got a taste of Western lifestyles, the race to the heavens was on. This urgency has birthed new technologies and construction methods—the Third Skyscraper Revolution—which has not only made buildings taller at less cost but also produced more internal sunlight, shrunk the core, and vertically moved more people in less time. Just as important, the Third Skyscraper Revolution is about the triumph of geometry. Developing nations crave an architectural vernacular that bridges their pasts with their futures. They want buildings that allow them to preserve a modicum of their historical identities, even as globalization wipes them away. Architects who design such towers bring to bear their eclectic sensibilities and storytelling gifts to give Asia its own storybook Postmodern skylines.

Taipei 101 (photo on page 122), for example, designed by Taiwanese architect C. Y. Lee, besides sporting the pagoda look, is also reminiscent of a bamboo stalk. But other references can be inferred from its design. As the building's *Wikipedia* entry states:

> Popular humor sometimes likens the building's shape to a stack of take-out boxes as used in Western-style Chinese food; of course, the stackable shape of such boxes is likewise derived from that of ancient money boxes. The four discs mounted on each face of the building where the pedestal meets the tower represent coins. The emblem placed over entrances shows three gold coins of ancient Chinese design with central holes shaped to imply the Arabic numerals 1-0-1. The structure incorporates many shapes of squares and circles to reach a balance between yin and yang.

FROM LEFT: Al Hekma Tower (2016) in Dubai,
King Power Mahanakhon ("Jenga") Tower (2016) in Bangkok,
and Merdeka 118 in Kuala Lumpur (2023)

Not everyone looks to the past, however, as there are also future-oriented builders who seek sci-fi renderings brought to life. Such structures include the Ping An tower, the Al Hekma Tower in Dubai, with a comic-book feel as "fiery" flares seem to shoot up along its corners, and the so-called Jenga Tower (formally the King Power Mahanakhon) in Bangkok, with a "pixelated" ribbon that runs around the façade. The Merdeka 118 in Kuala Lumpur has diamond-shaped façades giving it a funhouse mirror look. The building's spire, placed to one side, is meant to represent the outstretched hand gesture Malaysia's first prime minister, Tunku Abdul Rahman, made while he was shouting, "*Merdeka* [independent]*!*" when he proclaimed the independence of Malaysia on August 31, 1957.

And it's not just architecture that has changed. Up until the 1960s, if you wanted a skyscraper, you got a moment-resisting or rigid frame — the classic steel skeleton that holds up the Empire State and Chrysler Buildings. In the post–World War II era, you could get any supertall building you wanted, as long as it was a tube: a tube frame (Twin Towers), a braced tube (the John Hancock Center), or a bundled tube (Sears [Willis] Tower).

By the 1980s, however, the limits of the tube were revealed. The exterior columns tended to be too closely spaced together; windows were smaller, and less light spilled in. For that matter, the tube restricted what the architect could "say." This was readily apparent during America's Postmodernist phase, and even more so when China and Dubai started making requests for distinctive or weird architecture. Developers around the globe drew on the Western — particularly U.S. — Skyscraper Industrial Network, which has produced a "Chinese menu" of options. The technologies common today had been known since the 1970s, but America's retreat from building supertalls allowed Asia to take the lead.

There has also been a revolution in materials. Nowadays, most supertalls are composite designs. The core is a wind-resisting shear wall of reinforced concrete, while the horizontal floor beams and girders are steel, and the vertical load-bearing columns will be either concrete or steel. Concrete's asset is in its compressive strength, making it more efficient for columns and cores; while lighter steel has ductile or tensile strength from forces that pull buildings apart. When steel and reinforced concrete are put together, the building is both stronger and lighter.

And concrete can now do much more "heavy lifting." The quest for a high-strength variety began with the Petronas Towers. At the time, Kuala Lumpur did not have a developed steel industry, but it did have experience with concrete. To make the structure economically feasible, the developers pushed their concrete supplier, Samsung Corporation, to come up with a mix strong enough to hold up a record breaker. Its success was widely replicated; the Burj Khalifa is a nearly all reinforced concrete structure, as will be the Jeddah Tower, the currently stalled supertall, that if ever completed, will be the world's tallest.

Concrete, however, suffers from "creepage," the slow compression from its own weight. In fact, fifty years from now the Burj Khalifa will be two feet shorter as a result. The builders of the Empire State Building were made aware more quickly of a similar problem. In December 1930, the general contractor noticed that the building was six inches shorter than it was supposed to be. Upon investigation, it was realized that the weight of the steel on itself was the culprit. Once this was discovered, the installation of the elevators could proceed with only slight modifications.

In parallel have come new pumping technologies to get this concrete up to the top of the building before it sets—and in all kinds of weather conditions. For the Burj Khalifa, concrete had to be poured sixteen hundred feet in the sky, in a hot and humid desert no less. To slow down the hardening, the German chemical manufacturer BASF developed Glenium Sky 504, a "superplasticizer" that, once added to wet concrete, keeps it soft for three hours. To speed up the pouring process, engineers have designed formworks that can be easily lifted from one floor to the next: Build the forms, pour the concrete, raise the forms, repeat.

Whereas Fazlur Khan and the engineers of his generation relied on punch cards and mainframes, today architects and engineers have a vast arsenal of computing power and software that offers a Harry Potter's wand for creating new designs. The design software is linked to the engineering software, which can be linked to manufacturing software at the foundries. We are not quite at the stage of the AI-designed-3D-printed skyscraper, but perhaps someday.

Then there's the wind—arguably the biggest challenge to creating usable tall buildings. Besides a concrete core, most supertalls have one of several standard structural elements to help provide wind bracing. The most common structural "add-on" is the outrigger. In the nautical world, outriggers are flotation devices attached to the boat's hull by poles to provide support. In the skyscraper case, evenly spaced throughout the building are two or more so-called outriggers. Each one has a set of wide steel or concrete beams emanating from the core and is connected to the perimeter columns.

We can make an analogy to a skier. The core represents the skier's body. The outrigger beams are like the skier's outstretched arms, and the external columns are like the ski poles. When the wind blows on one side of a building, the other side can "push back" like the inside ski pole when the skier leans into the mountain.

Outriggers for skyscrapers were first used in the 47-story (190 m) Place Victoria Building (now the Stock Exchange Tower) in 1964 in Montreal. In the United States, the SOM team of Graham and Khan incorporated an outrigger in the U.S. Bank Center in Milwaukee, completed in 1973. As discussed earlier, Leslie Robertson also included them above the top floors of the Twin Towers. The outriggers are frequently supported by a belt truss, which wraps around the perimeter and connects the outrigger beams to add more stiffness.

In the 1980s, Adrian Smith, when at SOM, was hired to design a supertall in Chicago called the Dearborn Center. It was not built, but it contained a core-outrigger system that allowed Smith to create a Postmodern style. When Smith was awarded the Jin Mao Tower in Shanghai, he applied the technology and helped pave its widespread use in the East.

Outriggers can be used with most types of structural systems, such as tubes or moment-resisting frames. However, many outrigger buildings

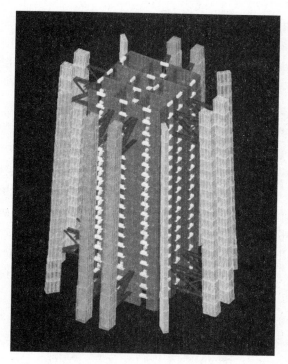

Shanghai Tower's structural system. The outriggers
run from the core to the megacolumns.

have megacolumns—very thick perimeter columns that are mainly
used to carry gravity loads, though they help with lateral loads. The
128-story Shanghai Tower (2015) uses this design, as does Taipei 101.
Megacolumns are valued because they reduce the number of perimeter
columns, increasing access to sunlight.

But wind is not just wind when it comes to skyscrapers. One problem
comes from gusts that "push" the building, causing it to sway. While no
skyscraper has yet to be knocked over by a storm, one came pretty close.
After the fifty-nine-story Citicorp Center was completed in Manhattan
in 1977, the structural engineer, William J. LeMessurier, was prompted
to revisit the building's wind bracing after a call from a graduate student,

who informed him that his professor said the building's columns were in the wrong place.

The structure's main columns had been moved, unconventionally, toward the center from the edges to allow for a church on the corner to remain below the tower, like an egg in the nest under its mother's belly. LeMessurier found that the steel installer, without his knowledge, had used bolts on the wind-bracing members as a cost-saving measure rather than welding them together. Normally this was not a problem, but given the unusual location of the columns, when LeMessurier recrunched the numbers he saw, to his horror, that if the wind blew at just the right angle and speed it could cause the skyscraper to collapse, producing a path of death and destruction on the streets.

The realization came in the early summer with hurricane season just around the corner. Putting aside his professional pride, he revealed the mistake to Citicorp, which worked quietly and quickly to shore up its building. Fortunately, we now have only an interesting historical gumdrop rather than a horrible tragedy or an inspiration for a Hollywood movie.

But hurricanes and gusts are not the only problems. Another issue is vortex shedding. When the wind blows at moderate speeds, the currents are split by the tower, creating two symmetric low-pressure eddies or vortexes. But at higher speeds, these vortexes spin or shed alternately from one side to the other, causing the building to sway due to differential air pressures.

A bigger problem emerges when the shedding sway rate matches the building's natural sway rate. In this case, even small amounts of vortex shedding can amplify the oscillations and lead to a collapse. "This phenomenon is similar to an opera singer shattering a wine glass by singing the right note exactly at the glass's natural frequency," notes architect and author Stefan Al.

And this brings us back to Shenzhen. On May 19, 2020, people were going about their lives when, as one headline reported, "Panic in Shenzhen as skyscraper starts to shake inexplicably." The building was evacuated and remained empty for weeks. Why it shook was a mystery. There were no reported storms, earthquakes, terrorism, or anything that might indicate a cause.

By July, inspectors found the culprit: "vortex resonance." The antennae masts were old, and their connection to the roof had weakened. When they started to sway, they matched the building's frequency and amplified the movement until it was fast enough to induce panic. Once the antennae were removed, life in the building returned to normal, but of course it's now the building with a "windy" reputation.

The key to wind engineering, though, is not to make the building perfectly stiff, which is too expensive. Rather, the goal is to slow the swaying so it's imperceptible to the occupants. Engineers have a rule of thumb to prevent sickness. The amount of lateral displacement should not be more than 2 feet (0.6 m) for every 1,000 feet (305 m) of building height.

But they don't always get things right. In the early 1990s, for example, my wife worked in a skinny skyscraper in Midtown Manhattan. On windy days, employees would feel the sway and hear the elevator cars screeching in their shafts. Many of her coworkers would instantly profess their motion sickness and abandon work for the day.

Besides concrete cores and outriggers, engineers can get ahead of the curve by using wind tunnel testing. After an initial building design is created, wood or plastic models are placed in wind tunnels, where they are subject to various types of wind forces to see how they withstand simulated storms, vortex shedding, and pedestrian turbulence.

One strategy is to refine designs to "confuse" the winds, so they don't blow around the tower. The notches on the corners of the International Commerce Centre and the uneven setbacks of the Burj Khalifa were added for this purpose. And wind tunnel tests can save lots of money. With the Shanghai Tower, Marshall Strabala has noted, "[t]hat twisted form creates these disorganized vortexes around the building that it breaks up the wind. . . . So we estimated it saved about $80 million in construction costs, which then paid for the second skin."

Another strategy is to employ a tuned mass damper. When I was in Shenzhen, I was able to see the Ping An's one-thousand-ton damper, a huge metal cube hanging from a steel A-frame. The damper is a counterweight that sways in the opposite direction of the tower's motion. In Hong Kong, engineers have cleverly placed swimming pools on the upper floors to act as liquid dampeners.

So, engineers can easily build up to 160 stories without occupants feeling the sway, but how do people get up there? The challenge is to minimize the so-called Pain Index—the total time it takes from once you hit the elevator button to when you arrive at your final destination. Most modern elevator systems employ computer algorithms and fuzzy logic to minimize travel times, using a Destination Dispatching System (DDS). In real time, the system analyzes the input data—where the buttons were pushed—and makes a list of whom to put in which cars and where the cars are to stop. DDS has cut travel times in half.

For very tall buildings, another trick is to use the shaft space more efficiently by having two elevators operate within the same shaft. One way to do this is to have one cab sit on top of another, creating a double-decker. Odd-floor travelers enter the bottom car, while even-floor travelers enter the top car after walking up a ramp. Recent installations run two independent cabs in the same shaft, such as at 50 Hudson Yards in Manhattan.

The suite of technologies has not only made passenger journeys faster and more pleasant but also freed a lot of otherwise wasted space that can now be used to generate income. By my estimate, the average number of elevators needed for a given skyscraper has fallen by about 4 percent per decade since World War II, so the typical skyscraper now uses half as many elevators as it did in 1980.

As buildings get taller, however, the amount of cable, or "rope," needed to connect the elevator car to the motor becomes that much longer. In very tall buildings, nearly 70 percent of the elevator's weight comes from the cable itself, and when the cable gets too long, it cannot support its own weight. Elevator manufacturers are in a race to develop new types of ropes that are stronger and lighter. With conventional ropes, the highest that one elevator car can travel is 1,640 feet (500 m). After that, going taller requires transferring to a sky lobby. The Jeddah Tower will install KONE's UltraRope, which has a carbon-fiber core, making it particularly light and strong, and which, in principle, can extend to 3,280 feet (1,000 m).

Height is one thing, but speed is another. "The human body has various internal sensors that are sensitive to external motion forces, noise, and vibrations," explains elevator engineer James Fortune. In particular, we are quite sensitive to acceleration and deceleration rates, which can cause ear discomfort due to rapid changes in air pressure. "However, ear comfort and pressure changes do not usually affect healthy elevator riders unless the descent speeds exceed 10 meters per second (33 feet per second/23 miles per hour) and vertical travel exceeds 500 m (1,640 feet)," says Fortune. For this reason, virtually all the latest supertall high-speed elevators might have "up" travel speeds near 70 feet per second but restrict "down" speeds to half that to keep riders satisfied. Some cutting-edge elevators, such as those installed at One World Trade Center, increase the air pressure on the way up to help prevent that annoying ear-popping sensation.

While there may be some discomfort in superfast elevators, maximum elevator speeds have been accelerating in the long run. A back-of-the-envelope calculation shows that from the Singer Building (1908) to the Shanghai Tower (2015), the maximum speeds have increased at an average annual rate of 1.78 percent per year.

Inside an elevator, you would not notice it, but when it comes to building services, skyscrapers are not really skyscrapers. Rather, they are more like stacked high-rises. Every twelve to forty stories is a mechanical floor that houses the equipment needed to make life safe and enjoyable. Given current technology, there is no way to distribute these services from one central source. Water and gas from the street mains don't have the pressure to naturally rise all that height. And pumps cannot push water up more than 984 feet (300 m). Thus, water is brought to storage tanks on each mechanical floor, which is left full to run the fire sprinklers. Alongside the tanks are the heating, ventilation, and air-conditioning equipment that controls the building's temperature and air quality.

Electricity has the opposite problem as water. The voltage from the mains is far too high for building operations, so each mechanical floor has a step-down transformer that lowers the voltage. In the mechanical closets, the electricity is reduced again to the 110 or 220 volts needed to power your iPhone or television. In the case of the International Commerce Centre, where there are trading floors one thousand feet in the air, high voltages can run directly up and be reduced as needed to power the trading floors. Stock traders and Instagram users also need access to the internet. Most tall buildings rely on a combination of wired and wireless connections, such as fiber-optic and Ethernet cables that are run through the building's risers and conduits, while the wireless connections are generated by Wi-Fi routers or cellular networks from antennae.

But mechanical floors have multiple uses. They enclose the outriggers, and since they can also be self-contained, they can house refuge floors, places where occupants can safely wait during a fire or other emergency until they can be evacuated. The Shanghai Tower, for example, is divided vertically into nine zones, each with twelve to fifteen floors. The inner cylinder sets back at each zone like a wedding cake. At the interface of the zones, a two-story floor houses the mechanical, electrical, and plumbing (MEP) equipment and serves as that zone's refuge area and is also used as a base for the atrium spaces discussed earlier.

THE BEDROCK MYTH REVISITED

All these technologies have been applied to going up toward the sky, but what about going down into the ground? There is also the issue of foundations. In some sense, foundation principles remain the same as ever: Stabilize the building so it doesn't lean, unevenly settle, or, for that matter, fall over. However, the Third Skyscraper Revolution has allowed engineers to use new technologies and new methods to hold up the world's supertalls in some of the worst geological conditions.

While the vast majority of skyscraper foundations are successful, the occasional screwup creates the perception that skyscrapers are inherently dangerous. A high-end apartment building in San Francisco, the fifty-eight-story Millennium Tower, has foundation problems, driving the press and public to call it San Francisco's Leaning Tower of Pisa. A 60 Minutes news story showed one homeowner placing a marble on the floor, which then rolled away.

The tower, as reported in The Guardian, "opened to fanfare in 2009 and its more than 400 apartments quickly sold out, for a reported $750m in total. But by 2016, the building had sunk 16 in (40 cm) into the soft soil and landfill of San Francisco's dense financial district." Engineers have reinforced the foundation by adding eighteen steel piles to the bedrock, but residents say they are not working.

More broadly, the "foundations-gone-haywire" story is one form of misperception that geological conditions can create a barrier against building tall. This idea originated decades ago in Manhattan, where, the story goes, skyscrapers are "missing" between Downtown and Midtown because the bedrock is far below the surface; as a result, developers avoided building in geologically unfriendly neighborhoods such as Greenwich Village. However, this is a confusion of correlation with causation.

The real reason there were few skyscrapers in the "dead zone" was that these neighborhoods were dense tenement districts crowded with low-income immigrants and factories, and in which there was no demand for high-end office buildings. New York later implemented zoning and required the low-rise neighborhoods to remain so.

Engineers at the end of the nineteenth century, however, had found a solution to the deep bedrock problem: the caisson, an empty, bottomless box filled with compressed air to keep out the water or wet sand. Workers would go inside and dig out the sand and the box would sink. When at bedrock, it was filled with cement and piers would be built to the surface to hold up the skyscraper. The costs of these foundations were high, but well worth it because the Downtown revenues were even higher.

Here we are in the twenty-first century and the idea that geology is a dominating force for tall buildings remains prevalent. I don't want to overstate the case. Of course, geology matters, but not in the way that most people think. If there's one lesson in the skyscraper's technological history, it's that barriers that seem to exist can be overcome. They are not cheap to be sure, but when the costs are placed in the larger context of the overall budget, they tend to be relatively small. If that were not the case, thousands of buildings would not exist.

Arguably, the best scenario is a lot with flat and strong bedrock, at depths of about 50 feet (15 m) below the surface, with the overlaying soil being sandy and dry. In this case, one could simply dig an open pit to the rock floor. In many coastal cities, however, the soil is waterlogged so one can't dig without causing a cave-in. In other cases, the bedrock is far below the surface or is easily crumbled and so anchoring a structure is not feasible. In other situations, on part of the lot the bedrock is optimal while on another part it falls off precipitously. If you are lucky to have a large site, you may be able strategically to relocate the building. This was the case with the Petronas Towers, which were shifted 200 feet (60 m) from their original spot to be over a more favorable geology.

Hong Kong's geological conditions along the harbor are arguably as bad as any around the world, as demonstrated by the International Commerce Centre. There was a metro tunnel 10 feet (3 m) to the east of the site, as well as a highway aqueduct 40 feet (15 m) to the west, neither of which could be disturbed through blasting or digging. There was good bedrock at 260 feet (80 m) belowground at one spot, but the rock floor rapidly dips down to 426 feet (130 m) nearby. Then there are possible earthquakes that could shift piles if the ground vibrates.

The foundation engineers Ove Arup & Partners determined that it was not feasible or safe to drill piles to the bedrock or use standard piles buried in the soil. After a detailed study, they concluded that "[i]n view of this, friction shaft grouted barrettes, although relatively new in Hong Kong, were considered the most feasible and viable option."

A barrette is a rectangular pile 9 feet (2.8 m) wide by 5 feet (1.5 m) long and 230 feet (70 m) deep. The advantage is that they have greater load-bearing capacity when additional industrial-strength grout is pumped in and around them. The pressure of the grout compacts the surrounding soil and helps keep the pile in place. The final foundation contains 241 barrettes and a bird's-eye view made the site look like a giant manhole cover. But the stock traders on the ninetieth floor and the hotel guests swimming 1,500 feet in the air know or care little about shaft-grouted barrettes—except that they work.

For that matter, below the world's tallest building, the Burj Khalifa, there is no useful bedrock, only weak sandstone. Plus, the water table rises to as high as 8 feet (2.5 m) below the street level. The solution was to drill 194 holes 140 feet (43 m) deep into the sandstone and fill them with reinforced concrete piles. On top of the piles was placed a 12-foot-thick (3.5 m) reinforced concrete mat. Since the groundwater is corrosive, with three times the sulfates and chlorides as seawater, the rafts and piles were waterproofed and contained corrosion inhibitors.

Without piles driven or poured to bedrock, however, the building will settle. But engineering software allows for a better understanding of by how much. Engineers determined that the maximum settlement would be about 3.15 inches (80 mm), and because the footprint is so large, this settlement would be a gradual curvature over the top of the Earth. Follow-up measurements proved them correct, as the actual settlement was very close to the prediction.

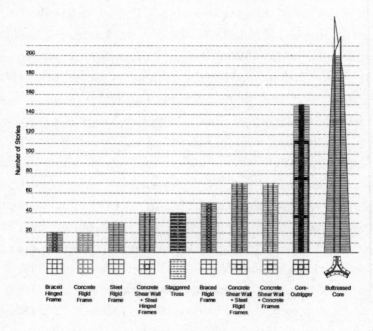

(a) Interior Structures

Different structural types and their efficient maximum heights

The technology of tall also means that the roof on height has been blown off. In a series of academic articles, written in the 1960s, Fazlur Khan illustrated—or advertised—different types of structures and the maximum heights at which their efficiency starts to drop off quickly. He estimated that the standard rigid frame with extra wind bracing would "max out" at around 60 floors. A truss, or braced, tube, like the John Hancock Center, would max out at 100 floors. The bundled tube, like the Sears (Willis) Tower, can go up to 110 floors.

Recently, two skyscraper scholars, Professor Kyoung Sun Moon of Yale University and Mir M. Ali of the University of Illinois

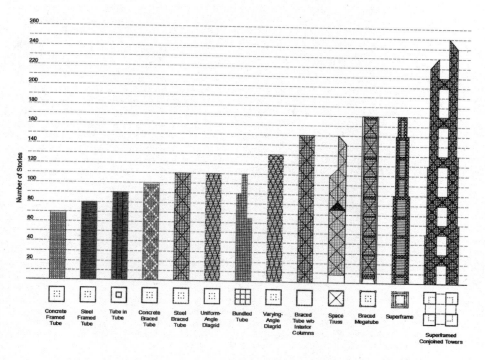

(b) Exterior Structures

Urbana-Champaign, updated Khan's structural forms to include those of the twenty-first century. In their analysis, they determined that it's economically feasible to build a concrete core-outrigger system with megacolumns to 140 stories, while current tube systems allow for buildings to efficiently rise to 140–180 stories.

The future of height, however, is likely to be a cojoined tower, which takes the stiffness of a tube or a core-outrigger system and enhances it by joining them together. The efficient maximum with this system, according to Moon and Ali, is over 200 stories.

I'll meet you at the observation deck!

CHAPTER 7

Oil-Rich Cities

Tales from the Arabian Heights

Burj Khalifa (2010)

THE BURJ KHALIFA

We stand together in the heavens, but we are very much alive. We are viewing a skyline of spires piercing through a blanket of cotton-like clouds. Encasing these structures is a dome of searing orange from the setting sun. Before you is the skyline from the sky—at 1,821 feet

(555 m) up—where we see nothing but a floor of white and a city of floating buildings. No roads up here. To travel from one building to the next would require cloud hopping or, better yet, winged flight. We stand on the observation deck of the Burj Khalifa.

By riding up the elevator and stepping out onto the viewing deck, it's as if we have entered a forbidden city—a modern Mount Olympus, where the gods drink their nectar and lord over the mortals below. The view also calls to mind a 1969 episode of *Star Trek*, "The Cloud Minders," where the crew of the USS *Enterprise* visits a society that lives in a dense cluster of Greek-styled, futuristic high-rises, built atop a puffy white cloud. There the people of Ardana, dressed in white togas, idly spend their days in intellectual and artistic pursuits.

Wiping away the clouds, however, reveals a city rising out of desert sands, where a capitalist chemical reaction has taken place in a crucible where East meets West, the product of which is the Burj Khalifa. Opened in 2010, at one half mile (828 m) tall, it is not only the world's tallest skyscraper but also the world's tallest human-made object. And, ironically, it has bones of stone—reinforced concrete walls—enclosed in the skin of aqua-blue glass.

Back on the ground, staring up at the massive tower, one might easily conclude that it is the result of excessive wealth, the craving for spectacle, and egos gone wild. While there are hints of all these, to say they were the driving forces behind the world's tallest structure is an oversimplification—an attempt to shrink the structure's gigantism to something we can comprehend. If anything, its creation is maniacal genius—having emerged from a clairvoyance that it would succeed when most people thought it a folly. The project's sheer boldness is reminiscent of the Empire State Building and the Eiffel Tower and is but one maniacal project in Dubai's long chain of them.

Having the world's tallest building, of course, by its very nature, is a product of competition. No one builds such a thing by accident, and everyone is keenly aware of the message it sends. When completed, it was not merely a few feet above the former world's tallest building, Taipei 101. Instead, it was 1,276 feet (389 m) taller, as if someone placed the Empire State Building on top of Taipei 101 and called it the Burj Khalifa, or Khalifa Tower, named after the former UAE president Sheikh Khalifa bin Zayed Al Nahyan.

However, the structure's history is complex and layered. Like all record-breaking skyscrapers, it was made possible by the alignment of interests and economics. First is rising real estate values, and for Dubai, before the 2007–2008 Financial Crisis, such was the case. Second is that technological innovations, materials prices, and supply chains must be available to realize grand dreams at a reasonable cost. The third is location. Such a project must be in a central place. And just as importantly, the city must be big and active, not only with global ambitions but also with global reach.

No one can deny that using skyscrapers to draw attention to Dubai has succeeded. The world's tallest building has helped to make it part of the international flow of people, information, and goods and services along the global highways and byways of commerce and consumption. The towers that transformed Dubai represent not only the power to harness resources for economic gain but also the power to alter perceptions and produce myths along with the real estate.

But Dubai as Dubai is the product of one ruling family, the Al Maktoums, and the city is their capitalist fiefdom. In a way, it is a nation that hews most closely to the client-patron states of old. The ruling Sheikh Mohammed bin Rashid Al Maktoum and his family are the ultimate patrons who bestow gifts on their clients in return for helping transform Dubai into a global city, while also earning a slice of the profits.

The story of the Burj Khalifa begins with Emaar Properties, a publicly traded company of which 22 percent is owned by the Emirate's SWF, Investment Corporation of Dubai. Founded in 1997, Emaar was charged with developing and managing real estate within Dubai. The company was the brainchild of Mohamed Ali Rashed Alabbar. He was selected by Sheikh Mohammed's father, Sheikh Rashid bin Saeed Al Maktoum, who ruled before him, to be a future leader. Alabbar was sent for his education to the United States, where he received his bachelor's degree in business administration from Seattle University in 1981.

When back home, Alabbar became the director of the city's Department of Economic Development and a member of the Dubai Executive Council, the supreme governing body that coordinates all growth initiatives in Dubai. Before leading Emaar, he created the Dubai Shopping Festival. In 1996, *Advertising Age* named him one of the "International Marketing Superstars of the Year."

In 1997, the United Arab Emirates merged the Dubai Defense Force into the UAE Federal Army, which freed up the Dubai army base. The 0.8-square-mile (2 km²) plot was now prime real estate near Dubai's new financial center and just north of the two skyscraper columns along Sheikh Zayed Road. As journalist Jim Krane chronicles, "Sheikh Mohammed wasn't going to build a trailer park there. In 2002, he handed the plot to Emaar. The conditions were tough. Emaar's chairman, Mohamed Alabbar, had to build a downtown that would command the world's attention."

Alabbar was inspired by the Petronas Towers project. "We looked at the success of KLCC [Kuala Lumpur City Centre]," Emaar executive Mark Amirault revealed. "Not only did they build the Petronas Towers, but they added in a major shopping center, a large man-made lake and park, [and] a hotel, and created the new center of Kuala Lumpur."

Emaar hired the master planner who had designed KLCC, David Klages of RNL, and began to envision something in Dubai along the same lines. The world's tallest tower—the Burj Dubai (Dubai Tower)—was going to be a centerpiece of Downtown Dubai. When Alabbar showed preliminary designs to Sheikh Mohammed, the meeting did not go well. "The Dubai crown prince asked for details of the world's tallest building, a tower in Taiwan called Taipei 101 [at 508 meters tall]: 'why is it taller? Are people there smarter than you?'" recounts Krane.

When Emaar initiated the architectural design competition for the Burj, the brief specifically requested the world's tallest tower of at least 550 meters (1,804 feet). Adrian Smith, then of SOM, produced the winning design that came in at 535 meters (1,755 feet) to the roof, with an additional 164-meter (538-foot) spire. When Alabbar returned to Sheikh Mohammed with the new rendering, it was the world's tallest—though not by enough. The sheikh's response: "Go a lot taller," Krane documents. As a result, the tower was raised to 682 meters to the roof and 808 meters to the spire's tip.

Originally Smith's team wanted the building to rise 804 meters, or a half mile. But the Chinese character for "four" sounds like the character for "death," and the team feared that the four would produce poor feng shui for potential Chinese apartment buyers. The height was thus raised to the lucky number of 808 meters, since the character for "eight" in Mandarin sounds like the character for "wealth."

And that was that—no zoning restrictions, no environmental impact statements, and no review by planning officials. The leader said, "Make it taller," and the developer made it so. There was never any pushback— why should there be? It would serve the goals of many and there were few technological, political, social, economic, or financial barriers to stop it from going forward.

Given the project was part of a retail, entertainment, and residential complex, Emaar preferred a mixed-used building rather than a pure office. This led to its key design feature: it would be tapered as it rose, shaped more like a pyramid than a box. The lower floors were to be used for a hotel, above that for offices, and above that for apartments. The very top was reserved for "luxury offices." The observation deck is on floor 124.

Smith's approach to the Burj was like that of the Jin Mao in Shanghai—find an architectural vernacular that would directly speak to the local culture and adapt it to a supertall. As Smith recalled:

I searched for elements within the existing context and culture of the area to reflect on and draw inspiration from. Within the Middle East and in Dubai, there are strong influences of onion domes and pointed arches, and there are patterns that are indigenous to the region, some of which are flower like with three elements, some with six and so on. Other influences range from spiral imagery and philosophy embedded in Middle Eastern iconographic architecture and motifs. These motifs have their origin in organic growth structures and plant materials.

As it turned out, the final height became 828 meters when the CTBUH's height measurement committee (discussed in the next chapter) determined that the building could be measured starting from the aboveground basement level—which had been raised up because of the high water tables—rather than the first floor, fortuitously providing an extra 20 meters (65 feet) to the official height.

As is common at SOM, like Bruce Graham and Fazlur Khan in the 1960s, architects work alongside a lead engineer. In this case, the team was Smith and engineer William Baker. Baker realized that to create this tapering "flower-like" design in an efficient and cost-effective manner, he could draw on a relatively new structural idea: the buttressed core.

Since the primary design is based on the "triaxial" geometric pattern, the form was to have three separate wings connected to a central core. The concrete hallway walls for each of the three wings act as part of the structure. Together the wings, which buttress the central core, make the building that much stiffer against the wind forces.

The Burj Khalifa was the "culmination" of the buttressed core idea that had been evolving since the 1970s. The Jeddah Tower, if ever completed, at one kilometer tall, will also use it. The two earliest precedents were Toronto's CN Tower (1976; 553.3 m, 1,815.3 feet) and Chicago's Lake Point Tower (1968). The CN Tower is not occupied but is an observatory and TV antenna, but it was the world's tallest human-made structure when completed.

The first "proto-buttressed core" residence was that of Chicago's Lake Point Tower (1968; 70 floors, 645 feet), which had a triangular core to add stiffness. It is a y-shaped glass-covered Modernist structure designed by the firm of Schipporeit and Heinrich for the developers, William Hartnett and Charles Shaw. The architects were students of Ludwig Mies van der Rohe. At the time of its completion in 1968, the 645-foot-tall (197 m) Lake Point Tower was the tallest apartment building in the world.

As reported in the *Chicago Tribune*:

It's often said—wrongly, it turns out—that Schipporeit and Heinrich based their Lake Point Tower design on Mies' visionary but unbuilt 1921 plan for a glass-sheathed skyscraper on a triangular site in Berlin. In fact, the architects initially conceived the skyscraper as a cross-shaped design with four wings, not three.

To make the project fit the budget, the developers lopped off one of the proposed wings. That led the architects to work out a three-winged, purely curvilinear design that was further distinguished by its sleek, continuous surfaces—a "skin" architecture as opposed to the X-braced "bones" of the John Hancock Center, which would make its debut in 1969.

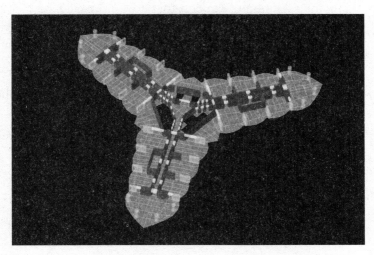

A cross section of the Burj Khalifa's buttressed core (© SOM, architect)

The buttressed core idea is a good example of how structural innovations unfold. Based on the success of the CN Tower and the Lake Point Tower, when an opportunity presented itself, SOM took the form to the next level. "The buttressed core represents a conceptual change in structural design whose evolutionary development began with Tower Palace III, designed by Chicago-based Skidmore, Owings & Merrill LLP (SOM)," write William Baker and James Pawlikowski. "Completed in 2004, Tower Palace III, located in Seoul, South Korea, promoted a new standard in high-rise residential development. Its tripartite arrangement provides 120 degrees between wings, affording maximum views and privacy. Although Chicago's Lake Point Tower set the architectural precedent." Smith planned to use a buttressed core in the Crown Las Vegas Tower, which was going to be a supertall hotel of 1,886 feet (575 m). After the financial meltdown in 2007–2008, the project was shelved.

And despite the universal conventional wisdom that record breakers don't pay, the Burj has been an economic success. On the cost side alone, it demonstrated that a supertall mixed-used tower could be built relatively cheaply. The buttressed core, along with innovations in high-strength concrete, formwork, and pumping, allowed Emaar to get its building for a fraction of the cost that it would have paid if such a building was completed in New York (the low-cost labor makes a huge difference).

One World Trade Center, admittedly expensive because of bureaucratic wrangling and the need to be terrorism-proof, cost $3.8 billion. New York's latest supertall office building, One Vanderbilt, at 1,401 feet (427 m) cost $3 billion. The Burj's construction cost came in with a price tag of $2.1 billion.

For that matter, the Burj is small. The Willis (Sears) Tower has 4.7 million gross square feet (440,000 m²). The Shanghai Tower has 4.5 million square feet (420,000 m²), and Taipei 101 has 4.0 million square feet (370,000 m²). The Burj has only 3.3 million square feet (309,473 m²), making it taller and skinnier. It also is the world's first record breaker

LEFT: CN Tower (1976), Toronto
RIGHT: Lake Point Tower (1968), Chicago

to be predominantly for residences. Perhaps that says something about the current and future nature of cities: less for work and more for fun.

But the cost is irrelevant if it does not generate revenue. Thanks to the booming housing market in Dubai, Emaar was able to presell 70 percent of the residences before completion, and, despite the Financial Crisis, it recouped most of its construction costs early in the process. In addition, the observation deck remains a cash cow, generating nearly $200 million a year in revenue. If the building were an observation deck alone it would have paid for itself in a decade.

Just as important are the spillover effects. Because Downtown Dubai was built entirely by Emaar it could reap additional profits from the increased land values nearby from the tower. By my estimate, a residential apartment within Downtown Dubai sells for about 15 percent more if it has a Burj view. The increase in surrounding property values alone more than likely paid for the tower.

Lastly is the impact of the Burj on Dubai itself. The tower's success in signaling the city's economic strength is undeniable. It remains a beacon to its can-do spirit. Was there ego involved? Of course. Sheikh Mohammed wanted the world's tallest building, and he got it. But was it an economically rational decision? Yes! Ego and economics are not mutually exclusive.

That's not to say that it's all roses and chocolate. While the Burj has been a moneymaker, there have been some downsides. One is the huge cost to maintain and operate. The apartment fees run in the tens of thousands of dollars each year, and from an investment point of view, the units are difficult to rent out because the income can barely cover the expenses.

Thanks to the hypersecurity, the building is essentially a fortress. It's isolated from the neighborhood by fencing, and to get to the observatory you need to enter through the mall on the lower level. One viral video on YouTube shows a resident needing ten card swipes to get to her apartment.

There's another chestnut that people love to bandy about. The Burj Khalifa was not hooked up to the municipal sewage system, which has prompted such grand headlines as "The Incredible Story of How the Burj Khalifa's Poop Is Trucked out of Town." Emaar Properties went with septic tanks since the city's sewage pipes were not equipped to accommodate the flow.

To critics, this is seen not only as a big waste (no pun intended) since removing it requires many trucks to ship the output to a treatment plant, but also as proof that the record breakers are silly. While it does suggest that Dubai is getting ahead of itself in terms of building upward faster than it can build its belowground infrastructure, the press and public love to telescope on this fact to conclude that tall buildings should not exist.

And, as will be discussed later, the Burj Khalifa was renamed from the Burj Dubai after Abu Dhabi bailed out Dubai during the Financial Crisis. The building emerged when the real estate market was overheated, and the Dubai government and investors overextended themselves. But like the Empire State Building, it will remain Dubai's beloved icon for many years to come.

But as the Financial Crisis was beginning to ebb, the Burj Khalifa officially opened with great fanfare and fireworks at midnight on January 1, 2010. The conception of the Burj during the real estate boom and its subsequent opening after collapse has led the skyscraper commentariat to point to the Burj as another example of the so-called Skyscraper Curse.

In 1999, an economist named Andrew Lawrence thought he saw a relationship between the business cycle and skyscrapers; he dubbed this the "Skyscraper Index," and it purports to demonstrate the "Skyscraper Curse," which is "an unhealthy correlation between the construction of the next world's tallest building and an impending financial crisis: New York 1930, Chicago 1974; Kuala Lumpur 1997 and Dubai 2010. Yet often the world's tallest buildings are simply the edifice of a broader skyscraper building boom, reflecting a widespread misallocation of capital and an impending economic correction."

It has proven a seductive idea and its tentacles have spread widely among the media and public. But the idea that the construction of the world's tallest building is a harbinger of economic doom is specious. It is an example of what I call Rorschach Economics. People see a relationship because they want to.

Economic downturns, panics, and/or crises happen very frequently, much more frequently than record-breaking skyscrapers. By my count, there have been at least twenty-eight panics, crises, or severe downturns in the last 125 years, over twice as many as record-breaking buildings. So it's quite easy to find a crisis and pair it with a tall building, proving the adage that even a broken clock is right twice a day.

The "Skyscraper Index" is not even an index, which is a set of measurements that represents the average value of something, such as the Consumer Price Index, which measures the cost of living, or the Dow Jones Industrial Index, which measures the value of thirty large-company stocks. The "Skyscraper Index," on the other hand, is simply a graphic montage that shows pictures of the world's tallest buildings over a timeline with some "nearby" financial crises.

The point of generating real indexes is that you can then use them to perform statistical tests to avoid conclusions based on "truthiness." This is just what I, along with two coauthors, Bruce Mizrach and Kusum Mundra, both at Rutgers University, did. First, as a very simple test, we looked to see where the announcement and completion dates of the world's record-breaking buildings fell within the U.S. business cycle.

While it is true that ten of these structures were announced during an upswing in the cycle, the range of months between the announcement and cycle peak is tremendous, varying from zero to forty-five months. Looking at the opening dates of the buildings shows a similar story. Only half were completed during the downward phase of the cycle, and furthermore, there is no pattern between when the building is opened for business and when the trough occurs. In short, there is no way to predict the business cycle from record-breaking buildings, based on either when a record breaker is announced or when it is completed.

In the second statistical analysis, we tried to do what the proponents of the Skyscraper Curse say you can do: predict changes in the economy from building heights. To this end, we tried to see if we could predict changes in a country's gross domestic product (GDP) for the United States, Canada, Hong Kong, and mainland China from the height of their tallest completed building each year, respectively. We could not. The strong evidence is that it is impossible to use building heights to make predictions about financial collapse. It shows that the Skyscraper Curse, despite its allure, is more puff than substance.

DUBAI'S FIRST SKYSCRAPER

The Burj Khalifa, however, gives the impression that Dubai was an instant city, in part because it was built in a region where Westernization supposedly passed by. The events of 9/11 and the actions of Saudi Crown Prince

Mohammed bin Salman Al Saud (MBS) help fuel this perception. The beliefs beg an interesting question: What was Dubai's first skyscraper?

It was, in fact, the Dubai World Trade Centre, constructed in 1979, only six years after New York's Twin Towers were completed. To many, this structure remains their favorite in the city, as it retains a quiet Modernist charm compared to the over-the-top futuristic and Postmodern structures that have risen recently.

Dubai's success is based on the historically tested notion that truly great cities are transportation and trading hubs. Once it built a World Trade Centre, Dubai was then linked to the other World Trade Centers around the world, whose mission was to foster global commerce and interconnections. Without trade and the investments that facilitate bringing people together, you can't have a great city. Be it eighteenth-century BCE Babylonia, fifteenth-century Venice, seventeenth-century Amsterdam, nineteenth-century Chicago, or twenty-first-century Dubai, the core principles are the same. The more trade, the higher the income, the greater the investments in art, culture, real estate, and pleasure.

Dubai's rise is all the more ironic since for millennia it was but a small village of Bedouin settlers, where fishermen and pearl divers would extract what they could from the sea. As *Dune*-on-the-Gulf, its Bedouin nomads lived a lean and mean desert life. Tribal sheikhs took power by being braver, wiser, or more generous.

Dubai's recorded history begins around 1800 when the Persian Gulf's strategic value was of interest to both Europeans and Ottomans. As Krane writes, "Britain . . . saw that it could not secure its lucrative trade lines to India without controlling the nearly landlocked sea. India lay just a few hundred miles across the Arabian Sea from the Gulf coast—easy striking distance."

But British rulers were not interested in running the place in the same way as Hong Kong or India. Rather, they made the Arab tribal chiefs their clients. The arrangement was to form treaties with each of the main local tribes, which became known as the Trucial States. The

TOP: Dubai World Trade Centre (1979)
BELOW: The subsequent rise of skyscrapers around it.

treaties stabilized the region by replacing tribal democracy with monarchies. The arrangement also meant that the monarchs now owned all the land and resources in their respective territories and could dole them out as they saw fit.

Around 1900, an opening presented itself, and Dubai made a small economic step forward. In that year, Iran raised taxes at its ports. As

Krane recounts, the ruler Sheikh Maktoum bin Hasher Al Maktoum "saw the low-hanging fruit. He launched a plan to make Dubai the most business-friendly port in the lower Gulf. Agents offered free land, a friendly ear at *majlis* [audiences with the sheikh], and hands-off government policy."

The incentives worked, and soon bustling wharves lined Dubai Creek, where cargo was reexported or strapped on camels and moved inland. In 1903 British steamships scheduled stops at Dubai, and by 1908 the city was home to ten thousand Arabs, Persians, Indians, and Baluchis. Trade was now its lifeline.

The modernization of Dubai began with Sheikh Hasher's son, Sheikh Rashid bin Saeed Al Maktoum (1912–1990), whose motto was "What's good for the merchants is good for Dubai." In the 1950s, the creek had become gummed up with silt. Rashid was determined to build a modern port. He raised money through assessments and donations and borrowed the rest from Kuwait. The creek was dredged, expanded, and shored up with retaining walls. When it reopened in 1961, one ship could deliver three times the cargo that Dubai imported in all of 1951.

What had originally looked like folly to many at the onset became Dubai's ticket to progress and the most accessible and important port in the region. Rashid repaid his backers ahead of schedule, and local merchants who pitched in were made extra rich through exclusive import licenses and business contracts.

Following the success of the creek expansion, Sheikh Rashid embarked on a series of large, risky investments. In the ensuing years, the ruler would build a new port for massive container ships, a smelting facility, and a huge dry dock for ship repairs. By sheer luck for the Emirate, the dry dock opened just before the Iran-Iraq War when, "[i]n a new twist on ambulance chasing, salvage tugs patrolled the Gulf and towed the [missile] victims to Dubai. . . . The dry docks grew so busy that damaged ships waited months for repairs," reports Krane. Taking a long-run view, one can say that big and bold investments were the DNA of Dubai.

Then there is the issue of oil. Compared to its neighbors, Dubai had very few reserves, which were found relatively late. However, by 1975, oil earnings were bringing in nearly two-thirds of its GDP. But by 1985, it slipped to 50 percent. By 2000, it was down to 10 percent. In 2006, it was a tiny 3 percent. Given that Dubai's oil discoveries were small, it depended on other sources of income, and the oil revenue was used to diversify its economy. In this way, oil helped finance what we can call Dubai, Inc., a series of state-owned businesses that propelled it into the twenty-first century.

And now, finally, we arrive at the story of how Dubai constructed its first skyscraper. But first, we must go back to New York City and see how, once again, it influenced global skyscraper history, this time, to the World Trade Center and the Twin Towers.

The original seed for its World Trade Center dates to 1946 when the New York State legislature created a World Trade Corporation to promote international trade. But it wasn't until 1957 when David Rockefeller, banker, and grandson of oil baron John D. Rockefeller, spearheaded the creation of the Downtown-Lower Manhattan Association (D-LMA) to help revitalize Lower Manhattan. The D-LMA commissioned SOM to create a master plan, which included a World Trade Center, and office and exhibition space near the East River south of the Brooklyn Bridge. The D-LMA turned to the Port Authority of New York as a natural agency that could spearhead construction.

The Port of New York Authority (today the Port Authority of New York and New Jersey) was formally created in 1921 and was conceived as a bi-state agency to coordinate the region's port activity. Its territory extended inside a twenty-five-mile radius around the Statue of Liberty. The hope was that the agency would rationalize and revitalize the port. Given the rising use of automobiles, however, it found itself being drawn into the construction of automobile tunnels and bridges, which were appealing, given the large toll income.

But with Rockefeller's proposal, the PA was nudged into real estate development. After protracted negotiations and "slum clearance," it took control of a 15-acre (6-hectare) site on Manhattan's Lower West Side. Tower 1 opened in 1972 and Tower 2 in the following year.

So, how did the project go from a World Trade Center to promote import-export businesses to the world's largest twin towers? The original SOM plan called for 5–6 million square feet (464,512–557,418 m²) of office and exhibition space in a series of towers. But once the project was under the control of the PA, its ambitious leader, Austin Tobin, expanded the project to 10 million square feet (929,030 m²).

At this point, there was no clear design for the towers. Lee K. Jaffe, a public relations expert on the planning team, circulated a memo in 1960 that included the remark: "Incidentally, if you are going to build a great project, you should build the world's tallest building." The idea took root. After all, Tobin wanted to go big, the Authority was freed from city zoning regulations, and the economics was less of a concern. So why not do it? It was a good public relations move.

Not satisfied with the early designs from the initial study team, the PA's chief on the WTC project, Guy Tozzoli, reached out to architect Minoru Yamasaki (1912–1986). Yamasaki was born in Seattle and studied architecture at the University of Washington. In part to escape anti-Japanese prejudice, he moved to New York in 1934. There he earned his master's degree in architecture at New York University and then joined the firm of Shreve, Lamb & Harmon of Empire State Building fame.

In the 1940s he started his own practice in Detroit, and after World War II he became a sought-after Modernist designer. Besides being known as the architect of the World Trade Center, he's infamous for designing the public housing project of Pruitt-Igoe in St. Louis, which was demolished in the 1970s because of its failures.

Tozzoli gave Yamasaki the general specs of the plan but left it up to him how to distribute the floor area between various buildings.

Yamasaki decided that instead of creating several evenly spaced and evenly heighted buildings, he would provide two eighty-story towers as the centerpiece, thinking that eighty was about as high as the PA should go, after considering the economics and the technology. However, his plan still did not have enough square footage as mandated by Tobin. He was pushed by Tozzoli to go taller.

Finally, in January 1964, Yamasaki's design was made public. The Twin Towers were each going to be 1,350 feet (411 m) tall, with 110 stories, and with 4.3 million square feet (399,483 m²) of space. To go so high meant that certain technological hurdles had to be overcome. As discussed in chapter 3, Yamasaki turned to Leslie Robertson, the young engineer, to make it all work.

Despite their destruction on September 11, 2001, the legacy of the Twin Towers remains strong. It was the first time that an American government agency — or likely any government agency the world over — directly developed and managed supertall skyscrapers meant to compete with the private sector. Historically, governments built tall buildings for their own needs. City halls competed with houses of worship to be the tallest in each city. But here was a regional governmental entity producing building space to earn a profit.

More importantly, it showed, over time, that placemaking via record-breaking skyscrapers was a viable option for cities, as the Twin Towers became instant icons of the Manhattan skyline. Just as important was their economic success, which created a new model: Build a record breaker with state support. If need be, fill it up with government agencies (or state-owned businesses outside the United States), give it time for neighborhood growth to kick in, and reap the returns.

That it took till 1998 for this strategy to surface in Asia — starting with the Petronas Towers in Kuala Lumpur — was due to the time Asia needed to catch up with its economic development and infrastructure. That it wasn't replicated in the United States after that was because by the end of the 1970s America's era of big government-funded urban renewal projects was over, while in Asia government-funded projects were just beginning.

As noted earlier, the WTC concept would help spawn World Trade Centers around the world, such as those in Chicago, Dhaka, Jakarta, Bahrain, and Dubai. The idea of using a skyscraper to promote trade is arguably one of their most natural uses. Each one says: "This is a house of trade; you are welcome here."

The idea of Dubai's World Trade Centre originated in a serendipitous meeting at its new airport terminal, designed and built by the British firm of Page & Broughton. "Travelers were greeted at once by Dubai's sophisticated airport and a display of British expertise that helped realize the airport and the city beyond," architectural historian Todd Reisz writes.

On March 14, 1974, a jet carrying Queen Elizabeth landed in Dubai. She was en route to Indonesia and asked her pilot to move the planned refueling from Bahrain to Dubai so she could get a glimpse of the new terminal. Once alerted to her arrival, Sheikh Rashid and architect and city planner John Harris provided a tour. Later that evening Harris was summoned to a meeting with Rashid. The queen's visit had convinced the ruler that Dubai needed exhibition facilities. Harris was commissioned to design them.

The original proposal was two interlocking six-story pyramids. "Rashid turned down the proposal. . . . He thought it was too understated," Reisz writes. "Rashid, bolstered by his recent $500 million windfall in oil sales, insisted on a skyscraper." And, as Reisz reveals:

After some more thought, Harris came upon a template for what Rashid wanted: a World Trade Center. He subsequently traveled around the world assessing the present state of the trade centre movement, visiting both the World Trade Center in Tokyo and the one in New York City, both designed by Minoru Yamasaki. The New York Project was dominated by the world's two tallest towers. . . . On the outside, New York

City's World Trade Center was an expression of financial might. Inside, it was a combinational structure of exhibition concourses, high-end office spaces, and convention halls. The World Trade Center, soon a global brand of corporate property management, packaged interiors as pampering hospitality and cushy privileges.

After deliberations about the site, it was finally chosen to be "out in the desert" where it would anchor a new business district. In October 1974, Harris handed Rashid "a tower proposal whose façade evoked the New York's twin towers' threadlike columns," Reisz writes. "In fact, earlier tower schemes even included twin towers. . . . Even the low-rise buildings had precedents in the New York scheme. The revised proposal was also featured on the cover of *Akhbar Dubai* as the 'tallest building in the Arab world.'"

The tower's height was set at thirty-three stories; however, as Reisz documents:

When the tower had reached eight stories, midway through 1976, the design and construction teams received news from Sheik Rashid: He wanted it to be taller. Rashid's sudden request might have resulted from news that Abu Dhabi planned an even taller building. . . . The project's engineers begrudgingly heightened the building based on what the foundation could carry. . . . Press releases announced a thirty-nine-floor tower but that counted the accessible rooftop as a floor. An added television mast helped the building top out at 175 meters, qualifying it to reign as Dubai's tallest building for at least twenty years.

Sheikh Rashid was warned by his advisors that the trade center was a waste of time. But the Middle East's tallest building had little trouble finding tenants, including IBM, Union Carbide, United Technologies, and British Petroleum. The skyscraper also hosted the U.S. consulate and as well as Dubai's local stock market.

Today its success is taken for granted and its stature is positively diminutive in Dubai's skyline. With over 1.3 million square feet of exhibition and event space, the Dubai World Trade Centre has hosted hundreds of trade events and millions of visitors. But on September 11, 2001, the New York Twin Towers and the Dubai World Trade Centre were linked once again by an act of unconscionable malice. The connection was not just that two of the hijackers were from the United Arab Emirates. Rather, the instant that United Airlines Flight 175 hit the South Tower, the terrorists handed the Arabian country an unintended victory for Western-style capitalism.

While the terrorists' goal was to put a stake in the heart of Americanism, they gave Dubai an economic boost that helped make it a hedonist and shopper's paradise. In fact, it's only a slight stretch to say that 9/11 created the Burj Khalifa, the ultimate symbol of capitalist striving. Why? In the post-9/11 U.S. climate, Gulf Arabs decided to pull out their billions in investments and assets to repatriate them. Arab-phobia in America was rampant, and few Middle Easterners wanted to take any chances. "In the Gulf, the September 11 attacks marked the start of a six-year economic boom that raged in gluttonous excess until finally losing steam at the end of 2008," Krane writes.

As a result, Krane documents, "[c]ash poured into Dubai, which became the poster child for the Gulf boom. Dubai's growth averaged a scorching 13 percent a year between 2000 and 2005, faster than China's. The emirate's population doubled between 2001 and 2008, reaching 2 million."

In the 1990s, Sheikh Mohammed, the then crown prince, who succeeded his father, Rashid, in 2006, had already turned Dubai toward consumerism and finance. The most famous example is the Burj Al Arab hotel, a blue skyscraper shaped like a ship's sail. Completed in 1999, at 1,053 feet (321 m), it fittingly replaced the World Trade Centre as Dubai's tallest building, as a symbol of consumption and leisure rather than ports and trade. It's an ultra-luxury hotel (falsely labeled as the world's only seven-star hotel) on its own artificial island, which helped brand Dubai as a luxury tourist destination.

Repatriation of funds timed nicely with Dubai's ambitions of becoming a residential real estate investment hub. In 2002, Sheikh Mohammed made arguably one of his most momentous decisions: permitting foreigners to own homes. "The decree unleased a typhoon of pent-up demand that was stronger than anyone knew. A gold-rush ensued. Expatriates jumped at the chance to buy. Investors followed, funneling cash into Dubai from ever farther away," Krane writes.

Within this frenzy, Downtown Dubai and the Burj Khalifa would rise, while between July 2005 and November 2008 residential prices increased by 250 percent. The economic and real estate boom was not without consequences, however. It produced a Wild West atmosphere. With little oversight from the municipality, developers from around the world rushed in and demanded weird and iconic structures from their architects, with little thought to how functional or efficient the buildings would be and how much they would cost to maintain.

And nearly overnight the Dubai skyline was born. Up until 2005, Dubai never built more than seven skyscrapers (328 feet or higher, 100 m+) in any given year. Then starting in 2006, over the next five years Dubai would erect 278. It was as if Heaven was getting acupuncture.

Then the Financial Crisis came. The market crashed and panic ensued. Developers were so eager to get out of town they were abandoning their cars at the airport. Until recently, a developer could not declare bankruptcy or legally default on a loan. If they did, they could wind up in debtor's prison.

In 2009, Abu Dhabi bailed out Dubai to the tune of $10 billion to stave off bankruptcy. Some of the money was used to rescue the state-owned real estate developer Nakheel Properties, which had plans to build a one-kilometer tower. As a token of gratitude, the Burj Dubai was renamed the Burj Khalifa, in honor of the white knight who saved Dubai.

But if you talk to industry insiders, they will tell you there was a silver lining to the collapse. Developers are more regulated. They are required, for example, to create escrow accounts before their projects begin. They are more likely to request "sane" designs from their architects that keep costs in line. And Abu Dhabi is watching more closely to make sure its investments are not squandered.

What was the result of Dubai's growth spurt? It is a thriving city, to be sure. It remains an international investment haven (for both legal and ill-gotten gains), and its economy is growing. As of this writing (September 2023), the news is once again broadcasting headlines like "'Spectacular' Dubai Property Bounce Likely to Continue, Knight Frank Says."

But few Americans realize the broader connections between the two places. In Dubai, everyone speaks English. The city is covered with malls and restaurants owned by star chefs. The currency is pegged to the dollar, and the planning is half Manhattan, half Phoenix, and half Las Vegas. I recall with amusement that one mall food court I visited for lunch had a stall for "New York Fries," next to a Baskin-Robbins and a Burger King.

And when you talk to a young Westerner who's traveled to Dubai, their first comment is how the place lacks soul as compared to New York, London, or Hong Kong. This is certainly true. Dubai feels plastic and sprawled out. The city is built around automobiles and not pedestrians, and it's a plain fact: car dependency robs cities of their energy. It's the same as Pudong, where Chinese planners created multilane boulevards and huge urban blocks. It has little of the urban vitality of the city across the river.

Dubai's over-the-top skyscraper architecture does exude a certain playfulness, but there's nothing like density and decades of use and reuse of a city and its buildings to generate a spirit and history to which you can connect. Ironically, the places where you can feel the urban vibe are in the old communities around the creek. When I visited the Al Fahidi neighborhood one Sunday morning, I was trapped in a narrow, ancient alleyway as a parade of Indian worshipers walked past. You could smell the incense as the women dressed in their traditional saris carried plates of food to the temple. However, the area is an ethnic enclave where workers hole up during their sojourns as temporary employees. It's not particularly welcoming beyond the gold and spice souks.

Modern Dubai was constructed for a purpose: to bring money to the nationals who could not depend on oil revenue. In this way, Sheikh Mohammed exploited Sheikh Rashid's bold project building and took advantage of its bright sandy beaches and turquoise water to create the ultimate vacation city, staffed by an army of migrant workers from India and the Philippines too afraid to step out of line, lest they instantly get deported. It makes the city safe and clean to be sure, but it also makes it a little uneasy.

There are thus three Dubais—Bling Skyscraper City, Arabia, and Migrantville. Will Dubai continue to grow and be part of the international economy? Yes. Will it ever get that soul that comes from the true mixing of people from around the world? I don't know, but let's see. Cities have a way of surprising you as they age into themselves.

THE JEDDAH TOWER

The success of the Burj Khalifa has made the world take notice, especially Dubai's neighbor Saudi Arabia. In August 2011, the Saudi billionaire Prince Alwaleed bin Talal Al Saud—aka the Warren Buffet of Saudi Arabia—unveiled plans to construct the world's tallest skyscraper, rising 1 kilometer (3,281 feet) high.

Though we won't dwell long in the land of the Saudis, it will pay to make a sojourn here as it provides some interesting contrasts and comparisons with its smaller but more cosmopolitan peninsula-mate. The country is facing the prospect of declining oil revenues and a stagnating economy filled with under- and unemployed young people. In fits and starts, Saudi Arabia is trying to embrace global capitalism and wants to use the Dubai model to help it out.

The tower is the brainchild of Alwaleed. It was designed to be the tallest building in three height categories of the CTBUH: the tallest architectural height (one kilometer), the tallest tip (just over one kilometer), and the highest occupied floor (167). Whereas the Burj Khalifa "grew" over its planning process, the Jeddah Tower was set to be at least one kilometer from the start. One kilometer sounds nice—it's clean, easily remembered, and, just as importantly, is significantly taller than the Burj. As Alwaleed said at the press conference announcing the tower:

> Building this tower in Jeddah sends a financial and economic message that should not be ignored. . . . It has a political depth to it to tell the world that we Saudis invest in our country despite what is happening around us from events, turmoil and revolutions even.

And like its neighbor, the skyscraper is to be the centerpiece of the newly constructed planned city—Jeddah Economic City, just north of historical Jeddah. But beyond becoming an anchor building and announcing the Kingdom of Saudi Arabia as a modern, international destination, the tower is, of course, meant to take the spotlight away from Dubai—to out-Dubai Dubai. Even the tower itself is nearly a replica of the Burj Khalifa.

Alwaleed is a grandson of Abdulaziz bin Abdul Rahman Al Saud (Ibn Saud), who founded the Kingdom of Saudi Arabia in 1932. The current king, Salman bin Abdulaziz Al Saud, is Alwaleed's uncle, and the crown prince, MBS, is his cousin. Alwaleed is the founder, chairman, former chief executive officer, and majority owner of the Kingdom Holding Company, created in 1980 and headquartered in Riyadh. It is an investment company with ownership stakes in a wide variety of companies and industries, including financial services, tourism and hospitality, mass media, entertainment, petrochemicals, aviation, technology, and real estate sectors. Over the decades, Alwaleed has purchased large blocks of stocks in many American companies, including Citicorp, News Corp.,

Time Warner, AOL, eBay, and Twitter. Though estimates differ as to his true net worth, *Forbes* has regularly listed him as among the world's richest men.

The Jeddah Economic Company (JEC) was formed as a private investment in 2009 to purchase the land and build it up. The marketing has pitched it as a neo-Dubaian:

> JEC's mission is no less than this: to envision, to design, to build and to manage—in short, to master plan in the fullest sense—an unprecedentedly vibrant urban center that will establish the city of Jeddah as a functional equal on the international scene of great modern urbanization, alongside the best new cities of the region and the world.

LEFT: The Jeddah Tower completed to date; RIGHT: Rendering of the tower (© Adrian Smith + Gordon Gill Architecture/Jeddah Economic Company)

The funny thing about the Jeddah Tower is there's hardly anything new about it—other than its height. It represents the next step in the buttressed core learning curve and is riding on the coattails of Dubai. In 2009, the JEC sent out its competition brief, which asked for a multi-use,

one-kilometer tower offering a five-star hotel, luxurious serviced apartments, state-of-the-art offices, and residential units, but with a maximum area of 3.1 million square feet (290,000 m²), 200,000 square feet
(18,580 m²) less than the Burj.

The brief was delivered only to a select group, including SOM,
César Pelli, and Adrian Smith, who had left SOM to start a new firm
with Gordon Gill, AS+GG Architecture. The competitors had only one
month to pitch their designs. The chief architectural technical director
of the project, Peter A. Weismantle at AS+GG, recalled to me:

> We got [the request] on June 30, got the materials together and the scale
> model, and shipped it to Riyadh. It was too tall for the room, and so
> they had to take the ceiling tiles out. It was a progression on the Burj
> Khalifah. When you have 30 days, you can't come up with a totally new
> idea. Five days later they said it looks too much like the Burj. Come
> back in two weeks to present a new version to Alwaleed and we came
> up with the scheme.

As is de rigueur, Smith needed to pair his building with a tale; to him
"the tower evokes a bundle of leaves shooting up from the ground—a
burst of new life that heralds more growth all around it. This symbolizes
the tower as a catalyst for increased development around it."

Just as important as the story was the orientation of the tower. One of
the three wings must point to Mecca, while a second to true north. This
orientation, however, produced trade-offs. It had improved views and
reduced pedestrian wind turbulence, but it made the building subject
to more wind forces than if the building was rotated by several degrees,
as was discovered in the wind tunnel tests. But the proper structural
adjustments were made to keep the client satisfied.

Alwaleed, like the owner of the fictional Pearl Tower in Hong Kong,
wanted a helipad. However, Adrian Smith learned something that
another Smith—that is, Al Smith of the Empire State Building—learned

in 1930. You can't use skyscrapers for the landing of lightweight flying craft. "The client asked for the inclusion of a helipad to be mostly used by the owner or visitors of the super-penthouse at level 157," Weismantle recalls. "However, further studies and consultation with experienced helicopter pilots and wind engineering consultants suggest that the helipad location would make taking off or landing maneuvers extremely dangerous." The helipad was made into a sky terrace.

The engineering was overseen by Robert Sinn, who after many years at SOM moved over to the engineering consulting firm Thornton Toma-setti. The tower has a structural design of which he is quite proud, due to both its simplicity and elegance. As he told me, the building is "simplicity but not simple." It is 100 percent reinforced concrete, and unlike the Burj, the Jeddah Tower has no outriggers. As Sinn recalled, "When I was working on the Jeddah Tower I always looked back at CN Tower as an inspiration . . . for what such a tall slender tower would be. It's probably a better comparison to Jeddah Tower than Burj Khalifa."

All the floors are 13 feet (4 m) tall to keep the concrete formwork the same while also giving a generous story height (in the Burj floors are about 10 feet [3 m] tall). This is an "easy" way to extrude towers while keeping the building area relatively small.

And when it came to the wind designs, there was another problem that came up. For nearly all supertall buildings to date, engineers could draw from easily accessible data about wind speeds, directions, and the frequency of such extreme events as typhoons or hurricanes. But as Sinn discovered, when it comes to wind conditions above 1,968 feet (600 m) there is hardly any climatological information to draw from. Like all engineers working on record breakers, he had to make predictions, in this case using weather balloon data and historical measurements. "We just wanted to make sure that what we were doing was conservative," he said.

Groundbreaking took place in April 2013, and everything proceeded apace. In 2016, the CEO of the JEC company, in a speech to industry professionals, proudly announced the company's slogan,

"It's happening." But what seemed to be a slick, confidence-building marketing catchphrase morphed into a cruel joke. As the building hit sixty-seven floors, the metaphorical earth shook beneath it.

In June 2017, MBS was officially made the crown prince of Saudi Arabia. MBS's rise to power was a confluence of serendipity and palace intrigue. He was the sixth son of King Salman bin Abdulaziz, who was the son of Abdulaziz bin Abdul Rahman Al Saud. "[King] Salman was the twenty-fifth of his father's thirty-six sons, which put him so low in the royal pecking order that, for most of his life, the prospect of his becoming king was remote. There were simply too many others ahead of him in line," recounts journalist Ben Hubbard.

But being so young in the family helped Salman succeed to the throne as his older brothers died off. And when it came time for him to choose his own heir, "[t]he sudden, untimely deaths of two sons threw Salman into deep mourning. While his older children were off pursuing careers and taking care of their own families, MBS, then 16, stuck close to his father in his time of pain, deepening the bond between them," Hubbard writes. The close relationship plus a series of ruthless and brash power-play moves in the Saudi Game of Thrones led ultimately to MBS being named the crown prince at the tender age of thirty-one.

Over the last several years, MBS has taken dramatic steps to loosen the grip of Islamic fundamentalists and the "religious police" who roamed the country enforcing strict adherence to Wahhabi Islamism. In September 2017, the kingdom finally passed a law making it legal for women to drive.

Just as important was MBS's launch of Vision 2030 in 2016. Vision 2030 is a strategic plan—created in large part by Western consulting firms—that aims to diversify the kingdom's economy and reduce its dependence on oil. The idea is to promote investments in health, education, infrastructure, recreation, and tourism. As Hubbard writes, the ambitious goal was that "[t]he kingdom would take advantage of its place in the Arab and Islamic worlds, transform itself into a global investment giant, and establish itself as a hub for Europe, Asia, and Africa."

The key paths to this are market liberalization and the creation of modern cities. And just as important is to get the nationals off the "oil dole." Seventy percent of economic activity is through the state. Citizens are given jobs with state-owned companies and with government agencies. The oil-soaked economy created a leisure-class nation.

To his detractors, MBS's actions are a disturbing consolidation of power. To his admirers, he is going to lead the kingdom into the future. Just as Vision 2030 was being launched and MBS was signaling his interest in moving the Saudis into a global future, two events shook the world's confidence and made people wonder if Saudi Arabia was really that interested in following through on its ambition.

Whether it was truly a power play, to root out rampant corruption, or some combination of both, MBS in November 2017 began mass arrests of many of the kingdom's richest residents. They were stripped of their cell phones, guards, and drivers and locked in the white-glove prison of the Riyadh Ritz-Carlton. Among those swept up in the dragnet were Prince Alwaleed and Bakr bin Laden, chairman of the Binladen Group, a major investor, and the general contractor for the Jeddah Tower.

"Alwaleed's detention was more mysterious than most," reported Bloomberg.com. "Of all the princes who were brought in, he alone hadn't served in the Saudi government, where kickbacks are considered common. And unlike other businessmen, he wasn't a government contractor and so couldn't have overbilled the state. He made most of his wealth transparently, in real estate and as an investor in public markets." Alwaleed was finally released eighty-three days later after paying a huge undisclosed sum.

Another shock came soon after. On October 2, 2018, the world-famous Saudi journalist and *Washington Post* columnist Jamal Khashoggi was brutally murdered in the Saudi Embassy in Istanbul by MBS's security detail. Khashoggi was a proud Saudi and close with many in the ruling family. He used his print media and social networking platforms to call for democratic reforms, but in 2017 he went into self-imposed exile after his writings critical of MBS. This evidently rubbed MBS the wrong way. Though MBS denies he ordered the murder, he bears responsibility since it was carried out by those in his charge.

When MBS rose to power, he was seen as a white knight who would make Saudi Arabia more economically friendly and open. This does not require democracy per se but does require an open and welcoming economy. Between the Purge and Khashoggi's murder, the world's perception of the kingdom has altered. MBS's decisions are being carefully watched to see in which direction he goes.

After the Purge, the Jeddah Tower was halted. As of this writing (September 2023), the Jeddah Economic City continues to be built, largely to avoid paying taxes on underutilized land. While the tower remains stalled, there are rumors that it will be restarted. One engineer I spoke with thought the delay was good since it's better to have the infrastructure in place that can handle the tower.

Another urbanization scheme, however, has emerged as a competitor with the JEC. MBS holds a special place for a new megacity called Neom, currently under construction along the Gulf of Aqaba. Neom is being designed as a model conurbation for Saudi's future. Parts seem reasonable while others seem the product of an unchecked oil prince with too much money. All told, Neom will also have seven cities, each with its own focus. The plans are nicely summarized by an October 2022 CNBC.com headline, "Flying taxis, robotic avatars and holograms — Saudi Arabia pushes ahead with its sci-fi city vision."

Oxagon, for example, will be a tech and industrial hub, with the aim of hosting seventy thousand jobs by 2030. Trojena, planned to open in 2029, will contain the world's largest elevated human-made lake. The water will be pumped from the Red Sea, treated, and deposited in the mountains where the lake is positioned. Surrounding the water body will be high-end hotels. In another part of Neom, fifty islands will be created from the sea for luxury resorts for the 1 percent of the 1 percent.

The most jaw-dropping project is called The Line, a titanic structure that will be 1,600 feet (500 m) tall, 660 feet (200 m) wide, and 110 miles (170 km) long, making this futuristic structure a horizontal skyscraper that aims to be both a building and a city under one roof. A within-building rail line or hyperloop will allow people to get from one end to the other in twenty minutes. At an expected price of $1 trillion, it is planned to house at least 9 million residents, similar to the population of New York City. Expressed in another way, The Line, if fully constructed, would be the equivalent of 9,000 Taipei 101s. The project is underway, and by 2027 it is expected to house 1 million residents who will find all their needs met within its walls.

I asked Professor Steffen Hertog of the London School of Economics, an expert on Saudi affairs, his take on the kingdom's future. He told me:

> MBS believes that Neom will be the new Saudi Arabia and could serve as a model for the reform of the rest of the country. I am not sure things will work this way. Other factors making new giga-projects attractive to leaders like MBS is that there is a big industry of consultants selling all sorts of innovations, plans, and promises and that the announcement of a large new project alone is sometimes seen as a success in itself, at least in PR terms, catering to the impatience of the leadership. Reforming existing structures is harder, slower, less visible.

The truth is, you can't build your way into (or up to) the twenty-first century overnight. You can *build* cities and skyscrapers, but societies grow through economic freedom, economic transparency, and strong property rights. The history of skyscrapers shows that they follow economic growth but do not magically cause growth to emerge where it does not organically happen. For Saudi Arabia, we'll have to wait several decades after the world finally weans itself off oil to see what happens.

PART III

A GLOBAL VIEW

PREFACE TO PART III

NOW THAT WE HAVE TRAVELED the world's cities observing their quests for skyscrapers and skylines, we are going to take a step back, or rather up, to a new kind of observatory from which we can take a global view.

As I have tried to document, global cities and skyscrapers go hand in hand. Yet skyscrapers remain controversial and shrouded in myths and misunderstandings. In part III, from our new vantage point, I take on broader social and economic issues to view the skyscraper's good, bad, and ugly in a larger context.

In the next chapter, I turn to their benefits and see why, despite countless predictions otherwise, the skyscraper remains an enduring building type. Next, I revisit their perceived deficits to separate fact from fiction and cause from effect. Finally, we get out our binoculars and try to get a glimpse of the future and where the tall building might be headed.

Ready? Let's go!

CHAPTER 8

Sky Prizes

The Value of Height

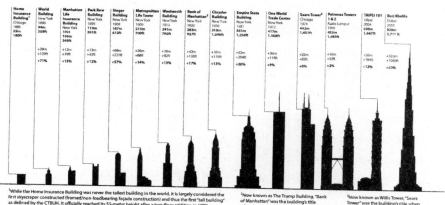

Evolution of the world's tallest building

THE HEIGHT JUDGE

In 1972, *New York Times* architectural critic Ada Louise Huxtable penned a piece on the "race" between the Sears (Willis) Tower and the Twin Towers, whereupon she opined:

> The peculiar drive for the title of tallest is a curious mix of emotion, structural engineering and economics. But it is a drive that will push the most programmatic developer as close to irrational behavior as the

cost-controlled real estate heart or computerized corporate soul can ever go. Call it status or immortality. Call it ego gratification. It seems to be programmed into the psyche of man.

Despite her conviction that the skyscraper was a product of unmoored mania, she turned to Lehigh University engineering professor Lynn S. Beedle (1917–2003) for more insight. He, however, was a bit more circumspect, citing the role of tall buildings in urban growth, as well as a mark of prestige.

Beedle was the head of the Joint Committee on Planning and Design of Tall Buildings, formed by the American Society of Civil Engineers and the International Association for Bridge and Structural Engineering, as Huxtable put it, to "deal with high-rise syndrome." Beedle helped found the committee in 1969, which was later renamed the aforementioned Council on Tall Buildings and Urban Habitat (CTBUH), of which, in full disclosure, I am a member. For many years, the group remained primarily of interest to structural engineers. Over the decades, under the leadership of Antony Wood, its current president, the CTBUH expanded into a broader organization for anyone with an interest (vested or otherwise) in tall buildings. Its current members are engineers, architects, suppliers, developers, and planners in equal measure.

Outside of the professional world, the CTBUH is known as the de facto arbiter of building height (there is no way, except maybe through some United Nations vote, to legally make it so). The media goes to it when they want precise measurements.

But such a thing is not easy to determine. Should spires be included? What about antennae? Where do you start, at the basement or at grade level? What if the building is on a slope so one side's entrance is, say, 20 feet (6 m) below the other side? These questions may seem silly, but the truth is, the world is watching. People demand certainty.

Interestingly, there was never a CTBUH committee charged with measuring heights. It didn't seem all that important. And the late 1980s was a quiet period for the organization. But that changed in 1993 when Petroliam Nasional Berhad (Petronas) announced its intention to build the world's tallest buildings. Suddenly the question became relevant after a two-decade dormancy.

As Daniel Safarik, director of Research and Thought Leadership at the CTBUH, told me, at that moment there was a feeling among the membership that it was time "to put the band back together." And the height committee was formed to answer the question, Will the Petronas Towers really be the next world's tallest buildings? But the committee found it difficult to reach a consensus. After all, César Pelli's Petronas Towers (eighty-eight floors) were only going to be the world's tallest because of their decorative spires. The highest floor was at 1,230 feet (375 m), while Sears (Willis) Tower's highest floor (110) was at 1,354 feet (413 m). Surely, this was a conundrum. But money, marketing, and bragging rights were at stake. To many, it seemed like Petronas was gaming the system.

In the end, the committee produced a set of conclusions. First, it did not matter the motivation; a building's official height—its so-called architectural height—would include decorative spires if they were part of the building's architecture. Broadcasting antennae would not count. But the final height would also be listed as part of an array of other measurements, such as the highest occupied floor and the tallest observation deck.

Because of the committee's professional credentials and the reputation of the CTBUH more broadly, its decisions became considered the final word. Ironically, however, the act of measuring height gave rise to more strategizing. Now that there were "official" height categories, developers had something by which to judge their buildings. And just as importantly, once developers knew that a spire would "officially" count, the sprint was on.

Competition has generated spire inflation among the world's tallest buildings. The spires on the Petronas Towers are 253 feet (77 m). The one on Taipei 101 is 230 feet (70 m). The Burj Khalifa's spire is 800 feet (243 m). If completed, the Jeddah Tower's spire will be around 1,080 feet (330 m), taller than the Chrysler Building!

It is also important to point out, however, that spire competition is neither systematic nor inherent. The Sears (Willis) and Twin Towers have no spires, nor does the International Commerce Centre. For that matter, the tallest floor of the Burj is at 1,921 feet (586 m), still taller than the Sears (Willis) Tower. So, the spire is long, but unlike the Petronas Towers, there's little controversy about it being the world's tallest.

When looking at all skyscrapers around the world that are 492 feet (150 m) or taller, the average "vanity" or spire height only adds about 10 percent more height. And when you consider that the rooftops often hold mechanical equipment and water tanks, the actual nonused part diminishes that much more.

But why do height competition and vanity height matter? Most people, like Huxtable, just assume it's about the outsized ego of the developers who want bragging rights. Yes, developers have big egos, but creating supertall landmarks also has economic, social, psychological, and aesthetic value for the wider public. People like monuments. And when monuments are spaces for living and working, all the better. Besides, a well-done spire adds elegance and beauty. No one complains about the spires on the Empire State or Chrysler Buildings.

I have, in fact, spent nearly two decades of my life researching the economics of tall buildings, and I have come to see that too much emphasis is placed on the "ego theory." It's true that developers and architects occasionally succumb to ego gratification, but a city's population and its GDP are the two most important predictors of how many—and how tall—a city's skyscrapers will be, making economics their fundamental driver.

And if you look at the height of cities' respective tallest buildings globally, they correlate strongly with the height of their second-tallest building (correlation coefficient = 0.94), suggesting that local developers who build the tallest buildings are not irrationally unmoored from the underlying economics.

Also, keep in mind, there are over 44,000 328-foot (100 m, 25 stories) or taller buildings on the planet; 50 percent are 394 feet (120 m) or less, and 90 percent are shorter than 558 feet (170 m). The super-supertalls, say over 1,000 feet (or 300 m), that everyone spends so much time talking about constitute a minuscule 0.07 percent of the world's tall buildings.

And what most people don't realize is that record breakers are, in fact, rational investments. Having the world's tallest building is a boon to the cities that host them. The current crop of Asian record breakers, for example, have all been built within larger planned developments, which has allowed the external benefits of the structure to be "captured" locally by the owners of surrounding properties, who are often the same developer.

The Petronas Towers, Taipei 101, and the Burj Khalifa were the centerpieces of new "downtown" neighborhoods that boosted local land values. The Petronas Towers emerged on the site of a former racing track, the Selangor Turf Club, which was underutilized land in a central area. In the 1980s, local officials initiated a plan to redevelop the site as a commercial center with shopping, offices, and park spaces. Today the Kuala Lumpur City Centre (KLCC) is a thriving neighborhood.

Taipei 101 was also built on underutilized land—a former military base—and has become the centerpiece of the Xinyi Planning District, near Taipei City Hall. As geography professor Sue-Ching Jou writes, "this newly created urban centre has been purposefully promoted and imaged by Taipei City government as a miniature of New York's Manhattan, a response to global-city competition and network-building." Similarly, as discussed in chapter 7, the developer of the Burj Khalifa was inspired to build the world's tallest tower as part of its 494-acre master-planned Downtown Dubai inspired by the success of KLCC.

But putting aside the focus on monumentality, let's turn to the value of skyscrapers to their occupants. Ultimately, if skyscraper builders are creating a service to humanity and if we want to understand these benefits, we need to look at the streams of revenue they generate. What do the "height consumers" pay for? To answer this, we can decompose the revenues as coming from at least five sources.

The first is its location. This is the price that occupants pay for the right to locate centrally. The second is the quality of the structure itself. Does it have ample sunlight; are the floor plates the right size; is the building wired for the latest technology? Third is the benefits that occupants get from being on higher floors, whether it's views or other perks.

Fourth is the "architecturality" or "iconicity" of the building. The goal of the developer is to provide something aesthetically pleasing and convey valuable information. Buildings that "sing" arias are worth more than their cacophonous counterparts.

Fifth is the so-called agglomeration benefit, the term economists use for the benefits of urban clustering that people or businesses don't get in less dense locations. When all these factors are present, the economics will generate a skyscraper.

Let's start with height itself. A key benefit of tall buildings is their height, plain and simple. Residing up in the clouds for many is something special (acrophobics excepted). It is this desire to get high, so to speak, that generates a height premium, the additional payment made to reside on a higher floor.

Only recently have academics—mostly economists—tried to understand building height's economic and personal benefits. Historically, researchers have downplayed their positives, and I think this has to do with an (often implicit or unconscious) academic bias against tall buildings. It's all too easy to telescope on their negatives when the pervasive perception is that they are wasteful monuments or when the demolition of high-rise public housing remains lodged in our collective consciousness. For that matter, outside of economics and business studies, it's considered unseemly to study those who seek profit. Research on tall buildings, for this reason, has been dominated by architectural historians because it's more "salable" to focus on aesthetics and ignore discussions of "greedy developers."

But when it comes to measuring the benefits from building height, if I may toot my own horn, I was one of the early people on this research train. In 2015, I was attending the conference sessions of the American Real Estate and Urban Economics Association (AREUEA), and the plenary speaker was discussing his research on the height premium. As he was about to give the audience his estimate for the average percent increase in office rents with each floor higher, I leaned over to my friend at the table and whispered into his ear, "zero-point-six." And then when the speaker concluded his sentence, he uttered the phrase "zero-point-six percent." I felt some pride when my friend smiled.

I knew this to be true because that was what I estimated for New York City offices while researching real estate in Manhattan. I was glad to hear he calculated a similar figure for the rest of the country. This means that, on average, businesses on the thirtieth floor are paying rent that is 6 percent higher than that of those on the twentieth floor, while companies on the sixtieth floor are paying 24 percent more than those on the twentieth floor. In other words, if a business is paying $50 per square foot for rent on the twentieth floor, another business on the fiftieth floor will typically be paying $60 for similar space.

Another study for Amsterdam found that Dutch companies are paying the same height premium as their American counterparts, and the Dutch—at least modern ones—are not known as cutthroat capitalists.

But what drives this premium? First is obviously the better views and access to more sunlight. Humans are programmed to like wide-open vistas. Looking at the city around you is pleasing—even enthralling. This is why observation decks are such moneymakers. Like millions of others, when I exit the elevators on the eighty-sixth floor of the Empire State Building it takes my breath away. It is a skyline symphony—a visual "Ode to Joy" laid out before you. Similarly, stepping out on the observation deck of the Burj Khalifa, you feel the awe of a skyline rising in the desert. Hong Kong's skyline from the top of Victoria Peak is jaw-dropping. Imagine working in an office with those views.

However, there's more at work than just views. If you take two floors up high with one right on top of the other, say on the thirtieth and thirty-first floor, respectively, they will likely have the same view and amount of sunlight, and yet, typically, the person or business on top will be paying a bit more. Same product, different cost? That can't be right. Something else must be going on.

Say you are the manager for an investment bank or consulting firm charged with finding new office space for your firm. You need to consider not only the horizontal location—the address—but also its vertical location. What are the potential benefits of renting on higher floors and are they worth the extra cost?

The first benefit is what economists call signaling—taking an action that requires paying a cost to convey specific information. We can imagine that potential clients do not have full information about different businesses. If, to a random client, one consulting firm appears the same as the next, then successful ones will use some of their revenues to rent the higher floors to convey their ability to would-be clients.

Managers of global firms feel compelled to rent higher floors in premium buildings. If they didn't their reputations would be harmed. Clients and suppliers would be left wondering, "What's wrong with this company? They can't afford to be in better digs?" As a result, there's a constant demand to be in the newest tall buildings to keep up confidence in the brand.

Employees also feel a sense of pride that employers are willing to provide this perk, and when clients come to visit they can show off their workplace-as-observatory. In 2018, I had an older student, named Edward Stellingwerf, in my urban economics course at Rutgers. He had a successful career in wealth management and had worked his way up on Wall Street starting in the 1980s without a college degree. But in the early 2010s, his company required that he have one, and so between his busy work schedule and in lieu of evening family time he squeezed in his education.

One day he invited me to give a presentation on New York City history to a group of midwestern farmers whom his company flew into town to pitch their wealth management plans. The meeting took place on the fifty-fifth floor of a shiny, new Midtown skyscraper.

For the talk, I sat at the head of the table, and behind me was an expansive panorama of New York City, with the Empire State Building over my right shoulder and the Wall Street skyline over my left. As I explained New York's history, I would point to key locations. It was a strange feeling of pride as for one moment I could show off "my city" to the group, who felt a palpable sense of wonder from nearly one thousand feet in the air.

After the pandemic, I caught up with Edward and asked him why he thought it was so important to bring prospective clients to the top floor. "In my line of work," he told me, "I meet people from all types of backgrounds, and when they brush up against this view for the very first time it brings them a sense of hope. The conversation that immediately follows after that initial view is very hopeful. They feel inspired. You can see it in their eyes and their body language, how joyful they feel at that moment."

But for those on the outside looking in, there's a perception that firms are being irrational or excessive by spending their hard-earned cash on higher floors. I think that may be the case once in a while, but overall, it's not a sustainable strategy. Companies are driven to maximize their profits, and if paying extra to be high up did not yield a benefit, their shareholders or owners would demand they move.

And a capitalist economy can't function without branding and signaling. Information is hard to come by, and productive firms are willing to pay some of their revenues to generate the information that consumers and clients crave. Not everyone wants or needs to be in the clouds. For some firms, it can hurt their business if they are seen as extravagantly paying too high a rent. A mid-level law firm, say, would then have to charge its clients more, potentially causing them to grumble that their high fees are being "wasted" on an unnecessary luxury. In a tall building, renters will sort themselves based on how much height adds to their bottom line or not.

But there is a social element to where businesses decide to locate. If one global trendsetting company, for example, moves to the top of a new skyscraper, competitors will feel compelled to follow so as not to be left behind. In this way, the "flight to height" can be like an arms race, where firms all move en masse and wind up paying higher rents but have the same revenues as before. So, there might be some coordination failures from time to time. But at the end of the day, people and businesses like the latest and greatest, and flexible cities cater to that need.

But businesses are not the only occupants who pay for height. Apartment dwellers and law firms are very different and yet the height premium is there for both groups. The residential height premium residual—that which remains after subtracting out the light and views part—must thus come from our inherent need for social status: to signal one's command of resources to more favorably place oneself within a social hierarchy, even if only in one's head.

In my own research for New York and Rotterdam, conducted with Professor Ilir Nase of the University of Manchester, we were able to measure the status effect in the two cities. In New York, for households living in a skyscraper, one on the fiftieth floor typically pays 5 percent more than another one living ten floors below, simply for the pride of being on top. In Rotterdam, that value is about 3 percent. In this sense, New York has two kinds of premia—one for height within the building and one for living in the city itself.

And, keep in mind, there are all sorts of costs associated with living higher up. There's more waiting time in elevators, longer escape times during emergencies, and possible building sway. But if these costs were not compensated by a suite of benefits, the tall building as we know it could not and would not exist. Yet tall buildings are getting taller and more common.

So, being on the inside is valuable, but what about the outside? What's the value of style? If you mention the word "iconic" to an architect, she will roll her eyeballs. Thanks to design software and innovations in fabrication and construction methods, there's been a great degree of icon inflation, particularly in Asia.

But what does iconicity do for the owners and occupants? Certainly, there are bragging rights to the owner—a sense that your building has something unique and is featured in the media and appears in coffee table books or on "skyscraper porn" websites. But developers are not typically in the habit of spending extra cash on a weird or novel design without some hope of it providing a return (despite what conventional wisdom would have you believe).

It does happen to be sure. Dubai and China are cases in point of "cowboy" developers rushing in and demanding crazy buildings without thought to their long-run profitability, but in time they get punished by the market. And iconicity is not a fly-by-night phenomenon. It started in the 1980s and is here to stay.

But if we want to determine the value of "iconicity" we need a measure of "icon-ness." One study of several Dutch cities looked at the impact on office rents of buildings' relative height as compared to those in the neighborhood. The authors found that the willingness to pay for being in a building of a given height is highly nonlinear. Up to 295 feet (90 m), the building height premium is relatively small, but after that, there's a dramatic rise in what tenants pay, irrespective of the floor they are on. In other words, businesses not only pay more to be on a higher floor but also will pay more to be in a relatively taller building. People "blame" the ego of the developer, but it's clear that there's a large push from the occupants.

Other studies look at the value—or not—brought by the architect. The global demand for iconicity has given rise to the "starchitect industrial complex" whose novel designs create instantly recognized images, from those such as Frank Gehry, Renzo Piano, Norman Foster, Zaha Hadid, Rem Koolhaas, Adrian Smith, and I. M. Pei, to name a few. And then there are the big firms: SOM and KPF are the most sought-after. Of the world's twenty tallest buildings, six were designed by KPF, five by SOM (or former partners), one by Gensler, and one by César Pelli.

Fortunately, for economists, measuring "starchitectnesess" is straightforward because the architecture world awards a handful of prestigious prizes and medals. Research in London and the United States confirms the market value of the starchitect. Tenants will pay more—between 5 and 17 percent—to be inside a prizewinning architect's building.

The problem here is that while we know who designed the building (or, more cynically, who initiated the blueprints), there are many things we don't know about what's driving the premium. It could be its artistic merit or its aesthetic je ne sais quoi, or it could be the social element. The building gets people talking (or posting on social media) about it and its special architect. My view: While some achieve great architectural beauty, they are for the most part branded buildings and people love brands because it helps shape their identities. The Coach bag, the Mercedes-Benz automobile, the Hadid-designed tower.

But just as important—beyond style and height—is the structure's location. In 1900, the architect Cass Gilbert argued that the tall building "was the machine that makes the land pay." By going tall, builders were acting rationally to recover the high costs of the land. But high land values are the value of geography itself, which is intimately tied to our social and economic endeavors. Being in the center confers many advantages. Firms cluster in "downtowns" because it means being part of a corporate ecology that makes their businesses more profitable. They have easier access to suppliers, financing, and customers, they can find workers more easily, and they can see and learn from the competition. Being in the center has other perks, such as access to culture, cuisine, parks, public transportation, and other people.

For residents, living in the center means less commuting and more time for other activities. Moving out to the suburbs has the advantage of cheaper land and housing. So, every business and household has to decide where they fall on the access-land balance. You get either more access and less space or less access and more space. For global or national firms and access seekers, the center's centripetal force dominates. And the more people and businesses are eager to be in the center, the higher the land values and the taller will be the buildings.

But the driving force from land values to height is not unidirectional. Height can drive land value increases as well. The reason is that the "correct" price of land is determined by the ratio of the income to the cost of producing that income. Innovations, like the framed tube or high-strength concrete, mean that more revenue can be generated for the same cost. And so, when buildings get taller because it's cheaper to build them, land values will go up. Buyers of nearby lots with lower-rise buildings will see what can be reaped and will bid up the land to a price that now reflects its "highest and best use."

This is not without controversy, because innovations, changes in tastes, or "flights to quality" can cause landlords with obsolete buildings to lose their investments through no fault of their own. However, building obsolescence is a cost of urban life. As I will argue in the next chapter, freezing or massively slowing down neighborhood evolution can ultimately do more harm than good. Creative cities can repurpose buildings—old offices can be converted into apartments, start-up incubators, or food courts. Or they can be torn down and replaced with something better. Good cities learn to manage and adapt to change.

GLOBALIZATION AND AGGLOMERATION

The big irony of the internet, telecom, and computing revolutions, however, was that they were "supposed to" destroy cities. First came fax machines and flip phones, then email and the internet, and now Zoom.

The population was freed to thrive in isolated suburban or semirural castles that were so natural to us. Central cities, on the other hand, were dens of crime, slums, noise, overcrowding, congestion, and frustration that drive the human sensory system bonkers. Hollywood films, like Neil Simon's *The Prisoner of Second Avenue* or Martin Scorsese's *Taxi Driver*, reflect our image of the dystopian city.

But the truth is that people wanted and want to be in cities because they are stimulating, profitable, and gregarious places, despite the headaches of traffic and noise. They are meet/meat markets for the young, cultural markets for the hip and curious, and money markets for the fortune seekers. Big cities are cool. Peter Rees, former chief planner of the City of London, after touring Frankfurt's skyscrapers and nightlife concluded that London has nothing to worry about. Frankfurt, he says, "is no fun." Good vibes, urban density, and economic growth mutually reinforce one another.

All the technology that was supposed to send us back to the woods actually made cities more important. New tech must be invented, funded, and improved upon. The dynamic stew that is a large city makes this possible. For that matter, the internet has allowed us to connect to many more people; we now have larger social and business networks, and eventually we want to meet up with some of them. The best places for that are in cities.

As the COVID pandemic began to wane, the mayor of New York, Eric Adams, urged residents to return to the office. "You can't stay home in your pajamas all day," he told an audience at an event announcing his economic development team. "That is not who we are as a city. You need to be out cross-pollinating ideas, interacting with humans."

He's right. The lynchpin for cities is that they generate spontaneous, unintended benefits: a new idea unwittingly slips out of your friend's mouth during happy hour; a recently hired worker brings her old experience to a new setting that then gives a business a competitive advantage; the desire to beat to the punch your competitors who reside in the same building urges you forward.

And it's not just, for example, that an aspiring stage artist moves to New York to get a gig on Broadway. But she becomes a better actor when mixing it up with other actors, directors, set and costume designers, writers, musicians, and composers. This is what economists call knowl-edge spillovers—cities not only allow us to do what we crave to do but also make us better at it because of all that magic in the urban ether. The best talent is drawn to the center, and in the process their talent rubs off onto others who become the best talent that rubs off onto others, ad infinitum.

In one important study, economists Edward L. Glaeser and David C. Maré looked at the wages of workers who moved into large cit-ies. As expected, they found wage increases over time as these workers gained more experience. But, just as importantly, those who then left for smaller cities showed no wage losses, on average, because the big city imparts substantial production bumps from the spillovers. When they leave, they take their skills with them. In this way, the metropolis is "spawning" additional productivity gains and passing them on to the rest of the nation. What happens in a New York skyscraper does not stay in a New York skyscraper.

Another interesting study conducted a thought experiment: What would happen if the City of London densified by simply shifting eighty thousand workers from other neighborhoods to the City. The report concluded that if London built more skyscrapers, average worker pay would increase by £2,500 a year simply because of the knowledge spill-overs and convenience of being in the center.

The mutual dependence between skills, knowledge, and city size has become even greater as we have built up the ship that is global capitalism. Just as important has been the rising importance of those with so-called noncognitive or "soft" skills, such as "grit," and the abil-ity to make interpersonal connections. In other words, the workplace increasingly values the ability of individuals to cooperate and collectively problem-solve, because the new economy requires teamwork to a greater degree than ever before.

In a fascinating study, one set of economists followed over 2.8 million men in Sweden between the ages of thirty-eight and forty-two from 1992 to 2013 who were previously drafted into the army (Sweden has mandatory military service). Each recruit had to sit for a psychological evaluation that, in part, measured their noncognitive skills such as social maturity, focus, perseverance, motivation, and emotional stability. This information was then matched to their subsequent wages. The authors found that

> [f]rom 1992 to 2013, the [economic] return [on] non-cognitive skill in the private sector roughly doubled, from about 7 to 14 percent. . . . Workers who have an abundance of noncognitive skills are increasingly sorted into occupations that are abstract, non-routine, non-offshorable, non-automatable, and social; this suggests that optimal skill mixes of given occupations have changed over time.

The premium for noncognitive skills is due to what people want to consume and how these products are created. Tech is more embedded in our lives, whether it's social media, the use of iPhone apps, streaming movie services, self-driving cars, AI, robotics, and so on.

The magic ingredient that allows businesses to create these new products is urban density. The former industrial coastal cities that used to belch pollution from factories, and whose products were shipped from Mafia-controlled ports, have not only retained their place in the global hierarchy but also become even more crucial. While they had lots of blue-collar workers, coastal cities also had a large corps of workers in finance, management, consulting, and legal services. Those industries attracted high-skilled workers, which generated more growth and attracted more high-skilled workers, and so on. Skyscrapers and factories were symbionts.

Most big cities around the world have found this connection to be true. Shanghai was an important trading and industrial node a century ago, and after its hiatus during Mao Zedong's rule it was able to regain its place in the pecking order. London, after hemorrhaging jobs in the 1970s, retained its centrality. In the mid-twentieth century, Dubai took advantage of its location at a time when there were few trading cities along the Persian Gulf. It has played the long game and only after the new millennium did those investments yield dramatically large—and tall—fruits.

This is not to say that geography is destiny, but it is to say that large commercial-oriented cities were always creativity hubs, and in the twenty-first century "hubbyness" has become increasingly important. Within its diminutive 23 square miles (60 m²) Manhattan Island, for example, accounts for 3.5 percent of the entire U.S. GDP, and that figure has been rising in the last two decades. Shanghai also accounts for 3.7 percent of China's GDP, while London generates a whopping one-third of the United Kingdom's GDP.

What does this mean for skyscrapers? High-skilled and "noncognitive" workers are put in team and group situations, which require that they work together for the greater good of the company. Since the "brains" enjoy views, sunlight, and the perks of modern, tall offices, developers are rushing to bring new ones online. My niece, Zoe Early, is a perfect example of this phenomenon. She graduated from the University of Pennsylvania in 2021 and went to work in healthcare systems consulting for a top U.S. company whose offices are in the brand-new, high-end Hudson Yards in New York. Like many of her generation, she worked at the company for two years then left for a better-paying offer.

While at the company, she spent most of her working hours with her team. "You win together, you lose together," she told me when I asked her how important teamwork was. "No one functions as a solo entity on anything; everyone's functioning as a team. If you mess up, it's not a reflection of me; it's a reflection of your company."

These new forms of work changed office spaces too. Starting in the 2010s, building owners and companies removed the "veal-fattening pens"—the tiny cubicles—and replaced them with open workspaces. Cafes were installed where small groups can work on their laptops, while the low-level employees work on their computers at long communal desks. Work is more socialized and young people need to signal their "noncognitivity."

Zoe went into her office two or three days a week for that purpose. "I would go in because I think I was more productive leaving my home. I would sit on floors with people with similar job titles. I'm also pretty chatty in general. And, I think it's important to network, especially early on. So, I would plan to grab coffee with somebody or, a lot of the time, I just feel like, 'Yeah, I know other people are going to be there and I'll bump into them.'"

The need for skyscrapers in the twenty-first century is the reason London became worried about its flat skyline and went on to embrace Cheesegraters, Walkie-Talkies, and Gherkins. London saw its future as the biggest and most dynamic city in Europe as facing competition and if it didn't start to plan or think strategically it could lose out. Other European cities, most notably Frankfurt—home to the headquarters of the European Central Bank—have been competing for a piece of the action. Then there's Dublin, just over London's shoulder. It probably was never a real threat, but here we are in a post-Brexit world, so the United Kingdom has imposed economic harm on itself. Then, of course, there is the rising Chinese Dragon, with Shanghai angling to become a top-tier financial city. And its old progeny, Hong Kong, is ever present.

In fact, when you look across the world, there are many ambitious cities vying not only to gain global status but also to become financial centers. These cities are also building lots of skyscrapers to welcome banks, investment houses, and stock-trading firms. Emerging metropolises, including Jakarta, Shenzhen, Kuala Lumpur, and even Istanbul and Mumbai (all Asian cities), have been adding to their skylines to compete with mature cities for business in the financial realm.

The reason: tall buildings are mini-economies unto themselves — within each tower is a mix of firms that depend on and learn from each other. On and around Wall Street, for example, where the skyscrapers reign supreme, only 21 percent of the office space is used by financial services firms; business services and government soak up most of the space. Traders trade on the lower floors, while the managers and executives make the deals higher up. The ambitious cities around the planet know this — they all want their financial districts to be the "Wall Street of . . ." Shanghai, Dubai, or Kuala Lumpur.

One can be a global powerhouse without tall buildings. Silicon Valley is arguably the example par excellence of one of the world's most productive areas. But its success is within car-based office parks sprawled out across San Jose. Silicon Valley shows that agglomerative forces, once sparked, can keep reigniting themselves.

In this case, the spark was the early semiconductor manufacturers, which had deep ties to Stanford University and kept attracting talent, even as its land use and real estate sprawled outward. So, it's clearly possible that once the agglomerative forces are ignited in an "Edge City," they can keep burning. But the question is not whether thriving Edge Cities can sustain themselves, but rather, whether it is the best or ideal configuration of real estate and transportation that provides the maximum productivity for the least cost. The problem is that we cannot create, or re-create, some hypothetical alternative reality, where we change San Jose zoning in, say, 1960 and see how an alternative high-rise, mass-transit version would have performed.

But we can look at cities around the world to get some clues on the relationship between skyscrapers and global competitiveness and to see if London is on the right path. To this end, we can review the Globalization and World Cities (GaWC) Project's Global Network Connectivity (GNC) index, which was created in 1998 and has been updated regularly for several hundred cities. By counting the number and size of foreign businesses in each city, the index indicates how economically connected it is to the rest of the world. The top-tier global metropolises will have local headquarters for many international firms, while lower-tier cities will have smaller representations or fewer foreign firms.

One key finding is that London is the global champion and has held the top position since the index was created. In 2000, after London the top four were New York, Paris, Tokyo, and Singapore. In 2020, the top five were London, New York, Hong Kong, Singapore, and Shanghai. Paris, not known for its skyscrapers, while still in the top ten, has slipped relative to the Asian cities. Also interesting is that in the early 2000s Dubai was not even in the top fifty; by 2020 it was ranked number seven.

But are skyscraper construction and global connectivity linked? The answer is yes. There is a strong positive relationship between the two. More global cities have more tall buildings than their less global counterparts, though London falls way below the trend line.

But just because there is a correlation does not mean there is a causal relationship. We don't know if, on average, global connectivity leads to more skyscrapers, more skyscrapers lead to greater global connectivity, or if the relationship is just a coincidence, driven by their connection to some other variable, such as a city's GDP.

But after performing a detailed statistical analysis, I found that sky-scrapers and globalness form a positive feedback loop. More skyscrapers enhance global connectivity, which increases employment and wages, which increases the demand for tall buildings, and so on. While skyscraper construction has its share of controversy and doubters, the evidence strongly suggests that cities are better off when they allow for needed tall buildings.

But there's another related question we can bring to the data — that of "leapfrogging." When we compare global cities around the world, we, ostensibly, see two different models. On the one hand, New York and Chicago's historical skylines emerged "spontaneously" as their land values hit thresholds, incentivizing the construction of tall buildings. This can be summarized as the "spontaneous eruption" theory or the "skyscrapers follow urban growth" theory.

On the other hand, some cities, especially in Asia, have seemingly used skyscrapers as a so-called Field of Dreams strategy—if you build it, they will come—in order to leapfrog over rival cities. Arguably, this began, as mentioned earlier, in Kuala Lumpur, with the Petronas Towers, in 1998. But perhaps no other city has so fully embraced the skyscraper as an economic development strategy as Dubai. Nonetheless, the Burj Khalifa is viewed as a pure "ego play" to try to get the world's attention. Then there's China's Skyscraper Fever and its centralized economic development strategy.

So, when we look at skylines around the world, we seemingly have two different models: "spontaneous eruption" versus "Field of Dreams." Can a country leapfrog its way to the top by building a supertall skyscraper?

We can look at the changes in the GNC rankings to see if there are dramatic leaps. In this case, I looked at five cities. The first three are Kuala Lumpur, Dubai, and Taipei; each has or had the world's tallest buildings. I then added Shanghai, with China's tallest skyscraper, the Shanghai Tower, and St. Petersburg, with Europe's tallest skyscraper, the Lakhta Center (2019; 1,516 feet, 462 m).

This exercise reveals that, on average, these five cities moved up in the global cities rankings between 2010 and 2020, but there were no major jumps, and each remained roughly in the same tier that it had been before. It shows that cities can use tall buildings to make relative improvements, but in no case do any of them see massive leapfrogging.

Thus, the Field of Dreams idea is more myth than reality. Rather, emerging cities with a global presence can use skyscrapers to improve their positions. But they cannot turn a small, isolated village into an urban juggernaut overnight. Instead, supertalls aid and abet the quest for status, but this is not possible without developing other economic and institutional factors first. In other words, you can't show up at the Olympics without first doing some heavy lifting.

CHAPTER 9

Cities and Civilization

Skyscrapers and Their Discontents

Billionaires' Row, New York City, in 2023

BILLIONAIRES' ROW

In 2010, New York developer Harry Macklowe visited the office of starchitect Rafael Viñoly, seeking a design for a supertall apartment building at the future address of 432 Park Avenue. Viñoly looked around the room. In the corner, he spotted a garbage pail formed by a latticework of flat metal strips. He walked over to it, flipped it over, and said, "Here's your building."

This garbage pail–as–apartment tower exudes over-the-top luxury. Most floors only have one or two units, and the advertisement for one on the market in April 2022—listed at $92 million—illustrates its credentials:

> Among the clouds, at one thousand feet, is the Floating Inner Garden. A one-of-a-kind Hiroshi Sugimoto–designed masterpiece. This serene full-floor residence offers 8,055 square feet (748 square meters) of living space, five bedrooms, five bathrooms, two powder rooms, unobstructed helicopter views in all directions, soaring ceilings, two private elevator landings, custom-built mechanical, electrical, plumbing, and HVAC systems, and a hand selection of the finest natural materials and finishes. Included in this offering are all custom-made furniture designed for the Floating Inner Garden by Hiroshi Sugimoto, site-specific permanent installation works of art by Hiroshi Sugimoto, two adjacent studio apartments, and two storage units.

The apartment building at 432 Park Avenue (on the left of the image on page 239) is part of the so-called Billionaires' Row, a string of supertall luxury condos that have been rising just south of Central Park. Their emergence is a result of the convergence of both supply and demand conditions. In 2017, I calculated the hypothetical return-on-investment to determine the profitability of a supertall condo development on 57th Street. While the project's estimated cost was $1.6 billion, its potential revenues from apartment sales came in at $2.76 billion. Developers are mining gold in the sky.

On the supply side, builders have benefited from the Third Skyscraper Revolution and are able to create ultrathin buildings that are protected against wind forces. The grid design and strength of 432 Park Avenue are made possible by its structure. The outer façade and the core are reinforced concrete tubes. Outriggers add rigidity, while tuned mass dampers slow the sway. The mechanical floors have no glass windows to reduce vortex shedding. "It's similar to making holes in the sail of a boat," explains Silvian Marcus, the lead engineer for the structure. "Instead of making the building even stiffer to overcome the movement, we flow with the wind."

On the demand side is the rise of the global class of billionaires who seek to park their savings and have a pied-à-terre in one of the world's greatest cities. Since the resident population is low, fewer elevators are needed, allowing the core to be that much smaller and apartments that much bigger. The use of interlocking "switchback" stairwells allows two staircases to be provided in the same space, helping to shrink the core that much more.

The structural innovations have also allowed skyscrapers to become ultrathin, as measured by the aspect or slenderness ratio, calculated by dividing the building's height by its width at the base. The Empire State Building's aspect ratio is 3 (that is, its height is three times its width); the Chrysler Building is 5, the Sears (Willis) Tower is 6.5, and the Burj Khalifa is 9.

A standard American ruler is 12 inches by 1 inch, hence an aspect ratio of 12. The crop of Billionaires' Row buildings tops this. The aspect ratio for 432 Park Avenue is 15. The new record holder for the world's skinniest skyscraper is the Steinway Tower on West 57th Street, nearly two rulers stacked on top of each other, at 23.5.

The New York zoning rules limit the total floor area but say nothing about ceiling height. In this way, Viñoly created a building where each floor was extra tall—15 feet (4.6 m) high—with nearly floor-to-ceiling glass, and yet still within the rules. If each apartment was only 12 feet (3.7 m) high, as per the norm, the structure would have been 20 percent shorter. Between the purchase of neighbors' unused development rights, a large lot, and generous as-of-right zoning, Macklowe built his tower without any need for planning permission.

New York zoning laws also allow an FAR bonus of up to 20 percent— that is, developers can add 20 percent more floor space to the building—if they provide a publicly accessible public space. Macklowe took

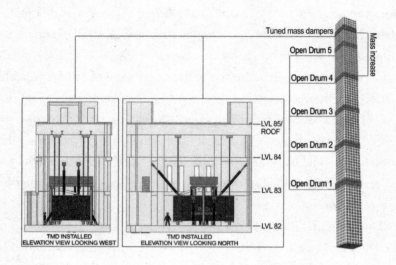

Tuned mass dampers in 432 Park Avenue

advantage of this rule to build eight and a half more floors, which likely netted $400 million in sales revenue. The cost of the plaza, on the other hand, was some trees and benches.

I've walked past the plaza at 432 Park Avenue a few times. Overall, it's well maintained, and during lunchtime workers sit there to eat their lunches. While not the most inviting of spaces—relaxing next to an ultra-luxury building is a bit intimidating—it's certainly not the worst in the city.

Over the years, developers have come under considerable flack for their less-than-stellar public spaces. A recent *New York Times* headline pithily reveals the problem: "New Yorkers Got Broken Promises. Developers Got 20 Million Sq. Ft." With little policing by the city, the spaces are often closed to the public, difficult to access, or, more commonly, not welcoming—they are either poorly designed or undermaintained. The failure to provide high-quality spaces outrages many New Yorkers, who see developers as taking advantage of the law.

The architecture of 432 Park Avenue, however, is much more elegant than Viñoly's clunky Walkie-Talkie in London. But his New York tower was also not without problems. Evidently, as the saying goes, mistakes were made. The megarich apartment dwellers have a laundry list of complaints. They are suing Macklowe for $125 million plus punitive damages in what seems like a Hollywood movie-in-the-making. "According to the [homeowners association] board, shoddy workmanship and poor planning have led to flooding, stuck elevators, electrical explosions, and 'horrible and obtrusive noise and vibration' caused by building sway," reported one outlet.

A recent sale, however, suggests that buyers are not too worried. In November 2022, one unit—the seventy-ninth floor—sold for $135 million. There's also a hearty rental market. In February 2023, the seventy-second floor was rented for $70,000 per month.

Despite their lure—and pitfalls—to the ultrarich, Billionaires' Row has become a lightning rod for the fury of New Yorkers, who see its buildings as causing gentrification, increasing wealth inequality, destroying street life, and throwing shade on their beloved Central Park. But do these buildings deserve such scorn? I don't think so. New Yorkers are drawing the wrong conclusions from these towers, which are mostly symbols but are hardly the cause.

There's even little new about the perception that the rich living in skyscrapers is bad for the rest of us. Nearly a century ago, the writer Eunice Fuller Barnard complained:

> Yesterday, money bought ostentation. Today it may buy immunity—complete detachment from the mechanics of life. The purse-proud Manhattanite of yore comparatively squatted on the ground, with his possessions spread out around him. Today he may live remote and unseen in the clouds, with no more furniture than five or six rooms can hold.

The neighborhood of which she speaks—the Upper East Side—is designated as an official historical district because of its contributions to the city.

While new and recycled complaints about skyscrapers continue to emerge, part of the debate is over. No one would suggest we lop off fifty floors of the Empire State Building. And both practical experience and economic analysis have produced a much stronger understanding that tall buildings are economically rational in places with high land values.

But, in another sense, the debate rages on. While urban residents love their old skyscrapers, they work to prevent new ones in their neighborhoods. They blame skyscrapers for all sorts of urban ills, and, in a way, a wider disconnect has grown between what economists and real estate professionals have come to know and what ordinary folks *feel*. The problem in the twenty-first century is that this disconnect is often driving local planning policies and creating a backlash out of proportion to the problem's magnitude.

That the rich can pay more for things really gets a lot of people's goats. There is a widespread sentiment to the effect of, "Someone obtaining such luxury that we can't have is not fair, and *their* giant, obnoxious buildings are casting shadows in *my* city." Certainly, when capitalism produces multimillion-dollar empty condos floating above a homeless man sleeping on the street, it is appalling and paradoxical.

And cities with many skyscrapers are expensive places to live. Take Hong Kong, which ranks among the most expensive in the world. Is it because of its skyscrapers? Many people seem to think so. In February 2021, I posted a blog discussing an academic research paper on building heights around the world that I wrote with two colleagues (discussed later). The aim of the paper was to look at why tall buildings are "missing" from some countries and yet seem to grow like weeds in others. One of the findings was that Ireland is the country with the most "missing" tall buildings. That is, given its wealth and urbanization, we would expect it to have more skyscrapers were it not so tightly regulated.

As it happens, I also have an Irish coauthor, Ronan Lyons, from Trinity College Dublin, with whom I work on other research and who has twenty-six thousand X, formerly Twitter, followers. He tweeted a link to my blog post with the comment: "We did it. We're number 1! Fair play to Mauritius, they put up a fight, but no country can match Ireland's skill at not building up. Remember: all new housing supply lowers housing prices. By not building up, we are pricing up."

This tweet was a proverbial shaking of the trees, and it brought out the Twitter birds who squawked with all sorts of opinions, especially from a particularly loud contingent of naysayers. Two comments to Ronan's tweet are relevant here.

One was: "Going by that 'logic,' Hong Kong, New York, Shanghai must have dirt cheap housing. . . ." And "high-rise housing can be 50% more expensive to build (than mid-rise) & is considerably more expensive to operate & maintain. Building up ~is~ pricing up."

Both tweets fall under the (false) logical chain: Tall buildings are expensive to build and maintain. Hong Kong has lots of tall buildings. Hong Kong is very expensive. Ergo, tall buildings must be the reason.

But just because high prices and tall buildings in Hong Kong coexist does not mean that tall buildings are the cause of high prices. Rather, tall buildings are a prime response to the high prices, not the other way around. So "blaming" tall buildings for Hong Kong's high cost of living is confusing correlation with causation.

It's true that some tall buildings can be more expensive to construct and maintain on a per-square-foot basis, but that is not necessarily the case when they are built with efficiency and good planning. When we think of skyscrapers, we tend to think of high-end luxury condos or splashy corporate headquarters designed by starchitects. But they are bespoke projects for those with big bank accounts.

Building medium- or high-rise housing for the middle classes need not be so pricey. When it comes to middle-class housing, there is no universal building height that minimizes the average construction costs, as much depends on local conditions. In some relatively less regulated countries with a fast-moving construction sector and low labor costs, taller buildings can be built more cheaply.

Also, much depends on the sizes of available lots. It's much more efficient to lay out whole communities. Ten tall buildings on one large lot can be cheaper on a per-unit basis than ten smaller buildings on ten lots. Contractors, for example, can buy in bulk and master-plan to use less plant and infrastructure.

A 2003 study of Hong Kong by two real estate professors found that the height with the lowest per-square-foot cost was about 328 feet (100 m or 30 stories). Hong Kong has actually figured out how to build tall buildings at a lower unit cost than shorter ones. A study of thirty-five Shanghai construction projects found that the lowest per-unit costs were hit around 79 feet (24 m, 7 floors). While in the United States researchers found the "bottom" point to also be seven stories, on average.

So, the idea that building up is pricing up because of higher construction costs is not true in principle. It's true in practice because global cities tend to build central city skyscrapers for the rich. But a tour through East Asian cities will show that the high-rise is the province of the middle class, where large housing estates with thirty- and forty-story structures are the norm.

Chinese residents think no more about living in a fifty-story building than a five-story one. To them, skyscraper living is as natural as suburban freestanding housing is in America. That's not to say that their large housing estates are utopias, but it is to say that East Asian countries have mastered the art of constructing middle-class high-rise housing.

A few years ago, when I taught a two-week undergraduate economics course at a university in Changchun in northeast China, I was invited by a junior faculty member to visit his home. He lived with his wife in a small one-bedroom apartment on the fortieth floor of a newly built high-rise. The building's hallways were poorly kept, but inside was pleasant and quiet, and he was proud to show me his mini castle in the sky. In fact, housing is so cheap in Changchun that he and his wife had purchased another place—no doubt with help from their parents—closer to her work to reduce her commute time. They were even thinking of buying a third unit near a good school for their future children. While high-cost cities like Shanghai or Beijing prevent residents from buying more than one unit there, they have been eager to snap up real estate in other cities as investments. A recent study found that nearly 42 percent of urban Chinese residents own two or more properties.

As a sidenote, the problem of American high-rise public housing was not one of cost—it was built at a very low cost—but rather its problems were related to concentrating the poor in declining cities and under-maintaining the properties, along with other issues including racism, urban flight, and poor provision of government services.

But just as importantly, costs in cities are not independent of the benefits. If a particular neighborhood needs and wants more housing, then it can be economically rational to build taller than minimum-cost housing to get the supply to match the demand. Tall buildings exist in a larger housing ecosystem, which constitutes a continuum from shanties to mansions and ultraluxury condos and everything in between. The supply and demand in each submarket are linked to the submarket just above and below, making all housing units and all neighborhood markets part of an interconnected web.

Growth in a particular submarket will then cause higher vacancies in the submarket below, which reduces their prices, making the lower-quality housing more affordable. This is called filtering, and it means that the best way to help lower-income residents is to build tons of middle-class housing and let the poor choose from the less expensive, former middle-class housing.

In one fascinating study, the economist Evan Mast investigated the impacts of 686 market-rate multifamily buildings recently completed in the centers of twelve large U.S. cities. He found that 67 percent of the new units in the central city are occupied by people already living in the metropolitan area. In New York, despite the belief that all new units go to jet-setting out-of-towners, 76 percent of the new-building occupants were from within the metro area and 68 percent were from within the city itself.

After locals moved into the new units, he looked at the income levels of those who moved into the "abandoned" units and did this for six rounds along the moving chain. Mast concludes that "[c]onstructing a new market-rate building that houses 100 people ultimately leads 45 to 70 people to move out of below-median income neighborhoods, with most of the effect occurring within three years. These results suggest that the migration ripple effects of new housing will affect a wide spectrum of neighborhoods and loosen the low-income housing market."

In plain English: New upper-class housing in central cities benefits those in low-income neighborhoods through the filtering process. We can't see it amidst the fog of our everyday urban experiences, but if you focus on filtering, it's there.

A related question is whether high-rise construction and gentrification drive the displacement of longtime, lower-income residents. You might not believe it when I say the evidence suggests that it does not drive mass displacement. This is not to say that no one gets displaced. Clearly, tenants are harmed when their building is torn down to make way for new construction. However, studies using cutting-edge methods of analysis reveal that displacement is much less than the average person thinks.

There are many reasons for this. First is that gentrifying neighborhoods tend to be dynamic places—people are moving out all the time. As some longer-term tenants move out for personal reasons—like retiring to another state or taking a job in another city—a younger, more affluent person might take their place, providing the appearance of displacement.

Also, by and large, gentrifying neighborhoods generate more supply responses. Developers see opportunities from the rising demand and build new in-fill units. Again, these new buildings help maintain prices for the "incumbents." Plus, lower-income residents see benefits to gentrifying neighborhoods, as the gentrifiers attract new stores and more investments in parks and schools (which is sad because they should have been there all along), and many people decide to stay, even if their rents increase.

But if supply lowers prices and makes more housing available why don't people recognize it? The problem is that housing supply and demand are locked in a perennial wrestling match. All great cities exist in a race between the two; when supply can't keep up with demand, housing becomes more unaffordable. In places like London, New York, Vancouver, and Hong Kong, people see luxury condos going up with the cost of living. To many, it must be the case that these luxury condos are causing rising prices.

But again, the truth is the opposite—the demand to live in these places is so great and the supply is so limited that global cities with international demand become like a game of musical chairs: the rich or their children get the pick of the litter, while the rest are steaming with resentment.

It's also important to keep these tall buildings in perspective. New York City, for example, has 3.6 million residential units, and only 5 percent of them are in buildings that are thirty stories or taller (and 1 percent in buildings fifty stories or taller). So, luxury high-rises are not driving the high cost of housing in New York.

A related beef about ultrarich skyscrapers is they are a great way to launder money. Real estate laws, in many countries, such as the United States, Canada, the United Kingdom, and Panama, frequently don't require purchasers to reveal their identities. Thus, a wealthy buyer will hire an attorney who forms a shell corporation and handles the transaction. The ill-gotten cash is slid from suitcase to shell corporation to condo suite and dirty money becomes clean.

In 2015, two journalists for the *New York Times*, Louise Story and Stephanie Saul, investigated the buyers at the Time Warner Center (now the Deutsche Bank Center), a fifty-five-story, twin-towered Manhattan office and condo skyscraper, designed by SOM and completed in 2004.

They found that over the decade transactions "have become increasingly opaque. In 2003, one-third of the units sold in Time Warner were purchased by shell companies. By 2014, that figure was over 80 percent."

The problem is that "[l]acking incentive or legal obligation to identify the sources of money, an entire chain of people involved in high-end real estate sales—lawyers, accountants, title brokers, escrow agents, real estate agents, condo boards and building workers—often operate with blinders on." As Rudy Tauscher, a former manager of the condos at Time Warner, told the journalists, "The building doesn't know where the money is coming from. We're not interested."

The skyscraper was home to at least seventeen billionaires on *Forbes* magazine's annual list of the world's richest people. Units were also owned by many celebrities, including singer Jimmy ("Margaritaville") Buffett, Tom Brady, the New England Patriots quarterback, and the talk-show host Kelly Ripa. But it's not simply the "honest rich" who dwell in its halls. As Story and Saul write:

> Units 72B and 51E are owned by the Amantea Corporation, which *The Times* traced to a mining magnate named Anil Agarwal. His company was fined for polluting a major river near a copper mine in Zambia, which sickened nearby residents. And judicial committees in his native India determined that his company had violated the land rights of an indigenous tribe near a proposed mine.

If there's one city with a housing affordability problem it's Vancouver, where Chinese nationals are known to gobble up high-end condos for investment properties. One study of British Columbia (BC) aimed to determine how money laundering might be affecting housing prices. They estimated that the higher housing demand from money launderers raised prices by about 5–7 percent for high-end units. So not a huge amount.

Across cities, the impacts depend on how responsive the supply is to rising prices. If rising prices (from money laundering or legal means) generate new supply quickly to cater to this demand, then the price effects can be neutralized. But arguably, the main concern is how money laundering affects the prices of the lower and middle classes. Here the connection is more tenuous. If money laundering raises the prices of superluxury high-rise condos, it will then raise the demand for those units below the ultraluxury level as some rich people decide to "downgrade." This will raise the prices for these units, which in turn increases the demand for those units below them, and so on.

But how far does the process go? I would argue it's not all that likely to spill far down to the middle-class housing in the outer parts of the city. Here, again, the real problem of affordability is not money laundering by the corrupt superrich, but that not enough housing is being built outside the central city where it is needed the most.

The problem of corruption is not the skyscrapers it may produce; rather, it's the source of the corruption. Stealing, enslaving, exploiting, and drug peddling are the real problems, and these should be stopped at the source, as hard as that is. Laws for real estate should not encourage or enable the world's grifters. No real estate transactions should be allowed through anonymous shell corporations, and laws should prevent using ill-gotten gains to buy real estate. The United States seems to be finally coming around to anti–shell corporation laws, though it remains to be seen if they will have a significant bite. However, if there is a "legal market" for supertall buildings, let them be.

Relatedly, in the discussion of skyscrapers people tend to confuse corruption with income inequality. No doubt there is a lot of overlap, but they are not the same thing. Income inequality has been rising throughout the Western world, particularly in Anglo-speaking countries. Economist Thomas Piketty's painstaking research documented in his 2013 book, *Capital in the Twenty-First Century*, shows that over the twentieth century, as nations became richer and government policies focused on social programs, income inequality fell across the developed world until around 1980, then reversed course.

The reasons for this are, of course, complicated and highly debated. Some point to the changing nature of the economy—such as the rise of high-tech and high-skilled jobs, winner-take-all compensation schemes, globalization, and outsourcing to the developing world—while others point to tax rate reductions that were originally initiated in the name of supply-side economics; while others focus on the political-economy side, where the rich have co-opted politicians to do their bidding. There's truth in all these things.

I believe that rising inequality in the West is bad. The traditional justification of inequality was that it linked effort with reward. The poor, it is argued, will tolerate poverty because they believe that with hard work and thrift, they or their children could rise into the middle class. But if poverty is simply a mire from which the poor never rise, then effort and thrift are decoupled from their rewards, which can ultimately lead to a downward economic and political spiral. U.S. administrations have been particularly bad about addressing inequality and, in fact, those on the right are exploiting it for their own political gain to the detriment of the commonweal.

The West, particularly the United States, needs to address income inequality by raising tax rates on the superrich, along with government programs for the poor, such as free job retraining or community college attendance, subsidies to move people from high-unemployment to low-unemployment regions, and better access to health- and childcare. To lower the cost of living and increase savings, there needs to be a more concerted effort to make housing more affordable. The best way to do this is to subsidize the construction of middle-income housing and eliminate burdensome zoning requirements.

Ironically, in the developing world, inequality is declining. The poor are moving into the middle class—and middle-class high-rises—and are eroding the traditional barriers between a small superrich and powerful elite and a large pool of poor and illiterate quasi-peasants.

When I look at the international data and crunch the numbers, I do not find that income inequality is a significant driver of skyscraper construction. Highly unequal societies are no more or less likely to overbuild than their more equal counterparts. Having said this, within the United States over time there is a relationship between income inequality and skyscraper booms. In periods during the highest level of income inequality in modern times—the 1920s, the 1980s, and 2010s—the nation has built more skyscrapers. The likely reason for this is, again, on the demand side. The more income at the higher end, the more demand for tall buildings, either from corporations that want to signal their economic strength or for the rich who want pieds-à-terre.

But flipping the question on its head: Do skyscrapers exacerbate income inequality? My answer is "perhaps." In the twenty-first century, the rich have consistently used their gains to make it that much harder to take them away. We can see this in real estate. Around the developed world, there has been a tremendous rise in housing prices over the last several decades. The blame, however, lies not only with the superrich but also with the middle classes, who have demanded that their leaders erect barriers to new housing construction.

NIMBYism is rampant at nearly all income levels, and, in fact, in places like New York and San Francisco, single-family homeowners have made common cause with apartment dwellers against new construction because they have jointly come to see developers as in league with the devil—allegedly ruining their neighborhoods through densification or gentrification.

Because it is very difficult to build in the suburbs, more demand for housing occurs in the center, which puts additional pressure on land values, which in turn incentivizes taller buildings. So those advocating suburban construction limits or caps on building heights in the name of "human scale" are in fact promoting the very high-rises they seek to ban.

Ironically, the only "place" in the market where new housing can be built on any systemic scale is on the upper end, where the rewards are greatest. The restrictions for densifying suburban neighborhoods are arguably tighter than in the central cities. But it's the restrictions on new housing that have given property owners monopoly power, which has increased their wealth. After Piketty's book was released, it was soon discovered that much of the gains driving wealth inequality, in fact, came from property ownership.

Pro-homeownership policies were meant to promote community and enhance personal savings, but they inadvertently pushed people to think more like a bank to preserve their return on investment. Skyscrapers, in and of themselves, are not the real drivers of income inequality, but rather it's the restricted property markets more broadly.

Ironically, if you look at the prices of ultraluxury condos in New York over the last decade, they have been flat. At the same time, condo prices throughout the New York metro region have increased by over 40 percent. The reason is that the high end is a competitive market on the supply side. Below that, not so much.

The money being funneled into high-rise condos around the world, however, has some perks. They add to the skyline's awe. I bet that twenty years from now Billionaires' Row in New York will be celebrated for its style of architecture and one that fits comfortably within its diverse panoply of towers. No doubt some will be landmarked by the city's Landmarks Preservation Commission. And, like the tales of the "ego-driven" developers of the Empire State and Chrysler Buildings in the Roaring Twenties, the "amazing tales" of latter-day robber barons and their Billionaires' Row will regale viewers on the History Channel.

And the reason that high-rise construction is so profitable is that their host cities are desirable places to be in because of the culture, culinary delights, social opportunities, and so on. The rich support these endeavors, and if they feel some connection to a city, however tenuous, they are more likely to donate to institutions, including museums, nonprofits, and charities. And they pay property taxes. Since they spend less time in the city, they likely pay more in taxes than they require in municipal services.

More broadly, the problem is not that some countries have too many skyscrapers but rather they don't have enough. Developing countries

have embraced skyscrapers because they are part of the suite of investments that go along with rapid economic growth. And when a country
seeks to grow, it builds infrastructure, improves its educational system,
creates favorable business climates, strengthens property rights, and
induces foreign direct investment. Skyscrapers are a natural extension
of this process—people need to live and work in central cities where
modern service-based economic activity takes place and where businesses want to signal their competitiveness.

But as developing countries turn into developed countries, they tend
to get stricter in their building regulations. Historical preservation, envi-
ronmentalism, and the desire for more green space rise in importance,
and city leaders turn toward quality of life over rapid growth. Laudable
goals to be sure but not a free lunch.

Research that I performed with two coauthors, Remi Jedwab, of
George Washington University, and Jan K. Brueckner, of the University
of California, Irvine, compared the number of tall buildings in each
country to what it "should" have if its real estate market was less regulated and more fluid. By this metric, we found the world is "missing"
six thousand Empire State Buildings. While this seems astronomically
high, our analysis also reveals that the rise in the global construction
gaps tracks very closely to the rise in global housing prices, suggesting
that these missing buildings are helping to fuel global unaffordability.

European countries are the most reluctant to build up. As noted
earlier, Ireland is the "winner"—it is the country that is "missing"
the most tall buildings, given its wealth and global importance. Regulations in Switzerland, for example, give strong veto power to those
opposed to skyscrapers, and, as a result, there are only five tall buildings
in Zurich, one of the world's wealthiest cities and a financial hub.
Interestingly, the United States makes it into the top twenty of the
most-likely-to-be-missing-skyscrapers list. The reason is California.
Despite its large wealth—its economy is larger than that of Mexico
and India, respectively—it has implemented stringent building height

regulations in the name of reducing congestion and improving the quality of urban life.

Just as importantly, we find that higher gaps correlate with more expensive housing prices, greater urban sprawl, more traffic congestion, and more air pollution, including carbon monoxide and nitrogen oxide. In short, overly restrictive nations are hurting themselves. For most people who see the trees, the skyscrapers, it's harder to see the forest, the skyline, but the health of the entire economic ecosystem is what matters.

WHAT ARE THE SOLUTIONS?

What's the solution to the housing affordability problem? The short answer that every economist will give is: eliminate overly burdensome regulations and allow the market to produce units based on the laws of supply and demand. If you look at Tokyo, for example, its population is rising, even if Japan's is not, and, by and large, housing is affordable because there is constant densification and construction of new units. It doesn't hurt that Japanese residents are seemingly content to live in apartments half the size that is acceptable to Americans. But it does show that when a metropolis embraces new supply policies, affordability can follow.

If adding new housing was so easy, however, every city would be doing it. At the end of the day, the problem is not economic; it's political and social. Paring building regulations, reducing excessive greenbelts, or evicting tenants to free up land is too controversial. But there are steps that cities can take, though there must be both carrots and sticks, as residents need incentives to switch from NIMBY to YIMBY and feel their neighborhoods will improve as a result.

Hong Kong, however, is in a particular pickle because of its unusual institutional background that limits land supply. Much of the non-developable land was converted to parkland in the 1970s. Though most of it is too steep for development, recent attempts to use some of it for housing have met fierce opposition. The government's "addiction" to land-lease revenue has also produced a "scarce land" policy to keep land-lease revenues higher. And the big four real estate companies have enormous reserves of rural land that they obtained from the government. But since they are not required to build, it sits undeveloped, as they wait to see where the Mass Transit Railway will eventually construct new rail lines.

When the Hong Kong airport was removed from Kowloon, hundreds of acres of airspace for tall buildings were freed up. But much of that was "withdrawn" in the mid-2000s when the city imposed restrictions preventing new buildings from blocking sight lines to the ridges on Hong Kong Island and northern Kowloon.

The government is taking steps to add more housing, however. It's planning to reclaim 2,500 acres (1,000 hectares) off Lantau Island with over 200,000 housing units for a population of half a million, along with a "work-live-play" central business district. Officials are also planning to construct a new town along the Shenzhen border, with as many as 926,000 homes for 2.5 million residents. But these projects are expensive, controversial, and will take years, if not decades, to complete.

If built, the so-called Northern Metropolis would weave Hong Kong and Shenzhen that much closer. As reported in one outlet, "China also hopes to speed the process by pulling part of the territory's core away from Hong Kong Island, which is distant and holds vestiges of British rule like Victoria Peak, a luxury residential district favored by Chinese executives."

To construct the Northern Metropolis and the Lantau Island project, the government plans to spend nearly $100 billion. I spoke to one Hong Kong planner about the plans, and as we chatted, his voice revealed a sense of exhilaration at what officials could achieve in Hong Kong—on a scale impossible in any U.S. city. If successful, the Northern Metropolis will create a bimodal city—the old Hong Kong along the harbor and "Shen Kong" along the border. Just as importantly, however, these projects suggest faith in Hong Kong's future and that it will remain vital, even if somewhat diminished.

SUCCESSFUL PLANNING

So, more broadly, what's to be done? I want to stress that I'm not arguing for eliminating planning or building regulations. I'm arguing for planning regulations that take "good" economics into account. Planners by their very nature seek to impose order and to "micromanage" a city to eliminate what they perceive as messiness and chaos.

The planners' visions in the past backfired because cities cannot be arranged like pieces on a chessboard. The overly stringent zoning regulations that "felt good" to planners in the mid-twentieth century are causing terrible affordability problems today because the politics of undoing them is too explosive, even though these regulations have been made obsolete with our vast improvements in health and technology.

If there's one lesson from urban economics: listen to the land values. As put succinctly by planner and writer Alain Bertaud, allocating land via the market

> sends strong signals through prices when land is underused or the use is unsuitable for its location; . . . provides a strong incentive to users to use as little land as possible in areas where there is a strong demand, in particular in areas well served by transport networks; and . . . stimulates innovation in construction; without land prices, there would have been no skyscrapers, no steel frames, and no elevators.

Here I lay out some steps, which I call the VEAM Principle. But the key fact we must remember is this: Cities are composed of dynamic interrelated systems. You cannot treat one neighborhood or one policy in isolation from the others; otherwise, policies can generate unintended consequences.

V: *The Value of Land*

Land values represent the value of geography. Central places are more valuable than suburban ones. So, there should be more tall buildings in the center and fewer tall buildings outside. In popular suburban neighborhoods, there should be the flexibility to build low- and mid-rise apartment buildings if need be. The suburbs don't need tall buildings if there is no demand, but let people vote with their dollars and feet.

New construction means that, occasionally, older buildings must go. Preservationists will squawk that this means the end of historical cities. One solution might be to reduce what can be saved (though that's not what people want to hear). Another option is to preserve the façades but let higher buildings rise in the middle of the blocks. Yet another option is to "enclose" the historical districts with surrounding high-rise districts. It's crucial to reiterate: If you limit supply in the most valued locations, you need to find places nearby to add it.

E: *Externalities*

The problem with dense development is that it creates a host of negative externalities or harms that affect other residents and visitors. Tall buildings can create shadows, and density can create congestion on the streets or strain local infrastructure. City planning needs to minimize the damage without harming the city in other ways. As a general rule, developers must be made to "internalize" the externalities to reduce them but not be forced to do so in a way that throws out the baby with the bathwater.

For example, using modern computing techniques, cities can assess the loss in surrounding property values when new buildings create shadows. If developers had to pay a "shadow tax" to compensate those harmed, they would have their architects produce skinnier or less darkening structures. With today's software, it's easy to determine where shadows will fall and for how long. One study of freestanding homes in Australia, for example, found that each extra daily hour of sunlight exposure was associated with a 2.6 percent increase in house prices. So, using this number, if a new building puts your apartment in the shadows for an hour more per day, the developer should pay you 2.6 percent of your home's value as fair compensation.

A: *Affordability*

In New York City, for example, rent stabilization laws—limits on rent increases—remain in effect if the citywide rental vacancy is less than 5 percent. But because rent stabilization reduces vacancies, the program self-perpetuates. Rather than saying, "Vacancy is too low; we need to implement price controls," cities need to imagine a world where vacancy is always at, say, 10 percent, with so much housing and so many choices that rents are inherently affordable.

The government needs to have more faith in the invisible hand, though that's not to say it can't wear a velvet glove to help from time to time. First, planners should reduce building restrictions as neighborhood vacancies fall below, say, 5 percent. Let demand dictate supply. Allow accessory dwelling units (ADUs) or the conversion of garages for apartments in the suburbs, allow taller buildings near rail lines, and allow for skyscrapers in the central cities.

Cities should buy up underutilized plots and sell the land leases to developers to densify them. This way, cities can actively encourage new housing exactly where it's needed and at an affordable price. Officials also need to simultaneously add social services, upgrade parks, and invest in transportation improvements as new units come online.

However, one of the biggest obstacles is the fear that homeowners will find their house values plummeting as the neighborhood redevelops. Ironically, a densifying community will see increased land values, which would help existing homeowners. But one proposal to mitigate NIMBYism has been put forth by William Fischel, Professor Emeritus at Dartmouth College, one of the world's foremost experts on zoning. His idea is that homeowners could take out an insurance policy that would pay out at the time of selling if their land values declined because of loosening restrictions. Since land values are determined by the nature and characteristics of the neighborhood and economic development more broadly, insurance can help assuage concern that changes will wipe out homeowners' equity through no fault of their own.

And what about public housing? Across the world, cities like Hong Kong, Vienna, and Singapore demonstrate that it can work. However, public housing needs to be open to all residents except the very rich, and money needs to be set aside for ongoing maintenance and upgrades.

But as America and Hong Kong have also demonstrated, public housing is not without pitfalls. Large public housing programs—especially in global cities—also mean dual housing markets. Those who get into government-owned units get a great deal. But people are much less likely to move, because moving would naturally increase their housing costs (even if they downsized). The waiting time for public housing in Hong Kong is nearly six years. For New York, since 2013, there have been more than 25 million applications submitted for roughly forty thousand units within New York City's public housing program. In Hong Kong, the people hurt the most are those at the bottom who must pay higher housing costs until their ship comes in. Public housing needs to be a complement to free-market housing, not a substitute.

M: Mobility

The goal of transportation policies should be to move the most amount of people with the least amount of delay by giving people choices and reducing congestion. All elements of the transportation system must be directly linked. Cars, buses, subways, commuter rail, walking, cycling, and scootering are all different forms of mobility and should be considered within a larger framework. The cost of using different parts of the system should be set simultaneously. For example, if there's too much road traffic, then jack up road congestion fees and reduce subway and bus fares in parallel. Strategically placed signs and transit apps can inform everyone of the costs and times of the different modes, and then people can decide what works best for them. If people had more choices, they would naturally eschew their cars, which would further enhance cities' dynamism.

A simpler, though less comprehensive, way to reduce car usage is through congestion pricing, where drivers pay a toll to enter the densest neighborhoods. The money raised is poured back into improving mass transit. Congestion pricing has been successfully established in London, Stockholm, and Singapore. Launched in 2003, the scheme for central London produced a 30 percent reduction in traffic congestion and increased car speeds by 30 percent for those who paid the fee. New York City is on the verge of initiating its own congestion plan for Manhattan south of Central Park. However, implementation is being delayed due to a "border war." The State of New Jersey is suing to prevent its residents from having to pay twice—first a toll to cross the Hudson River and then the congestion charge. The odds are that there will eventually be a resolution and the plan will move forward. But fear of car-addiction withdrawal is fierce.

At the end of the day, however, we must decide what we want—exclusive history museums like inner Paris or affordable future-oriented cities. They both have their benefits, but only one would be available to everyone and the VEAM Principle can make it so.

CHAPTER 10

Futureopolis

The Quest for the City of Tomorrow

The Brutalist Trellick Tower (1972) in London.
The council housing building, once infamous for violence and crime,
is now a trendy place to live and has landmark status.

CIVIL WAR IN THE SKY

Two miles east of St. Paul's Cathedral in London is a high-rise tower —
one of several built in the architectural style of Brutalism, a massive
gray concrete structure, which exudes the feeling of a giant bunker
with balconies.

With forty stories and one thousand apartments, it is designed for
middle- and upper-class residents to have all the latest conveniences. The

tenth floor is given over to a shopping concourse, with a supermarket, a liquor store, a hair salon, a swimming pool, a gym, and an elementary school. On the thirty-fifth floor are another smaller pool, a sauna, and a restaurant. The tower is surrounded by a large parking lot, so owners can easily drive from home to work. When the building was completed, the occupants moved in with heady optimism. The skyscraper was a machine for living, and they were going to have the modern lives to which they felt entitled.

Soon, however, strange things began to happen. Residents noticed that they had sorted themselves by floor level. Those with young children lived on the lower stories. Childless middle-class professionals lived on the middle floors, and the rich drifted to the top. This segregation nudged people to circle the wagons within their "zones." Tenants came to see those outside theirs as the enemy from within.

The changes started slowly—a dropped champagne bottle from up high, an elevator taken out of service, or some graffiti scrawl. But bit by bit, the residents blamed the other zones and engaged in retribution. Within three months the building had become a vertical *Lord of the Flies*. There was no longer any running water or heat. Furniture was used for barricades or firewood. The management abandoned the structure and residents stopped leaving. Gangs—made up of former lawyers, doctors, and filmmakers—roamed the stairwells beating up the unsuspecting from the other floors. Tenants held wild orgiastic parties, sending out looters to find alcohol to fuel their bacchanalia. When the food ran out, they ate the pet dogs and cats captured from the enemy. One by one, the weak were killed or died from wounds or starvation. The few who were left championed their feral lifestyle. The high-rise had collapsed from within.

So goes the story from the 1975 dystopian novel *High-Rise*, by British fiction writer J. G. Ballard. It was penned during a time when high-rise living was spreading to the masses in the Western world. Whereas before World War II high-rises were mansions in the sky for the wealthy; after the war high-rises were for all.

The great plans of the Modernist architects and their Corbusian utopian visions were finally being realized. And then reality followed. Living in the clouds was unnatural and isolating. It encouraged crime and social and economic harm. Fiction writers and filmmakers went into overdrive, presenting the world if carried to its logical extreme.

HAPPINESS AND HIGH-RISES?

In a way, we are confronted with a strange paradox. We are convinced that high-rise living is bad for us, and yet central cities throughout the world keep building up and up. Even the Netherlands, not known for its embrace of the skyscraper, is planning to build some two hundred high-rises in the ensuing decades. Even outside Asia, from Rio to Austin to Toronto to Sydney, middle-class high-rise apartments are increasingly being constructed.

No doubt it is because our future is an urban one. Nearly 60 percent of the world's population lives in cities, and in the next decades that figure is likely to reach 80 percent and we will continue erecting our urban habitat. The key argument of this book has been that we have our skyscrapers because we want and need them. Their existence is due to the underlying economics of cities: skyscrapers rise when the demand for certain locations exceeds the land's ability to accommodate it. The skyscraper is a geography-shrinking machine.

And yet we can't help but think that skyscrapers are bad for us. The press regularly reports about skyscrapers gone haywire, while critics complain of their scale and environmental impacts and the NIMBY crowds do what they can to keep them out of their neighborhoods.

So, what gives? We know they make economic sense, but do they make psychological and social sense? Do they make us happy? To be fair, there is research that suggests that high-rise living has (or had) its problems. In 2007, Professor Robert Gifford of the University of Victoria in British Columbia published an article titled "The Consequences of Living in High-Rise Buildings" in the journal *Architectural Science Review*, in which he reviewed about one hundred research articles on the psychological impacts of living in tall buildings. The results were not encouraging. Of the studies reviewed, only seventeen measured a positive outcome for the particular research question. Many studies found that people living in high-rises suffer from greater mental health problems, higher fear of crime, fewer positive social interactions, and more difficulty with raising their children.

On high-rise living and depression, Gifford reports:

> More serious mental health problems have tenuously been related to building height. In an English study, mothers who lived in flats reported more depressive symptoms than those who lived in houses. Rates of mental illness rose with floor level in an English study. Psychological symptoms were more often present in high rises.

And on child-rearing, he concludes:

> The problems range from fundamental child development issues to everyday activities such as play. For example, a Japanese investigation concluded that the development of infants raised above the fifth floor in high-rise buildings is delayed, compared to those raised below the fifth floor. The development of numerous skills, such as dressing, helping and appropriate urination was slower. Children who live on higher floors also go outside to play less often.

So the takeaway seems to be that high-rise living is "unhealthy." But probing a little more deeply suggests we should not be so hasty. In fact, in the last twenty years or so there has been an increasing stream of research that investigates the psychological and health impacts of tall buildings, especially in cities throughout Asia. And the findings are more sanguine than the ones that Gifford reviewed.

So how can we reconcile the differences? First, the studies in Gifford's article were mostly written in the 1970s and 1980s, a bad time for Western urbanism and arguably the worst time for public or low-income subsidized high-rising housing. The studies reflect not only the problem with the design and location of public housing but also the difficulty of living in cities with declining economic opportunities. The supply of low-income high-rises produced by the government got ahead of their natural demand.

High-rise living is bad when people are economically "trapped" and feel compelled to take cheap subsidized housing because they desperately need shelter they can afford. In this sense, the problem is choice—the ability to decide where to live and how high must be based on the weighing of the costs and benefits, along with the feeling that your housing choice conforms to the societal norm of "good" and "proper" housing.

On the other hand, in modern East Asian cities, high-rise living is typical. And when researchers started asking people about the quality of their lives there, the answers were that health, on average, was not that much different on higher floors than that of those living on lower floors. And people had great views and cleaner air.

In my own research, I have found that the building type that people live in does not affect their housing satisfaction once you consider, or control for, how they feel about other important elements. People are satisfied with high-rise living if their building is clean, well maintained, and safe. Just as importantly, they are happier if they feel their current housing choice is close to or matches their preferred option.

For the United States, the key lesson is that the market needs to have the freedom to work according to the laws of supply and demand and that people should have options. If residents *want* to live in the central city, then they will willingly face the key economic trade-off: higher prices and less space for greater access. If they prefer the leafier suburbs, then they should be able to live there in larger but cheaper spaces.

Ironically, public housing today in New York, while not a panacea, actually serves an important purpose. Since the 1990s, the New York economy has rebounded and crime has fallen, and central living again has its benefits. The truth is that without these units many low-income people would be forced to leave the city. In this sense, the city has finally caught up to its public housing.

STREET LIFE AND STREETSCAPES

According to the anti-skyscraperists, all that is socially good cleaves away from the skyscraper. Urbanists praise density but curse skyscrapers as "ruining the feel" of the streetscape. Architecture critic Justin Davidson says that "shiny towers are invasive species and they are choking our cities and killing off public space."

Jan Gehl—the godfather of "Human Scale" cities—is no fan. He points to the mistakes of mid-century planners as trying to create high-rise utopias. Then he proceeds to tell the world that to take their medicine they need to build Manhattan brownstones, low-rise walk-ups, and Parisian apartment buildings everywhere, regardless of the fact that imposing one or two building types across the city would be just another act of neo-utopianism. If there is one thing that economists have demonstrated, it's that ignoring the realities of how people respond to incentives generates unintended consequences that are often worse than the cure. At the risk of exaggerating, Gehl's philosophy is to save the city by ignoring the economics.

Let's be clear, I'm not saying there's no role for urban design, but I do want to stress that planners, economists, and other social scientists must work together to make sure design, quality of life, and economics work in harmony. The plethora of restrictions on new construction in the name of preservation and human scale are making global cities increasingly unaffordable for all but the very wealthy.

Having traveled the world, I can say that the idea that skyscrapers are inherently bad for urbanism is simply not true. High-rises that "engage" with the street level, through retail or encouraging pedestrianism and pleasing open spaces, can be as welcoming as low-rise neighborhoods. There are many exemplary residential neighborhoods around the world that can serve as models, like SoHo in Hong Kong, Manhattan along its High Line park, or Chicago's neighborhoods along the Chicago River and Lake Michigan.

Good cities are like playgrounds for kids of all ages; they are exciting and full of whatever kinds of activities you seek, and in good high-rise cities you can flow easily in both vertical and horizontal directions, providing truly three-dimensional experiences.

The biggest drag on cities, however, is the overreliance on automobiles. If we opened our streets to pedestrians and allowed for a panoply of other forms of transit, we would be that much better off. Automobile-centric cities mean large spaces devoted to moving, parking, and storing these self-powered boxes. They provide less ability for residents and visitors to interact with the city and other people.

But yes, some tall buildings can feel overwhelming. They are big, after all, and can give a sense of being a fortress. Over the last few years, social scientists have tried to understand better how building form can influence our emotional sense of peace or unease. The original research, begun in Japan in the 1970s, used the word 圧迫感 (*appakukan*), which translates into "to feel oppression" or "to feel overwhelmed." Researchers wanted to know what elements of streetscapes generate *appakukan*.

A 2012 study re-created, in a laboratory setting, the perspectives of pedestrians viewing a high-rise from across the street (although, in the lab, they are sitting in chairs). Using a wide-angle picture of a building on Hongo Street, a dense residential neighborhood in central Tokyo, the researchers rendered the image into a computer-generated one and then "covered" each image with regularly spaced dots. They counted the number of dots that fell on the building, the sky, and other features, such as trees. In this way, they had very specific measurements of what fraction of the view is taken up by different elements that a typical pedestrian might see.

Subjects then viewed different versions of the simulated images. Some had taller buildings, others had more open space, others had substantial tree coverage, and so on. Each of the subjects was asked to rate their perceptions of oppression (or unease), openness, and pleasantness. They found a strong positive correlation between the response to the oppression question and the height of the buildings. But they found that oppressiveness was moderated by adding trees on the street.

In another study, subjects observed pictures of actual buildings on the street and filled out a survey about how the views felt. Here they found that, after they controlled for the tree, sky, and ground area coverage, the building density had no statistical impact on oppressiveness. Again, this finding suggests that people's perception of unease from building form is moderated by the context in which it appears.

This research method offers a way to conduct highly controlled experiments to better understand people's emotional responses to different streetscapes. If we can measure streetscape pleasantness or *umami* versus *appakukan* and if the developers and architects employ these rules, it might give residents more confidence in new construction. People want to feel that the changes they see around them are helping to contribute to their life satisfaction or, at least, are not making things worse.

City officials, planners, architects, and developers need to be on the same page to provide not only better streetscapes and more housing but also more enjoyable housing. Factors that encourage people to remain in their buildings and get to know each other are helpful. In this regard, there is a certain benefit to "horizontality." Architects and developers must think more about enhancing this horizontality within their buildings, such as having unenclosed stairwells between floors or creating more common areas. Social spaces in the building are vital, such as playrooms for children, roof decks, or party spaces. Because of the COVID pandemic and the work-from-home movement, residential and commercial building owners are increasingly feeling the pressure to amenitize their buildings with these kinds of areas. This trend should be encouraged by cities since there is less incentive to provide them when they eat into otherwise valuable rentable space. Officials can give FAR bonuses for within-building public areas, so developers don't feel they are losing out. Or governments or nonprofits can rent the lower floors for community spaces.

Tencent Seafront Towers (2017), Shenzhen

Developers should be incentivized to provide public sky bridges that connect buildings either on a property or across properties. An interesting corporate example is the "vertical campus" of the Tencent Seafront Towers (2017) in Shenzhen. Tencent is the fourth-largest internet company in the world, after Google, Amazon, and Facebook. With its workforce growing rapidly, in 2011 Tencent held an international design competition for a new headquarters. Rather than building a sprawling suburban campus, like Apple Park in Cupertino, Tencent wanted a "vertical campus" in the city center. The winning design by the American architectural firm NBBJ comprises two towers — one fifty stories and the other thirty-nine — connected by three broad "street-scapes" or sky bridges.

The lowest sky bridge has restaurants, an auditorium, an exhibition space, and retail shops. The second bridge is called the health link and contains sports facilities, such as a track, a swimming pool, basketball courts, and a gym, along with a roof garden. The third bridge has meeting spaces and corporate training facilities. While at a construction cost of $600 million such a structure is available only to the largest corporate clients, it does offer a model to think more horizontally even as buildings grow vertically.

SUSTAINABILITY

Another belief is that skyscrapers are bad for the environment, particularly greenhouse gas emissions (GHGs). A case in point is the Bank of America (BoA) Tower, with 2.1 million square feet (195,100 m²) and fifty-five stories (1,200 feet, 365.8 m). Opened in 2009 in Midtown Manhattan with great fanfare, it was arguably the city's greenest office skyscraper ever built. Developed by the Durst Organization, it was the first high-rise tower to get Leadership in Energy and Environmental Design's (LEED's) Platinum Rating based on its suite of "sustainable" technologies.

The building includes a natural gas–powered 4.6-megawatt cogeneration plant, which produces 65 percent of the building's electricity and heating and cooling. For most buildings that tap into the electricity grid, the Environmental Protection Agency estimates that, on average, every unit of electricity consumed requires more than three times as much electricity to be produced. This is largely due to the inefficiencies of the power plant as well as losses during transmission. If energy is produced on-site, there is barely any loss. Cogeneration, one would think, is the wave of the future.

The building also includes a variety of other "green" features, such as an ice-storage system where ice is made at night and then used in the daytime for air-conditioning, solar panels on the façade, and a gray water recycling system to help minimize drawing water from the municipal system. The building's steel was made from 87 percent recycled metals, while the concrete was made from 45 percent recycled materials.

But then, in 2012, the truth was revealed after New York City passed a benchmarking law that required all large buildings to report their energy usage and greenhouse gas emissions. The BoA Tower was the worst energy user in Gotham. As reported in the *New Republic*:

> According to data released by New York City last fall [of 2012], the Bank of America Tower produces more greenhouse gases and uses more energy per square foot than any comparably sized office building in Manhattan. It uses more than twice as much energy per square foot as the 80-year-old Empire State Building. It also performs worse than the Goldman Sachs headquarters, maybe the most similar building in New York—and one with a lower LEED rating. It's not just an embarrassment; it symbolizes a flaw at the heart of the effort to combat climate change.

New York subsequently passed a law, Local Law 97, requiring all big buildings to reduce their greenhouse gas emissions or pay fines. This puts Durst Organization chairman Douglas Durst in a bind. As reported by *Bloomberg News*:

> At 77, Durst is one of the great characters of New York real estate, a terse conversationalist with a mordant sense of humor. Far from being elusive, he's happy to disclose the inner workings of his building. He says there's no mystery: Bank of America Corp. has five trading floors operating around the clock, packed with employees monitoring multiple computers at their desks. "A densely occupied building like this

is going to consume more electricity than a lightly occupied building,"
he says. To hear Durst tell it, Local Law 97 doesn't distinguish between
the two. "So a building that's vacant is going to get a better score than
a fully occupied building," he continues. "It makes absolutely no sense
whatsoever. That's the problem in a nutshell."

When the news of BoA Tower's energy use went viral, the press could
barely contain its schadenfreude-based glee—all running with some
version of the headline "Big Building Bites Back Big Apple." Regardless
of whether the tower itself gets a bum rap or not, its plight certainly
raises the issue of whether tall buildings are bad for the environment.

Thanks to the benchmarking law, New York has released data on
GHG emissions for thousands of large buildings across the city. This
has allowed me to look at the degree to which taller buildings are worse
than their less tall counterparts or not. My statistical analysis suggests
several conclusions. First, holding building area constant, if we compare
two buildings, but one is 10 percent higher than the other, it produces
1.3 percent more GHGs, on average. This means that taller buildings
do generate more GHGs but also do so at a decreasing rate. Adding one
floor to a ten-story building adds 1.3 percent more GHGs, but adding
one floor to a one-hundred-story building only adds 0.13 percent GHGs,
on average. If the same number of people occupy each floor, then on
a per capita basis, more height reduces per capita GHG emissions.

But I also find a larger role from the building area. Take two buildings that are the same height, but one is 10 percent larger; the second
one will produce about 6 percent more GHGs. Bulk is thus worse than
height. And when you take a skyscraper like the BoA Tower, you get
bulk and height—and energy-hogging traders—is there any wonder it
has trouble keeping its emissions down?

The finding that the size of the building matters makes sense. Large
buildings require more energy and fuel to power. Studies in Hong Kong
showed that for tall buildings about half of the energy usage was for

heating and cooling, 15 percent for lighting, and another 6 percent for elevators. But what is it about building height, per se, that affects energy usage?

First is the nature of its façade. Tall buildings are more exposed to the sun and elements. The greater the surface area relative to the volume, the greater its "interaction" with the environment, particularly when glass is involved. Before World War II most structures were clad in masonry and "punched" with windows. The reliance on masonry curtain walls actually provided a benefit for energy usage: the stone or brick walls added a cave-like property—keeping the building cooler from the sun in the summer and warmer from the cold in the winter.

But after World War II, the triumph of the glass box also meant a corresponding ratcheting up in energy usage. Whereas tall buildings completed prior to the war had between 20 and 40 percent glazing, postwar Modernist "International Style" buildings had between 50 and 70 percent glazing. They also tended to use fixed single-glazed panels, which had poor thermal and insulating properties. Without air-conditioning, the glass box could never have been built.

The energy usage was not only from the glass but also from its color. The preference of the day was black glass, which absorbs more of the sun's rays and requires extra cooling in summer. And less light penetrates deeper into the interior of the building, requiring additional artificial lighting. Black glass façades were fine as long as oil was cheap. And in fact, from 1946 to 1973 the real price of oil steadily dropped, masking the overreliance on cheap energy.

But the oil crises of the 1970s were a wake-up call (though long since forgotten), and architecture began to evolve. If you look at the American cities that went on a building spree in the 1980s, you see fewer all-glass structures and more reliance on masonry. In this way, the architectural zeitgeist of Postmodernism—which brought back souped-up forms of old building styles—was also partly driven by the economics of running a building, as well as boredom with the International Style.

But, still, glass is king. Occupants want light and views. And today's skyscrapers have returned to glass cladding in spades. The response has more efficient glass that reduces UV lighting but allows for visible light to pass through. Such windows are not just for new buildings, however. In 2009, when the Empire State Building refurbished sixty-five hundred windows with triple-glazed insulated panels, it reduced its annual electricity bill by $400,000.

Unfortunately, when it comes to glass, birds don't see things in the same way as humans. Bird strikes—particularly by migrating birds—are a worldwide problem. In the springtime in Newark, New Jersey, where I work, I often see dead birds on the ground from strikes, including the diminutive hairy woodpecker and red-eyed vireo. It's sad. Recent studies have estimated some 500 to 600 million bird deaths annually from strikes on all buildings in the United States. Though skyscrapers are a huge culprit because of their size, they only account for a quarter of deaths. A bigger culprit is outdoor cats, with one study estimating they cause 2.4 billion bird deaths alone (keep your cats indoors!).

It turns out that one simple way to reduce tall building strikes is to turn out the lights at night. Scientists found that on nights when half the windows of a large building in Chicago were darkened there were eleven times fewer bird collisions during spring migration and six times fewer collisions during autumn migration than when all the windows were lit. Still, cities need to work with building owners to devise better solutions. We want our cities to encourage biodiversity, not diminish it.

Though birds have wings, humans have elevators, and on any given day 7 billion elevator journeys are made around the world. Defying gravity means a significant use of energy. While buildings consume about 40 percent of the world's energy, elevators account for 2–10 percent of the building's energy consumption. During peak hours, elevators may drive 40 percent of a building's energy requirements.

Tall buildings are also more carbon-intensive to build, generating more of what is known as embodied carbon—the greenhouse gases created in the production and transportation of building materials. Concrete and steel require vast amounts of energy to produce, and since skyscrapers are mostly built from these materials, they are intensive indeed. Typically for a tall building, the steel and concrete will constitute half of the building's embodied carbon. One ton of steel produces up to 2.5 tons of carbon in production, while 0.25–0.50 tons of carbon are created per ton of concrete. The Shanghai Tower, for example, weighs 850,000 tons. Roughly speaking, it produced its own weight in embodied carbon!

Lower-rise buildings use more wood and less metal and concrete and thus generate less energy in manufacturing. So yes, skyscrapers do deserve some of the bad rap. And when we zoom in on their problems it's easy to see them. But we should be counting carbon at the city level, not at the building level. Focusing only on the tall buildings of the ultrarich or financial companies and concluding they are plagues is drawing general conclusions from a biased sample.

So, what are their net environmental impacts once you start putting them into context within the larger urban framework? The truth: They don't look so bad. Ultimately, lifestyle matters as much as anything. Cities that overly rely on freestanding houses and cars are worse than dense living, where high-rises are part of the equation.

Households who live in single-family homes tend to occupy more space per person. A four-person household in the suburbs might occupy, say, two thousand square feet, but the same household in a denser neighborhood might occupy fifteen hundred square feet. Excessive driving also spreads out suburbia far beyond what it would be if fewer people relied on cars.

Two scientists at the University of California, Berkeley, Christopher Jones and Daniel M. Kammen, created estimates of the average household carbon footprints for every zip code in the United States. They found that the benefits of central city population density contributions were offset by the profligate suburbs. While Manhattan is one of the greenest places in America, thanks to its small apartments, tall buildings, and extensive subway system, New York's outlying suburban areas have much higher carbon footprints.

My own review of the carbon footprints in the Jones and Kammen data for New York City shows that on average, high-rise residential neighborhoods are much better than single-family districts, though the "best" carbon-footprint neighborhoods are those with four- or five-story low-rise apartment buildings.

As a thought experiment, imagine we only dealt with lifestyle and transportation changes and ignored policies like taxing carbon. Say a new policy causes vehicle miles driven to drop by 10 percent, while average floors per building and total floor area both stimulatingly increased by 10 percent. Reducing vehicle miles traveled by 10 percent leads to a predicted drop of emissions by 2.73 percent. However, an increase in the average number of floors and total floor area by 10 percent increases emissions by 0.632 percent. Thus, on the net, GHG emissions would fall by about 2.1 percent. This number assumes that we hold the age of the housing stock and the number of units constant. But if densification is also associated with more units per building and newer structures, then the net impact will be even greater.

The anti-skyscraperists point to tall buildings as GHG factories, but, at the same time, we all go about our lives—driving, taking hot showers, eating beef, using computers, flying to vacation destinations—and think little about how these actions generate GHGs and abet climate change catastrophes. Every semester when I teach either Urban Economics or Introduction to Microeconomics, I poll the students to see how many decided not to drive to class on that day because they knew it would add carbon to the atmosphere. I don't think anyone has ever raised their hand in the affirmative.

Individually our contributions to the problem are small, but collectively they are huge. To blame skyscrapers—where millions of people work, live, and play—in this larger framework seems foolhardy. To reduce greenhouse gases, we must switch to green-produced electricity and to reduce energy usage. The process will require carrot-and-stick policies. But ultimately, since no one is willing to sacrifice their modern lifestyle, the solution will be through technological innovations that emerge out of both private and public incentives.

Developers are being incentivized to reduce carbon emissions both for good public relations and to lower production and maintenance costs. I can tell you that having attended the CTBUH's conferences in the last several years, I know the skyscraper community is very worried about reducing the carbon footprints from their buildings. Architects, engineers, and planners are working hard to create greener buildings. Not only are they personally worried about climate change, but their clients are asking for sustainable solutions also.

New technologies are being put to the task. Wind tunnel testing, for example, allows building design to be much more efficient, saving enormous quantities of material. Innovative strategies exist for positioning façades and adding overhangs to minimize direct contact with the sun in the summer. Double-skin façades can create "buffers" of air between glass façades to help better regulate building temperatures.

Besides recycled steel and concrete, mass timber buildings—where the entire structure is made of wood—are all the rage since, in theory, wood has a negative carbon footprint. Today the world's tallest mass timber building is a twenty-five-story apartment building in Milwaukee, though they are popular in Europe, appearing in Norway, Sweden, Austria, and the Netherlands, for example.

Improvements in elevator operation and equipment mean much more efficient elevator operations. The use of "regenerative drive" elevators produces energy and returns it to the grid as the cab descends, reducing net electricity consumption by up to 40 percent. The KONE UltraRope weighs 90 percent less than its steel variety and can save up to 15 percent of the elevator's energy usage.

Recent attempts at wind turbines and solar panels on buildings have not proved successful, however, and are seen as little more than "greenwashing." But developers shouldn't and won't give up on trying to use tall buildings to produce energy from wind and sun. At some point, the technology will be there and the more experimentation by today's builders means the faster will be the learning curve.

Taken together skyscrapers have become much more efficient on a per-square-foot basis—particularly at the supertall level where the criticism has been the fiercest. But economic growth and skyscraper demand mean more square feet being built overall and hence a likely increase in net GHG emissions. And rapid urbanization in the developing world means a huge demand for steel and carbon as these places build up their skylines. Thus, while the actions of individual building developers are good, collectively they will not be enough.

As a result, cities around the world, like New York with its Local Law 97 and London with its carbon taxes, are generating penalties for GHG-heavy building owners. This is good. Tax carbon and incentivize reductions in usage and switching to greener energy sources. I would argue, however, that New York's law, for example, does not go far enough. All households—not just those in large buildings—should face a carbon tax. If cities charged household "overproducers," and gave credits to "underproducers" based on their emissions, it would not only be fair—the rich would pay more in taxes—but it would also benefit those living in efficient medium- and high-rise buildings. A household carbon tax would also encourage denser, less-car-based lifestyles. If people want to live in freestanding homes and drive everywhere or if they choose to live in superslim skyscrapers that's fine, but they should pay for the harm they impose on society more broadly.

But other solutions must be pushed by national governments, which need to penalize CO_2 creation and reward alternatives that use less or no CO_2. For example, steel and cement producers need to pay for the carbon they generate, while R&D credits should be given to businesses that develop low-carbon products or production methods. Electricity providers need subsidies and incentives to switch over to wind, solar, and other clean energy forms, as well as to upgrade the grid.

And globally, the developed nations must help the developing countries to produce their skylines with low-carbon methods. Residents in developing nations want American lifestyles and feel that they should not make the sacrifices that the West never made. At the end of the day, solving the global climate crisis must be a global effort.

Overall, we are moving to a low-carbon world, and it is likely we'll get there in the ensuing decades (though not without a lot of suffering and damage along the way). But don't blame the skyscraper. CO_2 is the mother of all negative externalities and needs to be treated as such.

EVER UPWARD

Let's end this book on a high note.

In 1956, Frank Lloyd Wright unveiled a design for a mile-high skyscraper (1.61 km), called the Illinois. His presentation included a 26-foot-tall, 6-foot-wide rendering. It was to be built in Chicago and have 528 floors, with 12.3 million square feet (1.14 km²) of office space for 130,000 people. Commuters could choose from fifteen thousand parking spots after they arrived by one of four feeder highways. Two helicopter landing decks could accommodate fifty helicopters each. The building was to be served by seventy-six quintuple-deck elevators—that is, five elevators stacked on top of each other.

Ironically, Wright was, at best, ambivalent about skyscrapers. In 1923, after witnessing a devastating earthquake in Japan, he expressed his belief that "the skyscraper, never more than a commercial expedient . . . is become a threat, a menace to the welfare of human beings." He spent much of his career promoting his "Prairie Houses" and planned, decentralized communities, such as his Broadacre City.

But at some point, he seemed to have come around to the idea of skyscrapers. As the St. Louis Dispatch reported:

Frank Lloyd Wright revealing his
mile-high skyscraper, the Illinois, in 1956.

By bringing people together in such numbers [Wright] says, "the gregari-
ousness of man" would be satisfied, and he would be free to decentralize
his homes. Ten buildings like this on Manhattan Island would provide
all the office space needed, and the rest of the island could be open
landscape. "If we are going to concentrate mankind in skyscrapers,"
he says, "let's not build tall pens, boxes or bird cages. If we're going to
build high, let's build high—high and beautiful."

And thus, at age eighty-nine, he felt compelled to produce his
mile-high design. The building was, of course, merely a concept—an
imaginary figment of architecture. It was never meant to be built, as

the ability to construct and operate it was nearly impossible. But the octogenarian wanted to make one last splash to show the world that he was still there.

And, as Wright himself has rightly stated, "There is nothing so powerful as an idea," and when a man of Wright's stature proposes such a thing, it becomes part of the vast ocean of our collective consciousness. And just as importantly, it was produced by America's greatest twentieth-century architect when America reigned supreme in the world of skyscrapers. The medium was, in fact, the message.

Because it was a prototype, Wright could afford to be vague in his description of how it would be built and the technology it would contain. But in his mind, "[T]he whole will give the design impression of a great tree, with the floors radiating as limbs, and the sides hanging in suspension like leaves."

The gravity and wind loads were to be countered by a thick reinforced concrete central core, akin to the trunk. The foundation was to be like a taproot, a concrete inverted pyramid running deep into the ground. The floors were to be cantilevered outward from the core. The façade would be held by suspended wires.

The air on the upper floors would be pressurized for comfort, while the elevators were to run on nuclear power. Instead of cables, the cabs would move a mile per minute on teeth meshing into adjacent tracks. Wright's estimated cost was $100 million, which was overly optimistic by a mile, so to speak. To give a sense of this, the Sears Tower circa 1970 cost about $175 million.

Chicago's post–World War II, braggadocious builder Arthur Rubloff put it bluntly when he evaluated the economics of the building:

> The only thing wrong with the mile-high building . . . is that it is economically unsound, in Chicago or anywhere else. A building could be built a mile high by solving some engineering problems. But paying for it and tenanting it are something else again. The Prudential Building

cost $40 a square foot. Wright says he can build the Illinois for about $8 a foot. Why, it costs that to build a one-story building! My hat's off to Wright as an imaginative genius. The only trouble is he's poor at arithmetic.

Regardless of his motivations or his low-ball figures, Wright's renderings have launched a quest for the holy grail of skyscrapers—the mile-high. To build one is the burning ambition of many throughout the world, particularly in Asia. Whoever constructs it will beat the odds and grab ownership over something that was once purely an American phenomenon. After all, one mile—5,280 feet or 1,609 meters—is as arbitrary a length as anything, except that it's a unit of measurement in the United States.

Will such a structure ever be built? Yes.

How do I know? Well, first let's look at the history of building heights. Since 1900, the height of the tallest building completed each year has grown at an average annual rate of 1.2 percent, and, in fact, since 1980, when Asian countries started competing, the rate of increase has gone up to 1.8 percent.

As the impacts of the COVID pandemic wane, the world's tallest buildings will resume their upward trajectory. The tallest buildings' heights will likely double in forty to sixty years. In the early 1900s, typical tall build heights were around 328 feet (100 m). By the 1960s that figure was double that, and by 2015, 1,500 feet (457 m) was not uncommon. At some point, one-kilometer (3,280-foot) structures will be ordinary, and eventually the mile-high will arrive. Each generation of "growth spurts" sets of seeds for the next one.

The world's record holders have grown at a similar rate as the tallest completed each year. The only difference is the punctuated nature of record breakers. While not all record breakers seek to demolish the competition, frequently there are large jumps. For example, the Burj Khalif was 1,050 feet (320 m) taller than Taipei 101, and the Jeddah

Tower, if finished, will be 564 feet (172 m) above the Burj. Then "ordi-nary" supertalls "fill in" the gaps. After the Burj beat Taipei 101, a string of other towers came along that were in between the two, such as the Shanghai Tower and the Ping An Finance Centre. Taipei 101 is currently ranked the eleventh tallest in the world and its rank will continue to fall.

And, in fact, the one-kilometer tower (3,280 feet) is nearly a reality. The reason that it hasn't been completed has nothing to do with the technology or the cost but rather the political turmoil in Saudi Arabia. I predict that within the next two decades we will see at least two one-kilometer tower completions around the world.

The engineering knowledge to create a one-mile structure and to elevator it is here. The real problems are the economics and the needed technologies to cater to new issues that arise from the building being so tall. With current structural designs, the building will need to have several million square feet to generate the revenues to make it work. The Jeddah Tower, very thin by today's standards, will have 2.6 million usable square feet (243,866 km²) of floor area. Extruding this tower to one mile high would mean not only that its height is increased by 60 percent, but also its floor area will nearly quintuple. The "best" one-mile-high tower using today's know-how will have 12 million square feet—like Wright's tower.

If the Twin Towers—with a total of 10 million square feet—showed anything two decades ago, it was that putting that kind of square footage on the market will drive down prices for the foreseeable future. Good for buyers and renters, but lousy for the overall investment prospects. This price effect, however, could be mitigated in part by opening the building in stages, with the lower floors and the observation decks opening first and then the rest to follow as the demand warrants.

Another issue is the building's footprint. The base of a one-mile-high Jeddah Tower would be 80,000 square feet (1.8 acres; 7,432 m²). Finding an urban area that can accommodate or want a building this size would be difficult. If the structure is part of a larger greenfield development, then that may not be a problem.

Next is the expense of constructing such a building. While it can be done more cheaply on a per-square-foot basis than ever before, it will still be very expensive overall. Under the very best circumstances, the building can be designed, approved, and constructed in a decade. But such a project increases not only the financing costs but also the risk. The ups and downs of the business cycle mean that if construction of the building started in an upswing, there's a good chance as not it will open in a downswing.

Then there are some other hurdles that remain. They can be overcome, but since nothing like this has been done before it will take some time to figure out the issues. One of the biggest problems is the change in air pressure. The impact is the equivalent to a person going into a building on the ground floor in New York and exiting two minutes later at the top in Denver, possibly several times a day. How do you prevent altitude sickness?

For Wright that was easy: he simply announced that his building would be pressurized. But engineers in the near future will be tasked with figuring it out for real. Similarly, engineers will have to determine the wind behaviors thousands of feet up in the air and design their buildings accordingly.

At the end of the day, however, if "placemaking" skyscrapers have shown anything it is that the benefits of such a building extend far beyond the building itself. If the structure is part of a larger planned development, then it will increase land values nearby and offer a new landmark that puts its city on the radar screen. Likely this will be the driving force behind the one-miler, and if it can be done with net zero carbon, even better!

Ironically, when you track the height growth rates of the world's tallest skyscrapers, they compare poorly to that of the world GDP, which has grown at an average annual rate of 3.3 percent since 1960. If we assumed that the world's record breakers grew at the same average annual pace as GDP, this would suggest that the current record breaker should be 1.8 miles (2.9 km) high, 3.6 times higher than the Burj Khalifa. I thus think rather than asking why buildings are so tall, we should be asking why they aren't even taller.

A FUTURE OF MILE-HIGHS?

But are we likely to be living in a world populated by one-mile-high towers — the kind of city we might see in sci-fi movies? In theory, if building technology, zoning and planning regulations, and transportation technology (e.g., flying cars and superfast elevators) become such that building one-mile-high buildings is both cheap and practical, then it might be that some cities will build lots of them.

When you crunch the numbers, there's a certain appeal. Say a one-mile-high residential tower has 12 million square feet (1,114,836 m²) and say each person has an average of 400 square feet (37 m²). That means one tower could hold thirty thousand people. A city of 9 million (about the same as New York, London, or Hong Kong) could be housed in a mere three hundred buildings. If each one had a base of 80,000 square feet (1.83 acres), the entire population of this future city would only require 551 acres (223 hectares), less area than New York's Central Park or the City of London. Say we needed another square mile of land for offices, services, and retail within their own mile-highs. And, imagine that we moved all the city's buildings into one small area of, say, two or three square miles and turned the rest formerly used for buildings into parkland and nature.

Of course, our ability to erect such a thing is not prevented by technological hurdles, which can be overcome with the right motivations. It's not even economic — economic growth will mean taller buildings — and even mile-highs can become rational investments. Ultimately, it's social — if we find that living in the clouds lets us spend more time with nature and more time with each other, then we should do it!

But in the final analysis, skyscrapers must come with economic and social freedom. In the future, if we choose high-rise living because we enjoy it, then so be it. If not, that's fine too. The quest for skyscrapers and skylines can only work if it makes us better and more productive people.

If history is any guide, however, the journey will remain ever upward.

Epilogue

Cities and Skyscrapers in a Post-COVID World

IN EARLY FEBRUARY 2020, when news about the coronavirus began to percolate in America, I remember blithely quipping to my wife that by Christmas the whole thing would be forgotten. Little did I know what lay ahead.

A few days after the World Health Organization officially declared a global pandemic on March 11, my wife and I took a drive through Times Square and, like a scene in an eerie sci-fi movie, all that was left were the flashing neon lights. The Crossroads of the World was a ghost town.

People in America were fleeing central cities like rats from a sinking ship. Those who could get out did, while those who couldn't hunkered down as best they could. In other cities around the globe, residents were locked down and trapped, as if giant stone walls had magically risen around them. Hong Kong declared a "zero-COVID" policy and was sealed off for two years.

Like many, I thought it was the end of life as we knew it. I grew a beard and morphed into a scraggly mountain man. I taught my classes remotely, with my cat jumping on my desk just as I was about to make some important point.

But after much fear, sadness, and uncertainty, the clouds parted, and we could leave our homes and experience our lives again. And three years after such headlines as "The Pandemic Is Making People Reconsider City Living, Trading Traffic for Chickens," some things have changed while other things have returned to normal. We are back at restaurants, museums, teaching in the classroom, and, for the most part, work.

Deep down inside, I remained optimistic about the role of cities in our lives. From my studies, I have come to see that they are resilient entities. In 1975, New York City, for example, was on the verge of bankruptcy. The subway cars were scrawled with graffiti, its streets were strewn with garbage, and a dark cloud of despair encased a noir Gotham. Though big cities were left for dead in the 1970s, by the turn of the new millennium they were thriving, doing what they were always good at—providing jobs, knowledge, and fun.

As a more extreme case, two millennia ago the city of Rome was bursting at the seams with a million residents. When the empire collapsed, the Vatican was practically the only thing left. Though it took some time—one thousand years—Rome regained its million residents, and now has nearly three times that amount. It remains one of the world's great cities.

As the times change, a city may become outdated and forgotten, but the kernel of its greatness always remains like a quiet tabernacle flame. Cities are *ideas* as much as locations, and they inherently have within them the power of rebirth and renewal.

Despite this lofty idea, however, pitfalls remain in a post-COVID world. In the United States, work from home has taken deep root. People found they didn't have to commute, and they could get things done all the same. Today's headlines are paradoxical. Housing unaffordability remains at an all-time high, while a looming office foreclosure apocalypse threatens to implode the metropolis. And though work from home has some great features, it's not all win-win. People can become more socially isolated and miss out on those spontaneous moments of insight or joy that come from being around other people.

Landlords are trying to lure back workers by adding all sorts of goodies to their buildings, including pickleball courts, climbing walls, cafes, and restaurants. One Manhattan office building ad, for example, provides all the right buzzwords for its new floor: "An amenity space that caters to all your business and social needs. A truly collaborative space boasting comfy seating and large communal tables, perfect for brainstorming and networking, as well as a bar and stylish dining area. Whether you're closing deals, sharing ideas or simply relaxing, this amenity floor caters to every need."

Nonetheless, people are not going to return to work in droves if they must commute an hour each way. The low-hanging fruit is to allow more mixed uses within buildings and to convert as many offices as possible into residences. The postwar towers with sprawling floor plates are difficult to convert and must be repurposed or demolished. And the high cost of housing keeps young people from joining the mix. Meanwhile, city planners are moving glacially to rewrite the old, outdated rules.

But a look at office cycles over the last century suggests that what's happening in America is a crisis of degree, not kind. After the Roaring Twenties boom, vast acres of office space lay dormant for a decade and a half. The oil crises of the 1970s and then the office glut of the late 1980s were each followed by rebounds. Some busts took longer to recover from, but they all dissipated just the same. The reason: populations rise and markets work. As prices fall, construction slows down, gluts eventually become shortages, and the market grows again.

And while working from home has changed where people spend much of their time, it has not changed as much what people do or what they want out of life, and the things that power our economy have not changed. We are still in a high-tech, knowledge-based world. As nicely put by *New York Times* columnist and Nobel Prize–winning economist Paul Krugman:

> Americans probably aren't going back to the office full-time. But they will continue to work together, maybe even more than before. And some

of this work will still need to be done face-to-face, which will mean that people will still want to live in or near big cities.

In fact, there's some preliminary evidence that working from home is, in some ways, actually making urban life more attractive: People who don't have to commute to the office every day spend more time frequenting local shops, restaurants and so on, improving the quality of their neighborhoods.

And just as importantly, cities are growth engines, which creates more employment. So, while each worker might go into the office fewer days per week, at some point the office market will benefit from all the new jobs created, and the net effect will be to wipe away the losses.

So, what does a post-COVID environment look like for the world's skyscrapers and skylines? As long as the city endures so will the sky-scraper. And despite the ups and downs, the trials and tribulations, the city will endure. It is too important in our lives to be lost.

Skyscrapers, like all forms of real estate, grow or shrink according to the laws of supply and demand, and I believe their demand will remain strong for the foreseeable future. In fact, as I write this, looking at the data suggests that 2023 will be a bumper year, with completions similar to before the pandemic. And while a new world record is still some years away, the Merdeka 118 tower in Kuala Lumpur has recently been completed; at nearly seven hundred meters, it is now the world's second-tallest building (knocking down a peg all the other former record breakers).

But the key to everything—the sine qua non of the skyscraper—is economic growth. Planet Earth has put all its chips on global capitalism, and as I have argued here, urbanization and capitalism are two sides of the same coin. Economic growth creates the need for skyscrapers for working, living, and playing.

While in Asia high-rise living is the norm, North America remains in love with the freestanding single-family home. But there's reason to believe this will change. An increasing number of people see suburban living as wasteful and not sustainable. They also see driving and traffic as a chore (and preventing their constant use of social media). NIMBYism is putting homeownership out of reach for all but the richest households. Skyrocketing home prices mean there's ample opportunity to provide more housing in tall buildings. The developing world has a rising middle class, and many of them will opt for living and working in tall buildings. As our world moves toward Terranism, global cities will have increasingly global real estate to cater to the demand, and tall buildings will be part of the solution.

A decarbonizing world might mean fewer tall buildings without cheap fossil fuels. And this is a perfectly reasonable response. But I suspect, as we adjust to climate change, the tall building will, in fact, be more important. Coastal cities, with rising sea levels, will see their urban footprints shrink. This will put pressure on land values, which will incentivize tall buildings in other parts of the city. Tall buildings will likely prove more resilient. Plant and equipment can be placed on higher floors, and if properly designed the ground floors can better withstand flooding. It will often be cheaper to erect new buildings than to retrofit older ones for a post-carbon world.

In the big scheme of things, better cities will emerge when politicians, planners, architects, developers, engineers, residents, and social scientists engage with each other to craft policies that work for the people. But this requires collaboration, compromise, and consensus, which unfortunately remain in short supply in today's political climate.

But I am an optimist by nature. I believe we can and will solve the challenges that lie ahead if we maintain our lofty ambitions.

Acknowledgments

I am deeply grateful to all those who have generously provided their help, knowledge, and support throughout the book-writing process. Without my family, friends, colleagues, and those I interviewed, I could never have completed this work.

I would first like to thank Colin Harrison, my editor at Scribner. I appreciate the lunches spent pouring over iterations of the manuscript, and I'm indebted to him for his patience, enthusiasm, and wisdom. I am also grateful to my literary agent, Chris Kepner of the Kepner Agency, for his belief in the project and his dedication to helping bring the book to fruition.

I would also like to thank the friends, colleagues, and students who read all or parts of the manuscript drafts. Troy Tassier of Fordham University provided many probing and detailed comments along with deep friendship and encouragement. Jan K. Brueckner of the University of California, Irvine, Thomas Leslie of the University of Illinois Urbana-Champaign, and my former master's student Julia Sinitsky offered excellent comments that helped improve the manuscript. Julia's help in tracking down the image permissions was invaluable. My graduate student Ang Liu was diligent with his valuable research assistance.

I am honored to have had the opportunity to work with amazing coauthors on research projects about skyscrapers and cities, including

Troy Tassier, Jan Brueckner, Remi Jedwab, Jingshu Luo, Gabriel Ahlfeldt, Ilir Nase, and Peter Weismantle. I also want to acknowledge my colleagues in the Economics Department at Rutgers University–Newark, who have provided a genuinely supportive environment to pursue my quest to understand skyscrapers and skylines.

Many people graciously provided their valuable time for interviews. I want to thank them for answering my many questions and providing insights from their areas of expertise: Stefan Al, Mir M. Ali, Simon Allford, William Baker, Sara Beardsley, Scott Bloom, Ibrahim Bostan, Paul Cheshire, Richard Dennis, Roy Denoon, Christopher Deutsch, Peng Du, P. Martin Dufresne, Zoe Early, Donald Friedman, Adam Gee, Sudeep Ghosh, Michael Hebbert, Vic Huang, Mehdi Jalayerian, Leonard M. Joseph, Gerald Larson, Thomas Leslie, L. H. Li, KK Ling, Ang Liu, Peyman Askari, Peter Rees, Mark Richards, Daniel Safarik, Tom Schnell, Ro Shroff, Robert Sinn, Roger Ridsdill Smith, Edward Stellingwerf, Steve Watts, Peter Weismantle, Kelvin Wong, and Charlie Q. L. Xue.

I would also like to thank the archivists who welcomed me into their temples of history, including the Hagley Museum and the Ryerson and Burnham Libraries at the Art Institute of Chicago, with a particular shout-out to JT de la Torre, who went above the call of duty in helping to identify valuable documents about William Le Baron Jenney and his colleagues.

Any errors in the book, of course, are my responsibility and mine alone.

Finally, without the support of my family, I could never have realized this project. I give heartfelt thanks to my in-laws, Bill and Ann O'Connor and Mary Jean Hughes, as well as to my mother, Marjorie Barr, and my sister, Stephanie Early.

Most of all, I would like to thank my wife, Kathy, and my son, Will, for their patience, encouragement, and love. I've enjoyed my "research" trips with Will to Manhattan's observation decks and our quest for the ultimate skyline photograph.

I dedicate this book to Kathy and Will, along with the memory of my father, Sheldon Philip Barr (1935–1996). Learning about and observing my dad's journey, from his childhood in the Bronx to his career in Manhattan, to our residing on Long Island, and to his ultimate return to living (and dying) in New York City, unwittingly—yet profoundly— seeded my fascination with cities and skylines.

Notes

INTRODUCTION

xiii *energetic business community*: New York Times (1929), Aug. 30; Tauranac
(1995), p. 131.

xiii *ten blocks to the north*: New York Times (1929), Nov. 19.

xiii *international travel*: New York Times (1929), Dec. 12.

xiv *". . . with the mast"*: Ibid.

xiv *". . . to the near-by buildings"*: New York Times (1930), Dec. 17.

xiv *generated $1 million*: Financials of the Empire State Building from the 1930s
to the 1940s are in the archives of the Hagley Museum in Delaware. See
"Empire State, Inc. Operating Statement, May 1, 1931 to April 30, 1932," du
Pont papers, Box 183.

xv *in its market value*: Barr and Ahlfeldt (2020).

xvi *and technology change*: Throughout this book, I do not give a firm definition
of a "skyscraper." Here I take the general position that a skyscraper is a relatively tall building used to house economic activity and is built with modern
technological methods, such as having a steel or concrete frame, and includes
an elevator. Having said that, in the twenty-first century, when needed for
simplification, depending on the context, either 100 meters (25–30 floors) or
150 meters (40–45 floors) or taller will be considered a "skyscraper."

xvii *has 163 stories*: Throughout this book, data on skyscrapers comes from the
Council on Tall Buildings and Urban Habitat (CTBUH) database and Empo-
ris, which was formerly a skyscraper database that was purchased by CoStar
and folded into their database. Both data sets contain information on heights,
use, year completed, and location. The statistical results and analyses on
skyscrapers are derived from these data.

xviii *". . . a like faith in others"*: Shultz and Simmons (1959), p. 12.

xix *and more automobile-based sprawl*: Ahlfeldt and Barr (2022); Bertaud and Brueckner (2005); Jedwab et al. (2022); Barr et al. (2022).

xxi *you a patron, as well*: Watson (2017).

xxi *the Warwick Business School*: Prynn (2017).

CHAPTER 1 **Chicago**

4 *". . . if this building is any good?"*: Ducat & Lyon, "To the Editor of the Engineering Record," *Engineering Record* 24 (July 11, 1896):103. The story was provided at the request of Jenney by Ducat & Lyon, the firm that survived after Ducat passed away in January 1896. Jenney's letter to the firm requesting help in the battle to claim to be the first is housed in the Chicago Art Institute archives. A version of the story is also provided by Jenney in A. C. Ducat's memoirs, published in 1897 (Ducat, 1897, pp. 65–67).

5 *". . . at the earliest date possible"*: Ducat & Lyon (1896), p. 103; Ducat (1897), pp. 65–67.

5 *was not the first one*: That Jenney was not the inventor of the skyscraper is now well known in architectural and skyscraper history circles. I claim no originality in this argument. The modern debunking of the Jenney myth began with Larson and Geraniotis (1987), who were the first to provide an updated forensic reevaluation of the Home Insurance Building's structure. In 2019, I attended a one-day symposium of architectural and engineering historians, organized by the Council on Tall Buildings and Urban Habit (CTBUH), to discuss which building was the "first skyscraper." Among the crowded room of experts, only one person argued for the Home Insurance Building. The vast majority of attendees rejected the premise that one could even declare a single building the "first skyscraper."

6 *Western Union Building (1875, ten floors)*: *Chicago Tribune* (1883), Feb. 25, p. 9.

6 *were nine stories or taller*: Building database in Leslie (2013).

7 *columns, beams, and girders*: Reinforced concrete skyscrapers appeared after the turn of the twentieth century. The Ingalls Building (1903, sixteen stories) in Cincinnati is considered the first one.

7 *pure skeletal structure*: Larson (2020A, 2020B).

8 *uneven manner*: Jenney (1885).

8 *were connected to iron beams*: Friedman (2014).

8 *Manhattan Building in Chicago*: Barr (2017), Oct. 7.

9 *". . . established themselves"*: Personal conversation, Sept. 2020.

9 *that "buildings fall down"*: Personal conversation, Jan. 2021.

10 *". . . to study the problem"*: Peck (1948), p. 35.

11 "... *promise of its future greatness*": Hoyt (1933), p. 7.

12 *2.5 million, respectively*: Knapp (1924).

12 *from the hinterland*: Cronin (1992); Cain (1998); Hartshorne (1926).

13 "... *United States and Europe*": Hartshorne (1926), p. 274.

13 *in human history*: Hoyt (1940).

13 *own "dismal swamp"*: All told, downtown Chicago is fifteen feet higher than when first settled due to its efforts to raise the grade (see Peck 1948).

14 "... *into our windows*": Letter reproduced in Bluestone (1991), p. 114.

14 "... *express wagons*": Ibid.

14 *attorneys rose from 629 to 4,421*: Bonshek (1985); Bonshek (1988).

15 *tall buildings*: Ahlfeldt and McMillen (2018).

16 *new architecture*: Schaffer (2012); Bonshek (1985).

17 *Italian Renaissance styles*: Landau and Condit (1999).

17 "... *iron framing*": Condit (1964), pp. 84–85.

19 *degree in architecture*: Brooks Estate (2022).

19 *real estate development*: Berger (1992).

20 "... *found to erect them*": Condit (1964), p. 52.

20 "... *island of Manhattan*": Weis (2010).

20 *lost everything*: Leslie (2013); Larson (2020), Sept. 6.

20 "... *most profitable investment*": Condit (1964), p. 66.

20 "... *first 'skyscraper'*": Shultz and Simmons (1959), p. 23.

21 *many revelatory letters*: The Brooks records and letters had been preserved up until at least 1969. At some point after that, they were discarded by the company that inherited Aldis's portfolio. Fortunately, some scholars were able to view the letters before they were destroyed, and their diligent research provides a glimpse of Chicago's real estate past.

21 "... *purchase it*": Reprinted on p. 52 of Condit (1964).

21 "*eight stories. . . .*": Condit (1964), p. 52.

22 "... *much consideration*": Ibid., p. 53.

22 "... *must be*": Ibid., p. 54.

22 *viewers "agog"*: Berger (1992), p. 30.

22 *three hundred occupants*: Korom (2008).

22 *valuable farmlands*: Kuhn (1970).

22 *rented for offices*: Berger (1992); Kuhn (1970).

23 *conflagration hit*: Tullis (1978).

23 "... *be with good men*": Ibid., p. 10.

24 *four instances*: Home Insurance Company (1903).

24 *their visitors*: *The Insurance Journal* (1886).

24 *lighting technology*: *The Telegraphic Journal and Electrical Review* (1885).

24 "... *done in the city*": *The Irish Builder and Engineer* (1886).

24 *". . . telephonic communication"*: Gass (1886).

24 *elevator shafts*: Jenney (1885).

25 *". . . Opera House"*: Blackall (1888).

25 *". . . excellent class": Chicago Tribune* (1888), July 29, p. 7.

25 *father of the skyscraper*: For example, on June 23, 1907, the second paragraph of the *Chicago Tribune's* obituary states: "Jenney invented the skeleton structure and revolutionized city building" (part 6, p. 29). The *Washington Post* and many other newspapers reproduced the article in toto.

26 *". . .-F.T. Gates"*: Gates (1896).

26 *win the title*: Jenney letters at the Art Institute of Chicago archives.

27 *". . . first to accomplish"*: Burnham (1896).

27 *in the 1850s*: There was also the balloon framing of houses using wood two-by-fours, which began in Chicago in the 1830s. Further, Jenney first used iron columns to help reduce the thickness of masonry in his First Leiter Building (1879), so iron to share exterior loads wasn't novel by 1885. See Leslie (2013).

28 *". . . above the first floor"*: Sanderson et al. (1932).

CHAPTER 2 **New York City**

31 *in the world: New York Times* (1957).

31 *an architect*: Wermiel (2006).

32 *vice president: New York Times* (1932).

32 *Company of Canada: New York Times* (1965).

32 *a wheelbarrow*: Shultz and Simmons (1959), p. 167.

33 *Midtown Manhattan*: Friedman (1998).

33 *". . . get back in": New York Times* (1965).

33 *floors per week*: Shultz and Simmons (1959), p. 167.

33 *". . . stacked three high"*: Friedman (1998), p 37.

34 *looking for a new location: New York Times* (1928), Dec. 23; *New York Times* (1929), March 10.

34 *Manhattan office buildings: New York Times* (1955).

35 *for the times*: Shultz and Simmons (1959), p. 165; Tauranac (1995).

35 *sale was final*: Tauranac (1995), p. 121.

36 *father's savings bank: New York Times* (1942).

36 *with assets valued at $300 million*: https://en.wikipedia.org/wiki/Chatham_Phenix_National_Bank_and_Trust_Company_of_New_York (accessed Sept. 2023).

36 *from the bank: New York Times* (1929), June 4.

36 *owners a mortgage*: Tauranac (1997), p. 121.

39 *additional income*: du Pont archives at the Hagley Museum.
39 *Manhattan skyscraper*: *New York Times* (1951).
39 *about $2 billion*: Barr and Ahlfeldt (2020).
41 "*... per cubic foot*": Heights of Building Commission (1913), p. 19.
41 "*... such congestion*": Price (1916).
43 *limit supply*: Willis (1995).
43 *130 feet (40 m, 10 floors)*: Nichols (1923); Willis (1995), pp. 50–51.
43 *the height limit*: See chapter 9 of Schwieterman and Caspall (2006).
43 "*... taller one*": *New York Times* (1902).
43 *volume of the main structure*: Schwieterman and Caspall (2006). Also see Willis (1995), pp. 50–65, and Weiss (1992), p. 207.
44 *mind for decades*: Nichols (1923), p. 14.
44 *lower than that*: Nichols (1923), p. 27.
44 *concluded Shultz and Simmons*: Shultz and Simmons (1959), pp. 286–287; Barr (2013).
46 *banning skyscrapers*: See Barr (2016).
49 "*... floor plans*": Bascomb (2003), p. 64.
51 *a bit different*: The creation of the FAR goes back to the efforts of one advocate, Robert D. Kohn, a now-forgotten architect and housing reformer, who pushed for FAR limits as early as 1935. From there, his contemporaries and their disciples spread out to the rest of the country and helped enact the zoning code reforms across the country. The FAR was implemented in cities across the United States in the 1940s; New York ironically was late to its own party. See Barr (2022), Aug. 9.
52 *less than 3*: Brueckner et al. (2017).
52 *higher than twenty-five feet*: Maki (2019).
53 *high as 30*: Lainton (2011); Brueckner and Sridhar (2012).
53 *strong ones*: Ahlfeldt and Barr (2022).
53 *extra-legal means*: See Cai et al. (2017) in the case of China.
53 *rise seventy stories*: Brenzel (2018).

CHAPTER 3 **The American Century**

56 *on the planet*: *Chicago Tribune* (2000).
56 *spans 50 miles*: Khan's papers at the Chicago Art Institute; theskydeck.com (2023).
56 *(... Iceland at the time)*: World Bank (2023).
56 *thirteen countries*: *New York Times* (1970), July 28.
57 *office tower*: Pridmore (2002).
57 *or even two*: Willis (2019).

57 *reported the* New York Times: *New York Times* (1970), Oct. 18.

57 *13.5 million square feet!:* Ibid.

58 *real estate consultants:* Pridmore (2002), p. 20.

58 *recounts Pridmore:* Ibid., p. 22.

58 *". . . Khan understood immediately":* Ibid., p. 25.

59 *writes Pridmore:* Ibid., p. 28.

59 *". . . space race is silly":* New York Times (1970), Oct. 18.

60 *to its creditors:* Feder (1994).

60 *for $110 million:* Greenberg and Pacelle (1997).

60 *the main creditor:* New York Times (2003).

60 *a Chicago skyscraper:* de la Merced (2015).

60 *for upgrades:* Fortune (2015).

60 *$2.85 billion:* Grant (2021).

61 *elevators and tech:* Roeder (2022)

61 *was 95 percent rented:* Hughes (2018); Roeder (2022).

61 *181,000-square-foot space:* Hammill (2017).

61 *$918 million:* Using CPI values from Officer and Williamson (2023).

62 *the demand:* Real Estate Board of New York (1964).

63 *". . . machines and equipment":* Fisher (1967), p. 3.

64 *called the Economic Height:* Willis (1995); Clark and Kingston (1930).

64 *truly been mastered:* Barr and Weismantle (2023).

66 *graduated from MIT:* Adams (2007).

66 *". . . Bunshaft and Graham":* Ibid., p. 11.

67 *". . . various systems":* Baker (2001), p. 482.

68 *". . . tradition that he created":* Baker (2014).

68 *". . . cost too much":* Stegmann (1975), 14–17.

69 *from the masonry:* Robertson and Teen (2005).

69 *per square foot:* Baker (2001).

69 *look like bamboo (discussed in chapter 6):* Dubey (2016).

70 *". . . understood the principle":* Personal email correspondence, Aug. 2021.

71 *". . . Brunswick downtown":* Ibid.

72 *". . . for the windows":* Baker (2001), p. 482.

72 *". . . Chicago skyline":* Petroski (1999), pp. 17–18.

73 *revolutionize the industry:* Bernstein (2021).

74 *". . . rental agents":* Robertson (2017), pp. 113–114.

74 *more incredible:* Magnusson (2021).

74 *adjustments followed:* Robertson and Teen (2005).

75 *". . . psychophysical alarm bells":* Glanz and Lipton (2002).

77 *". . . at the time":* Khan (2004), footnote 29, p. 385.

77 *". . . individual or a team":* Robertson (2017), pp. 114.

CHAPTER 4 **London**

83 *long as the Shard*: Smith (2008).
85 *a review and negotiations*: Personal conversation with Peter Rees, former chief planner for the City of London, Feb. 2022.
88 *skyscraper its trademarked name*: Eileen (2016).
88 "*. . . significant stakeholder*": Watson (2017), p. 126.
88 "*. . . one-acre site*": Sellar (2015), p. 139.
89 "*. . . than the Qataris*": Watson (2017), p. 203.
89 "*. . . guide to New York City*": Bagli (2005).
90 *for $3.95 billion*: The Guardian (2008).
90 *for a huge loss*: Mafi (2019).
90 *$300 million profit*: Given the global appetite for iconic buildings, it does indirectly contribute to the construction of more skyscrapers than otherwise. Larger skyscraper market values will induce speculative construction to those who can then "flip" them to global investors. The long-run size of this effect, however, is not clear, as overbuilding will generate gluts and pullback.
90 *building was completed*: Prynn (2017).
90 "*. . . Because it's profitable*": Sellar (2015), p. 143.
91 *are cases in point*: Čamprag (2015); Sciocolone (2012).
93 *five English residents*: http://www.demographia.com/dm-lon31.htm (accessed Sept. 2023).
93 *one or the other*: Porter (2011).
93 *French Renaissance style*: Landau and Condit (1999), p. 62.
95 *first apartment buildings*: Cromley (1990).
95 "*. . . already 100 feet high*": Dennis (2008), p. 234.
95 "*. . . in case of fire*": Ibid., p. 235.
96 "*. . . MBW rejected them*": Ibid., p. 236.
96 "*. . . would produce*": Ibid., p. 237.
97 *in the complex*: Watson (2017), p. 45.
97 "*. . . Queen Anne's gate*": Dennis (2008), p. 240. London folklore has it that the height ban was due to Queen Victoria's displeasure when from Buckingham Palace she saw Queen Anne's Mansions rising. I asked Professor Dennis about this and his response: "I can only confirm what I said in our talk online that I have seen no direct evidence of Queen Victoria's involvement in the case of Queen Anne's Mansions. I see that Wikipedia and various blogs make this claim, but as far as I can see, they all derive from a debate in the House of Lords on 4th July 1972, when Lord Reigate claimed that 'When it was put up in the 1870s it caused Queen Victoria very great annoyance because it obtruded on the view from Buckingham Palace . . . The fact that one of its wings was

only 100 feet high was largely due to the intervention of Queen Victoria.' I suppose that the Queen may have expressed her dismay in her private correspondence, and I confess I have not looked at biographies or publications related directly to the Queen; but there is no evidence of any influence on the Queen's part in any of the official documentation I consulted, either in parliamentary papers online, or in the press, or in the documentation of the Metropolitan Board of Works in the London Metropolitan Archives" (email correspondence, Oct. 2022).

97 *business communities*: Kaika (2010), p. 459.
98 *offices to let*: Barras (2009), chapter 6.
98 *trustworthiness and profitability*: Summerson (1977).
98 *between 1866 and 1914*: See Barras (2009), table 6.2.
99 "*. . . by at least 50%*": Ibid., p. 195.
99 *turn of the twentieth century*: Ibid., table 6.3.
100 *down to 59,000*: https://en.wikipedia.org/wiki/City_of_London (accessed Sept. 2023).
101 *of space (353,032 m²)*: Professor Barras was kind enough to share his office construction data.
101 *during this period*: Devaney (2010).
101 *about 4 percent per year*: Turvey (1998), p. 8.
102 *adjacent to the Twin Towers site*: Krummeck and MacLeod (2015); Fainstein (1994).
104 *or tall buildings*: See McNeill (2002), pp. 328–329, on reforms.
104 "*. . . whole national economy*": Quote reproduced in McNeill (2002), p. 327.
105 "*. . . feature in the City*": Personal conversation, Feb. 2022.
105 *Londoners were convinced*: Charney (2007).
106 "*. . . concrete high-rise boxes*": Charney (2007), p. 200.
106 "*. . . since the Luftwaffe*": Quote reproduced in Charney (2007), p. 198.
106 "*. . . London's visual image*": Quote reproduced in Charney (2007), p. 201.
106 *most expensive pickle*: *Daily Mail* (2007); https://en.wikipedia.org/wiki/30_St_Mary_Axe (accessed Sept. 2023).
108 *Swiss Re in 1998*: Johns (1997).
108 *author Ken Powell*: Powell (2006), p. 40.
108 *dodge a bullet*: Watts and Langdon (2013).
109 *according to one outlet*: Saini (2015).
109 *up in flames*: Lallanilla (2013).
109 "*. . . secondary thing*": Quirk (2013).
110 "*. . . diagram of greed*": *The Guardian* (2015).
110 *valuable "prize"*: Cheshire and Dericks (2020).
111 "*. . . of £148 million*": Ibid.

CHAPTER 5 **Hong Kong**

114 *ultimate tree of money and power*: The movie script says: "Ladies and gentlemen, I give you a 6.5 billion dollar chimney." I guess that means USD and
not HKD, but $6.5B is absurdly high for a skyscraper. 6.5 HKD is too low. A
building like this would probably cost around $3-4 billion USD. See Thurber
(2017).

114 *a movie theater, and a hotel*: Brayson (2021).

115 *actual Pearl skyscraper*: https://en.wikipedia.org/wiki/Skyscraper_(2018_film)
(accessed Sept. 2023).

116 "... *the Reno of China*": Director's commentary on the *Skyscraper* DVD.

117 *Li Ka-shing*: Heng (2021).

117 *Hong Kong Stock Exchange*: Poon (2011).

118 *total energy consumption*: Bogle (2011).

118 *towers' energy consumption*: Killa and Smith (2008).

119 *located in an open field*: Tomlinson et al. (2014).

121 *a curse on the city*: Du (2018).

121 *Lower Manhattan*: Fusscas (1992).

121 *its economic success*: Bunnell (1999).

122 "... *point of takeoff*": Mydans (1996).

122 "... *look at you differently*": Ibid.

123 "... *people around the globe*": Bradsher (2004).

123 *the same coin*: Here I looked at buildings that were 328 feet/100 m or taller. I
regressed ln(city's tallest building height) on ln(# skyscrapers) and looked at
the residual. The correlation of ln(tallest) and ln(# skyscrapers) is 0.75. Data
were from the Emporis.com database.

124 *and their cities*: *South China Morning Post* (2016). Jiangyin is Tier 4 and
Zhenjiang is a Tier 3 city, as is Yinchuan.

125 *a "super transport node"*: Malott (2010).

125 *the developer told KPF*: Tang (2016B).

126 *Canton (or Cohong) System*: Carroll (2007).

127 "... *to seize Hong Kong*": Ibid., p. 15.

128 *were ... changed forever*: Nissim (2022); Lai (1998).

128 *Hong Kong's competitiveness*: Legislative Council Secretariat (2020).

129 *3 to 12 percent of total exports*: Shuyong (1997).

129 *from 549,000 to 907,000*: Ibid., p. 589.

130 *buildings are residential*: 328 feet/100 m or taller.

131 *1,619 per acre (4,000 per hectare) is obtained*: Shelton et al. (2013), p. 4.

133 *colony's landmass*: Carroll (2007); Shuyong (1997).

133 *dunes, and pumps*: Hoeksema (2007).

133　*territory is landfill*: Shelton et al. (2013), p. 3.

133　*100,000 per month*: Xue (2016).

133　*Charlie Xue*: Ibid., p. 9.

133　*makeshift shelters*: Shelton et al. (2013).

134　*Xue describes*: Xue (2016), p. 11.

134　*". . . new form of urbanism"*: Shelton et al. (2013), p. 74.

134　*". . . in the 21st century"*: Xue (2016), p. 23.

135　*aviation restrictions*: shenzhenshopper.com (n.d.).

137　*". . . down by Foxconn officials"*: Merchant (2017).

138　*". . . betray socialist principles"*: Bach (2017), p. 24.

139　*professor Ezra Vogel*: Vogel (2017), p. xiii.

139　*Vogel reports*: Ibid., p. xii.

140　*". . . silenced the room"*: Shen and Xu (2012), p. 91.

140　*China's skylines*: Rithmire (2015).

141　*". . . utilize land rents"*: Qiao (2017), p. 192.

141　*at the same time*: Wu (1997).

142　*development annually*: Janvatanavit (1993).

142　*". . . one year ago"*: BBC (2022).

142　*was allowed to run*: Maizland (2022).

CHAPTER 6 **China**

146　*completion (discussed later)*: The B1M (2020).

146　*the International Commerce Centre*: Work and Ursini (2022).

147　*". . . typhoon-prone area"*: CGTN (2020); Chengxi (2020).

148　*". . . live in harmony"*: http://www.chinaknowledge.de/Literature/Daoists/
　　daodejing.html (accessed Sept. 2023).

150　*". . . two iconic landscapes"*: Song (2020).

150　*at its own game*: Brook (2013).

153　*GDP is $830 billion*: Pudong's GDP is from https://en.wikipedia.org/wiki/
　　Pudong (NYC's GDP is from https://www.bea.gov/data/gdp/gdp-county-metro-
　　and-other-areas) (accessed Sept. 2023).

154　*launched in 2015*: Flannery (2013).

154　*". . . much to the public"*: Turk (2017).

154　*(. . . script for a Hollywood movie)*: Chen (2018).

154　*Pudong office market*: Yang (2008); Fong (2017).

154　*pandemic was in full swing*: Lewis and Son (2021).

155　*had little expertise*: Ren (2018).

155　*officer of Gensler*: Turk (2017).

156　*"'. . . worthy of their trust'"*: Ren (2018).

156 *Allianz, and* BNP *Paribas*: CGTN (2020); Jing and Ying (2022).

157 *". . . economic triumph"*: *Asia Times* (2019).

157 *high-tech and green industries*: Dai (2019).

157 *circumference of Earth*: Jones (2022).

158 *compared to the United States*: Barr and Luo (2017).

159 *". . . World Trade Center"*: *Asia Times* (2019).

160 *buildings than otherwise*: Barr and Luo (2021).

160 *real estate chain*: Yu (2014).

160 *building each year*: Barr and Luo (2021).

161 *units are occupied*: Alesha and Jarryd (2023).

162 *"boy who takes a dump"*: Told to me by Peter Rees in Feb. 2022.

162 *"no more weird architecture"*: Howarth (2014).

162 *". . . novelty and strangeness"*: Zuo (2021).

163 *who were prosecuted*: See figure 1 from Zhao et al. (2020).

163 *who replace them*: Chen and Kung (2019).

164 *". . . capacity of their locations"*: Li (2021).

165 *". . . yin and yang"*: https://en.wikipedia.org/wiki/Taipei_101 (accessed Sept. 2023).

167 *a record breaker*: Kim and Lee (2004).

167 *slight modifications*: For the Empire State Building, see Friedman (1998), p. 35. For the Burj Khalifa creepage, see Al (2022), p. 42.

167 *soft for three hours*: Al (2022), p. 38.

168 *add more stiffness*: Alhaddad et al. (2020). Note there are several types of systems in use today not discussed in the book. Another common structural system is the diagrid, with diamond-shaped members externally placed around the building. These diamonds will redirect the wind loads to the ground. For a fuller treatment of current structural systems, see Ali and Moon (2018).

170 *a Hollywood movie*: Morgenstern (1995).

170 *architect and author Stefan Al*: Al (2022), p. 69.

170 *". . . shake inexplicably"*: *Global Construction Review* (2021).

171 *a "windy" reputation*: The most famous example of wind-induced collapse is that of "Galloping Gertie," the Tacoma Narrows Bridge. Because it was so narrow relative to its depth, it was poor at resisting the twisting forces. Four months after it opened in 1940, a suspension cable slipped, lowering one side of the bridge. As the wind blew, it started to twist, generating a vortex, which drove the bridge to twist in phase with it and helped contribute to its collapse.

171 *of building height*: Al (2022).

171 *pedestrian turbulence*: Engineers also have to try to mitigate the stack effect, which is cooled air running downward in the building on summer days and

cold air running upward in the winter. It can make opening doors difficult
and can rattle the elevators, among other impacts.

171 *". . . the second skin"*: Interviewed in Chengxi (2020).

172 *act as liquid dampeners*: AI (2022).

172 *final destination*: Smith and Gerstenmeyer (2020).

173 *engineer James Fortune*: Quoted in Barr (2019).

174 *atrium spaces discussed earlier*: Xia et al. (2010).

175 *". . . dense financial district"*: Beckett (2022).

175 *to remain so*: Barr (2016).

176 *favorable geology*: Baker et al. (1998).

177 *426 feet (130 m) nearby*: Davies et al. (2004).

177 *". . . and viable option"*: Ibid.

177 *giant manhole cover*: Tang (2016A).

177 *close to the prediction*: Russo et al. (2013).

178 *can go up to 110 floors*: Ali and Moon (2007).

179 *those of the twenty-first century*: Ali and Moon (2007); Ali and Moon (2018).

CHAPTER 7 Oil-Rich Cities

183 *interests and economics*: The road to supertall skyscrapers is littered with the
fevered dreams of narcissistic madmen, who could wallpaper entire imag-
ined cities with their plans. In the Roaring Twenties, these dreamers wanted
to outdo the Empire State Building, which got there before the economy
tanked. Donald Trump spent his career proffering record breakers but to no
avail. He paid for renderings for the world's tallest building in Manhattan in
1984 and again in 1985. On September 11, 2001, his agents were in the Chicago offices of the SOM planning the next world's tallest building. In 1987,
a developer named Harry Grant released drawings for a 121-story tower in,
of all places, Newark, New Jersey. Then, during the real estate boom of the
2000s, the Nakheel Tower for Dubai was offered up at one kilometer (3,300
feet) to surpass the Burj. Even Emaar had ambitions of building something
to overtake its own tower. But then came the financial collapse, and it was
iced. In short, it's one thing to dream, but quite another to accomplish.

184 *". . . Superstars of the Year"*: Bhoyrul (2013).

184 *". . . the world's attention"*: Krane (2010), p. 160.

184 *". . . Kuala Lumpur"*: Halpern (2007).

185 *Krane documents*: Krane (2014), p. 161.

186 *". . . plant materials"*: Smith (2008).

187 *". . . its debut in 1969"*: Kamin (2018).

188 *". . . the architectural precedent"*: Baker and Pawlikowski (2012).

188   *4.0 million square feet (370,000 m²)*: The Taipei 101's tower is 2.1 million square feet, but the entire structure is 4 million square feet because of the podium surrounding the tower.

189   *$200 million a year in revenue*: Smith (2021). Also see the interview with Smith in Dupré (2008).

189   *a Burj view*: Data was generously provided by LuxuryProperty.com in Dubai.

190   *get to her apartment*: Makhlouf (2022).

190   *". . . out of Town"*: Meinhold (2014).

191   *Skyscraper Curse*: Mansharamani (2016).

191   *". . . economic correction"*: Reuters (2012).

191   *record-breaking buildings*: https://en.wikipedia.org/wiki/List_of_economic_crises (accessed Sept. 2023).

192   *U.S. business cycle*: Barr et al. (2015).

193   *more generous*: Krane (2014), pp. 9–10.

193   *". . . easy striking distance"*: Ibid., p. 14.

195   *". . . hands-off government policy"*: Ibid., p. 22.

195   *". . . is good for Dubai"*: Ibid., p. 75.

195   *reports Krane*: Ibid., p. 92.

196   *Brooklyn Bridge*: Grutzner (1960).

197   *". . . world's tallest building"*: Gillespie (1999), p. 46.

198   *of space*: Stengren (1964).

199   *Todd Reisz writes*: Reisz (2020), p. 274.

200   *". . . cushy privileges"*: Ibid., pp. 276, 278–279.

200   *"'. . . in the Arab world'"*: Ibid., p. 281.

200   *". . . at least twenty years"*: Ibid., p. 297.

201   *". . . reaching 2 million"*: Krane (2014), pp. 119–120.

202   *Krane writes*: Ibid., p. 121.

202   *increased by 250 percent*: Hepşen and Vatansever (2012).

203   *". . . Knight Frank Says"*: Mathew (2022).

205   *occupied floor (167)*: Weismantle and Stochetti (2013).

205   *". . . revolutions even"*: NBCNews.com (2011).

206   *". . . region and the world"*: Hammoud (2015).

207   *". . . up with the scheme"*: Personal conversation, Oct. 2022.

207   *". . . increased development around it"*: Quoted in Weismantle and Stochetti (2013), p. 15.

208   *". . . extremely dangerous"*: Ibid., p. 24.

208   *". . . than Burj Khalifa"*: Sinn (2020).

208   *". . . was conservative," he said*: Ibid.

209   *"It's happening"*: Hammoud (2016).

209   *recounts journalist Ben Hubbard*: Hubbard (2020).

209 *Hubbard writes*: Ibid.
210 "*. . . Europe, Asia, and Africa*": Hubbard (2020).
210 "*. . . investor in public markets*": Schatzker (2018).
211 "*. . . sci-fi city vision*": Procter (2022).
212 "*. . . less visible*": Email correspondence, April 2022.

CHAPTER 8 Sky Prizes

218 "*. . . psyche of man*": Huxtable (1972).
220 *fundamental driver*: Another trope is that supertalls are so-called white ele-
     phants, "gifts" bestowed by the Great Leader to enhance his cult of personality.
     My deep dive into the data reveals that autocracies, contrary to conventional
     wisdom, are no more likely to "overbuild" than democracies. One paper by
     Gjerløw and Knutsen (2019) finds that autocracies build more skyscrapers,
     but my review of their data shows that when you exclude China and limit
     the sample to a more recent time period, the results go away. My analysis of
     the data suggests that one needs to control for the strength of property rights
     and corruption control, rather than autarky, since the former two are stronger
     predictors of skyscraper growth than the type of government.
221 *in a central area*: Ibrahim and Leong (2015).
221 "*. . . network-building*": Jou (2005).
223 *as cutthroat capitalists*: Liu et al. (2018); Nase et al. (2019).
226 *decide to locate*: Weber (2019).
226 *even if only in one's head*: Dorfman et al. (2017); Barr and Nase (2022); Ben-
     Sharar et al. (2023).
227 *taller building*: Koster et al. (2014).
228 "*. . . makes the land pay*": Gilbert (1900).
230 "*. . . interacting with humans*": Fitzsimmons (2022).
231 *into large cities*: Glaeser and Mare (2001).
231 *being in the center*: British Property Federation (2008).
232 "*. . . changed over time*": Edin et al. (2018), p. 1.
234 *in the financial realm*: Hsu and Chan (2014).
235 *most of the space*: https://zip-codes.cybo.com/united-states/10005_new-york
     -city/ (accessed Oct. 2023).
235 *several hundred cities*: Barr (2022), March 28.

CHAPTER 9 Cities and Civilization

239 *432 Park Avenue*: Pristin (2009); Clarke (2023).
240 "*Here's your building*": Hudson (2015).

240 *". . . two storage units"*: https://www.cityrealty.com/nyc/midtown-east/432-park
-avenue/apartment-79/cqWOUpShA (accessed Oct. 2023).

240 *gold in the sky*: Barr (2017), Nov. 26.

240 *slow the sway*: Marcus (2018).

241 *". . . with the wind"*: https://www.wsp.com/en-us/projects/432-park-avenue
(accessed Sept. 2023).

241 *at 23.5*: World Record Academy (2022).

242 *sales revenue*: The lot area is 34,470 ft². The FAR was 10, with plaza bonus
of FAR 2, which gives 68,940 ft² of space. Each floor is about 8,000 ft². I
assume $6,000 per square foot of sales based on sales between 2015 and 2017
on StreatEasy.com.

242 *advantage of the law*: In my opinion, the FAR plaza bonus should require
that the city take over the open space via a long-term lease and the space gets
folded into the domain of the Parks Dept. The lot owner then must pay the
city for its upkeep. This way, the land is effectively publicly owned.

243 *reported one outlet*: Avery (2021).

243 *$70,000 per month*: https://streeteasy.com/sale/1560050; https://streeteasy.com/
rental/3820459 (accessed Sept. 2023).

243 *". . . rooms can hold"*: Barnard (1928).

244 *two colleagues (discussed later)*: Brueckner et al. (2021).

245 *". . . we are pricing up"*: https://twitter.com/ronanlyons/status/136926624825784
3201?s=20 (accessed March 2022).

246 *(24 m, 7 floors)*: Blackman and Picken (2010).

246 *stories, on average*: Eriksen and Orlando (2022).

247 *more properties*: Huang (2023).

248 *the city itself*: Mast (2023).

249 *housing in New York*: Statistics are from the New York City Primary Land Use
Tax Output (PLUTO) file 2022 version 3.

250 *". . . We're not interested"*: Story and Saul (2015).

250 *housing prices*: Maloney et al. (2019).

251 *significant bite*: Frank (2021).

252 *their bidding*: Moretti (2012); Piketty (2013); Stiglitz (2012).

254 *property ownership*: Spector (2015).

254 *not so much*: Richter (2021).

255 *Empire State Buildings*: Jedwab et al. (2022).

256 *new units*: Lee (2016).

257 *fierce opposition*: Davis (2019).

257 *decades, to complete*: Lin (2023).

257 *". . . Chinese executives"*: Kihara (2022).

258 *". . . no elevators"*: Bertaud (2018), p. 15.

260 *house prices*: Fleming et al. (2018).
262 *paid the fee*: Tri-state Transportation Campaign (2018).

CHAPTER 10 **Futureopolis**

266 "*. . . in high rises*": Gifford (2007).
266 *that Gifford reviewed*: Ng (2017); Je and Lee (2010); Yuen and Yeh (2011).
268 "*. . . killing off public space*": Davidson (2018).
269 *regularly spaced dots*: Asgarzadeh et al. (2012).
272 *grow vertically*: Gagne (2018).
273 *45 percent recycled materials*: Durst (2015).
273 "*. . . combat climate change*": Roudman (2013).
274 "'*. . . problem in a nutshell*'": Leonard (2022).
274 *keeping its emissions down?*: Barr et al. (2022).
275 *6 percent for elevators*: Cangelli and Fais (2012).
275 *never have been built*: Oldfield et al. (2009).
276 *bill by $400,000*: Alpen Co. (2016).
276 *(keep your cats indoors!)*: Loss et al. (2015).
276 *windows were lit*: The Guardian (2021).
276 *energy requirements*: Al-Kodmany (2015).
277 *in the United States*: Jones and Kammen (2014).
279 *elevator's energy usage*: Reina (2013).
281 "*. . . welfare of human beings*": Quoted in Levine (2016). p. 134.
282 "*. . . high and beautiful*": Quoted in McCue (1956).
283 *collective consciousness*: Fort Worth Star-Telegram (1956).
283 "*. . . suspension like leaves*": Quoted in Buck (1956).
284 "*. . . he's poor at arithmetic*": Quoted in McCue (1956).

EPILOGUE

290 *returned to normal*: Kelly and Lerman (2020).
291 "*. . . caters to every need*": Industry email blast regarding 2 Grand Central
      Tower, May 30, 2023.
292 "*. . . quality of their neighborhoods*": Krugman (2023).

Bibliography

Adams, Nicholas. *Skidmore, Owings & Merrill: SOM since 1936*. Phaidon Press, 2007.

Ahlfeldt, Gabriel M., and Jason Barr. "The Economics of Skyscrapers: A Synthesis." *Journal of Urban Economics* 129 (2022): 103419.

Ahlfeldt, Gabriel M., and Daniel P. McMillen. "Tall Buildings and Land Values: Height and Construction Cost Elasticities in Chicago, 1870–2010." *Review of Economics and Statistics* 100, no. 5 (2018): 861–875.

Al, Stefan. *Supertall: How the World's Tallest Buildings Are Reshaping Our Cities and Our Lives*. W. W. Norton, 2022.

Alesha and Jarryd. "Tianducheng—China's Strange City of Paris." *NOMADasaurus* travel blog, January 15, 2023. https://www.nomadasaurus.com/tianducheng-chinas-strange-city-paris/.

Alhaddad, Wael, Yahia Halabi, Hu Xu, and HongGang Lei. "A Comprehensive Introduction to Outrigger and Belt-Truss System in Skyscrapers." *Structures* 27 (2020): 989–998.

Ali, Mir M., and Kyoung Sun Moon. "Structural Developments in Tall Buildings: Current Trends and Future Prospects." *Architectural Science Review* 50, no. 3 (2007): 205–223.

Ali, Mir M., and Kyoung Sun Moon. "Advances in Structural Systems for Tall Buildings: Emerging Developments for Contemporary Urban Giants." *Buildings* 8, no. 8 (2018): 104.

Al-Kodmany, Kheir. "Tall Buildings and Elevators: A Review of Recent Technological Advances." *Buildings* 5, no. 3 (2015): 1070–1104.

Alpen Co. "Empire State Building Becomes More Energy Efficient than New Construction," March 2016. https://thinkalpen.com/wp-content/uploads/2016/03/Alpen-Heat-Mirror-Empire-State-Building-Project-Profile.pdf.

Asgarzadeh, Morteza, Anne Lusk, Takaaki Koga, and Kotaroh Hirate. "Measuring Oppressiveness of Streetscapes." *Landscape and Urban Planning* 107, no. 1 (2012): 1–11.

Asia Times. "China Now a Kingdom of Tall—Empty—Towers," May 28, 2019. https://asiatimes.com/2019/05/china-now-a-kingdom-of-tall-empty-towers/.

Avery, Dan. "Embattled Billionaire Skyscraper Developer Sued for Shoddy Construction." *Architectural Digest,* September 27, 2021. https://www.architectural digest.com/story/432-park-avenue-lawsuit.

Bach, Jonathan. "Shenzhen: From Exception to Rule." In *Learning from Shenzhen: China's Post-Mao Experiment from Special Zone to Model City,* edited by Mary Ann O'Donnell, Winnie Wong, and Jonathan Bach, 23–38. University of Chicago Press, 2017.

Bagli, Charles. V. "Arab Royals Buy 2 Pieces of the Skyline." *New York Times,* November 10, 2005. https://www.nytimes.com/2005/11/10/nyregion/arab-royals-buy-2-pieces-of-the-skyline.html.

Baker, Clyde N., Jr., Elliott Drumright, Leonard M. Joseph, and Ir. Tarique Azam. "Foundation Design and Performance of the World's Tallest Building, Petronas Towers." *Proceedings: Fourth International Conference on Case Histories in Geotechnical Engineering* (1998): 175–187. https://scholarsmine.mst.edu/cgi/viewcontent.cgi?article=1831&context=icchge.

Baker, William F. "Building Systems and Concepts." In Tall Buildings and Urban Habitat: Proceedings: 6th World Congress of the Council on Tall Buildings and Urban Habit (2001): 481–493. https://global.ctbuh.org/resources/papers/1202 -Baker_2001_StructuralInnovation.pdf.

Baker, William F. *Tall Building Lectures, Princeton Engineering Lectures,* February 5, 2014. https://www.youtube.com/watch?v=cSShh6bOFMk&t=17s.

Baker, William F., and James J. Pawlikowski. "Higher and Higher: The Evolution of the Buttressed Core." *Civil Engineering Magazine Archive* 82, no. 9 (2012): 58–65.

Barnard, Eunice Fuller. "Towers of Luxury Rise on Manhattan: New Hotels Are the Visible Symbols of a Change in the Ideals of the Wealthy American." *New York Times,* January 8, 1928. https://www.nytimes.com/1928/01/08/archives/towers -of-luxury-rise-on-manhattan-new-hotels-are-the-visible.html.

Barr, Jason. "Skyscrapers and Skylines: New York and Chicago, 1885–2007." *Journal of Regional Science* 53, no. 3 (2013): 369–391.

Barr, Jason M. *Building the Skyline: The Birth and Growth of Manhattan's Skyscrapers.* Oxford University Press, 2016.

Barr, Jason M. "The Birth of Height: What Was the World's First Skyscraper?" *Skynomics Blog,* October 7, 2017. https://buildingtheskyline.org/birth-of -height/.

Barr, Jason M. "Manhattan Profits (Part II): Return on Investment for a Superslim Skyscraper." *Skynomics Blog*, November 26, 2017. https://buildingtheskyline.org/manhattan-profits-2-roi/.

Barr, Jason M. "The Technology of Tall (Part II): The Need for Speed." *Skynomics Blog*, September 24, 2019. https://buildingtheskyline.org/skyscraper-technology-2/.

Barr, Jason M. "Skyscrapers and Global Connectivity: Which Causes Which?" *Skynomics Blog*, March 28, 2022. https://buildingtheskyline.org/skyscrapers-and-globalization/.

Barr, Jason M. "The Birth and Growth of Modern Zoning (Part II): The FARsighted Great Depression." *Skynomics Blog*, August 9, 2022. https://buildingtheskyline.org/floor-area-ratio-2/.

Barr, Jason M., and Gabriel Ahlfeldt. "Boon or Boondoggle? The Long Run Economics of the Empire State Building." *Skynomics Blog*, August 17, 2020. https://buildingtheskyline.org/empire-state-building-economics/.

Barr, Jason, and Jingshu Luo. *Economic Drivers*. CTBUH Research Report (2017).

Barr, Jason, and Jingshu Luo. "Growing Skylines: The Economic Determinants of Skyscrapers in China." *Journal of Real Estate Finance and Economics* 63 (2021): 210–248.

Barr, Jason, Bruce Mizrach, and Kusum Mundra. "Skyscraper Height and the Business Cycle: Separating Myth from Reality." *Applied Economics* 47, no. 2 (2015): 148–160.

Barr, Jason, and Ilir Nase. "Game of Floors: The Determinants of Residential Height Premiums." Working Paper, Rutgers University-Newark (2022).

Barr, Jason, Shaojie Wang, and Ujjaini Desirazu. "High-Rises versus Sprawl: The Impacts of Building Sizes and Land Uses on CO_2 emissions." In *Sustainable High-Rise Buildings: Design, Technology, and Innovation*, edited by Khir Al-Kodmany, Peng Du, and Mir M. Ali, Institution of Engineering and Technology and the Council on Tall Buildings and Urban Habitat, 2022.

Barr, Jason, and Peter A. Weismantle. "The Economics of Record-Breaking Height." *CTBUH Journal* 1 (2023): 36–43.

Barras, Richard. *Building Cycles: Growth and Instability*. John Wiley & Sons, 2009.

Bascomb, Neal. *Higher: A Historic Race to the Sky and the Making of a City*. Crown, 2004.

BBC. "Hong Kong National Security Law: What Is It and Is It Worrying?" June 28, 2022. https://www.bbc.com/news/world-asia-china-52765838.

Beckett, Lois. "Sinking Feeling: San Francisco's Millennium Tower Is Still Leaning 3in Every Year." *The Guardian*, January 10, 2022. https://www.theguardian.com/us-news/2022/jan/10/san-francisco-millennium-tower-sinking.

Ben-Shahar, Danny, Deng Yongheng, Eyal Solganik, Tsur Somerville, and Zhu Hongjia. "Vertical Status: Evidence from High-Rise Condominiums." Working Paper (2023).

Berger, Miles L. *They Built Chicago: Entrepreneurs Who Shaped a Great City's Architecture*. Bonus Books, 1992.

Bernstein, Fred A. "Leslie Robertson, Who Engineered the World Trade Center, Dies at 92." *New York Times*, February 11, 2021. https://www.nytimes.com /2021/02/11/nyregion/leslie-robertson-dead.html.

Bertaud, Alain. *Order without Design: How Markets Shape Cities*. MIT Press, 2018.

Bertaud, Alain, and Jan K. Brueckner. "Analyzing Building-Height Restrictions: Predicted Impacts and Welfare Costs." *Regional Science and Urban Economics* 35, no. 2 (2005): 109–125.

Bhoyrul, Anil. "Mohamed Alabbar: The Only Way Is Up." *Arabian Business*, March 31, 2013. https://www.arabianbusiness.com/mohamed-alabbar-only-way-is-up-495767.html.

Blackall, C. H. "Notes of Travel." *American Architect and Building News* 23, no. 635 (February 27, 1888): 88–91. (Google Books) https://www.google.com/books/ edition/The_American_Architect_and_Building_News/dCNLAQAAMAAJ.

Blackman, Ivy Q., and David H. Picken. "Height and Construction Costs of Residential High-Rise Buildings in Shanghai." *Journal of Construction Engineering and Management* 136, no. 11 (2010): 1169–1180.

Blair, Kamin, and Thomas A. Corfman. "Sears Tower to Stand Tallest in Antenna Race." *Chicago Tribune*, February 16, 2000. https://www.chicagotribune.com/ news/ct-xpm-2000-02-16-0002160355-story.html.

Bluestone, Daniel M. *Constructing Chicago*. Yale University Press, 1991.

Bogle, Ian. "Integrating Wind Turbines in Tall Buildings." *CTBUH Journal* 4 (2011): 30–33. https://global.ctbuh.org/resources/papers/download/293-integrating -wind-turbines-in-tall-buildings.pdf.

The BIM. "Why Shanghai Tower Failed." YouTube, April 1, 2020. https://www .youtube.com/watch?v=JgkgBZfLu2I.

Bonshek, Jane. "Skyscraper Property Development in Chicago, 1882–1892. Doctoral Thesis, University of Reading, 1985.

Bonshek, Jane. "The Skyscraper: A Catalyst of Change in the Chicago Construction Industries, 1882–1892." *Construction History* 4 (1988): 53–74.

Bradsher, Keith. "Taiwan Close to Reaching a Lofty Goal." *New York Times*, January 11, 2004. https://www.nytimes.com/2004/01/11/world/taiwan-close-to-reaching -a-lofty-goal.html.

Brayson, Johnny. "The Real (and Very Tall) Buildings That Inspired Skyscraper's Pearl." *Bustle*, March 5, 2018. https://www.bustle.com/entertainment/is-the-pearl -in-skyscraper-a-real-building-the-hong-kong-tower-is-a-sight-to-behold-9703615.

Brenzel, Kathryn. "JPMorgan to Buy 50K sf of Air Rights—and Maybe 505K more for 270 Park Avenue." *TheRealDeal*, June 28, 2018. https://therealdeal.com/new-york/2018/06/28/jpmorgan-to-buy-50k-sf-of-air-rights-and-maybe-505k-more-for-270-park-avenue/.

British Property Federation. *The Economic Impact of High Density Development and Tall Buildings in Central Business Districts* (September 2008). http://www.ctbuh.org/Portals/0/People/WorkingGroups/Legal/LegalWG_BPF_Report.pdf.

Brook, Daniel. "Head of the Dragon: The Rise of New Shanghai." *Places Journal*, February 2013. https://doi.org/10.22269/130218.

Brooks Estate. "History of the Brooks Estate." Accessed September 14, 2023. https://brooksestate.org/history/.

Brueckner, Jan K., and Kala Seetharam Sridhar. "Measuring Welfare Gains from Relaxation of Land-Use Restrictions: The Case of India's Building-Height Limits." *Regional Science and Urban Economics* 42, no. 6 (2012): 1061–1067.

Brueckner, Jan K., Remi Jedwab, and Jason M. Barr. "Cities without Skylines: Worldwide Building-Height Gaps, their Determinants, and Their Implications." VoxEU, February 28, 2021. https://cepr.org/voxeu/columns/cities-without-skylines-worldwide-building-height-gaps-their-determinants-and-their.

Brueckner, Jan K., Shihe Fu, Yizhen Gu, and Junfu Zhang. "Measuring the Stringency of Land Use Regulation: The Case of China's Building Height Limits." *Review of Economics and Statistics* 99, no. 4 (2017): 663–677.

Buck, Thomas. "Sky City Plan No Idle Dream, Says Wright." *Chicago Tribune*, October 17, 1956.

Bunnell, Tim. "Views from Above and Below: The Petronas Twin Towers and/in Contesting Visions of Development in Contemporary Malaysia." *Singapore Journal of Tropical Geography* 20, no. 1 (1999): 1–23.

Burnham, Daniel. "To the Editor of the Engineering Record." *Engineering Record* 34 (July 28, 1896): 145. (Google Books) https://www.google.com/books/edition/_/kk81AQAAMAAJ?hl=en&gbpv=0.

Cai, Hongbin, Zhi Wang, and Qinghua Zhang. "To Build above the Limit? Implementation of Land Use Regulations in Urban China." *Journal of Urban Economics* 98 (2017): 223–233.

Cain, Louis P. "A Canal and Its City: A Selective Business History of Chicago." *DePaul Business Law Journal* 11 (1998): 125.

Čamprag, Nebojša. "Frankfurt and Rotterdam: Skylines as Embodiment of a Global City." *CTBUH Journal* 1 (2015): 26–32. https://global.ctbuh.org/resources/papers/download/2068-frankfurt-and-rotterdam-skylines-as-embodiment-of-a-global-city.pdf.

Cangelli, Eliana, and Lukia Fais. "Energy and Environmental Performance of Tall Buildings: State of the Art." *Advances in Building Energy Research* 6, no. 1 (2012): 36–60.

Carroll, John M. *A Concise History of Hong Kong.* Rowman & Littlefield, 2007.

Charney, Igal. "The Politics of Design: Architecture, Tall Buildings and the Skyline of Central London." *Area* 39, no. 2 (2007): 195–205.

Chen, Frank. "Risks Remain Months after China's Tallest Skyscraper Passed Fire Safety Inspection." *Asia Times,* October 26, 2010. https://asiatimes.com/2018/10/risks-remain-months-after-chinas-tallest-skyscraper-passed-fire-safety-inspection/.

Chen, Ting, and James Kai-sing Kung. "Busting the 'Princelings': The Campaign against Corruption in China's Primary Land Market." *Quarterly Journal of Economics* 134, no. 1 (2019): 185–226.

Chengxi, Yang. "Has World's 2nd Tallest Building Failed? The Pros and Cons of Shanghai Tower's Unique Design." CGTN, September 1, 2020. https://news.cgtn.com/news/79416a4e32514464776c6d636a4e6e62684a4856/index.html.

Cheshire, Paul C., and Gerard H. Dericks. "'Trophy Architects' and Design as Rent-Seeking: Quantifying Deadweight Losses in a Tightly Regulated Office Market." *Economica* 87, no. 348 (2020): 1078–1104.

Chicago Tribune. "New York Gossip," February 25, 1883.

Chicago Tribune. "Chicago Real Estate," July 29, 1888.

Clark, William Clifford, and John Lyndhurst Kingston. *The Skyscraper: A Study in the Economic Height of Modern Office Buildings.* American Institute of Steel Construction, 1930.

Clarke, Katherine. *Billionaires' Row: Tycoons, High Rollers, and the Epic Race to Build the World's Most Exclusive Skyscrapers.* Crown Currency, 2023.

Condit, Carl W. *The Chicago School of Architecture: A History of Commercial and Public Building in the Chicago Area, 1875–1925.* University of Chicago Press, 1964.

Cromley, Elizabeth C. *Alone Together: A History of New York's Early Apartments.* Cornell University Press, 1990.

Cronon, William. *Nature's Metropolis: Chicago and the Great West.* W. W. Norton, 1992.

Dai, Sarah. "President Xi's Dream City of Xiongan Pushes Ahead with Smart City Infrastructure Aimed at Covering All Areas." *South China Morning Post,* September 16, 2019. https://www.scmp.com/tech/innovation/article/3027415/president-xis-dream-city-xiongan-pushes-ahead-smart-city.

Davies, John, James Lui, Jack Pappin, K. K. Yin, and C. W. Law. "The Foundation Design for Two Super High-Rise Buildings in Hong Kong." *Proceedings: CTBUH 2004 Seoul Conference* (2004): 10–13.

Daily Mail. "City Gherkin Building Sold for Record £600m," February 5, 2007. https://www.dailymail.co.uk/news/article-433970/City-Gherkin-building-sold-record-600m.html.

Davidson, Justin. "Why Glass Towers Are Bad for City Life — and What We Need Instead." TED Conference, February 5, 2017. https://singjupost.com/justin-davidson -why-glass-towers-are-bad-for-city-life-and-what-we-need-instead-transcript/.

Davis, Hana. "Explainer | What You Should Know about Hong Kong's Country Parks . . . and Are They under Threat in City's Thirst for Land?" *South China Morning Post*, May 9, 2019. https://www.scmp.com/news/hong-kong/society/ article/2189241/what-you-should-know-about-hong-kongs-country-parks-and-are.

de la Merced, Michael J. "Blackstone Group Purchases Landmark Chicago Tower: New Owner for Willis Tower." *New York Times*, March 17, 2015. https://www .nytimes.com/2015/03/17/business/blackstone-group-purchases-landmark -chicago-tower.html.

Dennis, Richard. "'Babylonian Flats' in Victorian and Edwardian London." *London Journal* 33, no. 3 (2008): 233–247. https://discovery.ucl.ac.uk/id/ eprint/14487/1/14487.pdf.

Devaney, Steven. "Trends in Office Rents in the City of London: 1867–1959." *Explorations in Economic History* 47, no. 2 (2010): 198–212.

Dorfman, Anna, Danny Ben-Shahar, and Daniel Heller. "Power and High Stories." Working Paper, Alroy Institute for Real Estate, Tel Aviv University (2017).

Du, Juan. "How I.M. Pei's Bank of China Tower Changed Hong Kong's Skyline." CNN, January 8, 2018. https://www.cnn.com/style/article/100-years-of-i-m-pei- bank-of-china/index.html.

Dubey, Parul. "The Man Who Saved the Skyscraper." *Informed Infrastructure*, August 2016. https://informedinfrastructure.com/25510/the-man-who-saved -the-skyscraper/.

Ducat, Arthur Charles. *Memoir of Gen. A. C. Ducat.* Chicago: Rand, McNally, 1897.

Ducat & Lyon. "To the Editor of the Engineering Record." *Engineering Record* 24 (July 11, 1896): 103. (Google Books) https://www.google.com/books/edition/_/ kk81AQAAMAAJ?hl=en&gl=us&sa=X&ved=2ahUKEwiI5sDNwKyBAxU-Flk FHaXZDQoQre8FegQIIRBg.

Dupré, Judith. *Skyscrapers: A History of the World's Most Extraordinary Buildings.* Black Dog & Leventhal, 2nd ed., 2008.

Durst, Alexander. "Efficient Energy Production for High-Demand Tenants of Tall Buildings." *Proceedings: 2015 CTBUH Conference* (2015): 40-47. https:// global.ctbuh.org/resources/papers/download/2436-efficient-energy-production -for-high-demand-tenants-of-tall-buildings.pdf.

Edin, Per-Anders, Peter Fredriksson, Martin Nybom, and Björn Öckert. "The Rising Return to Non-cognitive Skills." Working Paper no. 2018: 15, Depart- ment of Economics, Uppsala University (2018). https://www.econstor.eu/bit stream/10419/197667/1/1042325294.pdf.

eileen. "Iconic Glass Structures—the Shard." *Glass Point Blog*, October 2, 2016. https://glasspaint.com/iconic-glass-structures-the-shard/.

Eriksen, Michael D., and Anthony W. Orlando. "Returns to Scale in Residential Construction: The Marginal Impact of Building Height." *Real Estate Economics* 50, no. 2 (2022): 534–564.

Fainstein, Susan. *The City Builders*. Oxford: Blackwell, 1994.

Feder, Barnaby J. "Trust Gets Skyscraper from Sears." *New York Times*, November 8, 1994. https://nyti.ms/45RWopD.

Fisher, Robert Moore. *The Boom in Office Buildings*. Report No. 36, Board of Governors of the Federal Reserve System, 1967.

Fitzsimmons, Emma G. "Can Eric Adams Cheerlead New Yorkers past the Pandemic?" *New York Times*, March 20, 2022. https://www.nytimes.com/2022/03/20/nyregion/pandemic-recovery-masks-nyc.html.

Flannery, Russell. "China's Tallest Skyscraper Marks Big Step toward Its 2015 Finish." *Forbes*, August 3, 2013. https://www.forbes.com/sites/russellflannery/2013/08/03/chinas-tallest-skyscraper-celebrates-big-step-toward-its-2015-finish/?sh=46a1ad671781.

Fleming, David, Arthur Grimes, Laurent Lebreton, David Maré, and Peter Nunns. "Valuing Sunshine." *Regional Science and Urban Economics* 68 (2018): 268–276.

Fong, Dominique. "Shanghai Tower Fails to Meet High Leasing Hopes." *Wall Street Journal*, January 3, 2017. https://www.wsj.com/articles/shanghai-tower-fails-to-meet-high-leasing-hopes-1483462332?mod=djemRealEstat.

Fortune. "Former Sears Tower in Chicago Has a New Owner." March 16, 2015. https://fortune.com/2015/03/16/sears-tower-chicago/.

Fort Worth Star-Telegram. "New Concept of the 'Tree' Skyscraper Revealed by Frank Lloyd Wright." October 17, 1956, p. 2.

Frank, Thomas. "Treasury Wants to Crack Down on Shell Companies, Corruption with New Rule." CNBC, December 7, 2021. https://www.cnbc.com/2021/12/07/treasury-wants-to-crack-down-on-shell-companies-corruption-with-new-rule.html.

Friedman, Donald. "'A Story a Day': Engineering the Work." In *Building the Empire State*, edited by Caroll Willis and Donald Friedman, 33-46. W. W. Norton, 1998.

Friedman, Donald. *Structure in Skyscrapers: History and Preservation*. Self-published, 2014.

Fusscas, Andrew Francis. "The New York World Trade Center: A Performance Study." Master's Thesis, Massachusetts Institute of Technology, 1992.

Gagne, Yasmin. "Inside Tencent's New $599 Million Shenzhen Headquarters." FastCompany.com, October 29, 2018. https://www.fastcompany.com/90244981/inside-tencents-new-599-million-shenzhen-headquarters.

Gass, John B. "The Godwin Bursary: Portions of Report of a Visit to the United States of America and to Canada" *Sessional Papers Read at the Royal Institute of British Architects* 2 (1886): 145–162. (Google Books) https://www.google.com/books/edition/Transactions_of_the_Royal_Institute_of_B/EQgtAAAAYAAJ?hl=en&gbpv=0.

Gates, F. T. "To The Editor of the Engineering Record." *Engineering Record* 34, no. 4 (June 27, 1896): 71. (Google Books) https://www.google.com/books/edition/_/kk81AQAAMAAJ?hl=en&gbpv=0.

Gifford, Robert. "The Consequences of Living in High-Rise Buildings." *Architectural Science Review* 50, no. 1 (2007): 2–17.

Gilbert, Cass. "The Financial Importance of Rapid Building." *Engineering Record* 41 (1900): 624.

Gillespie, Angus Kress. *Twin Towers: The Life of New York City's World Trade Center.* Rutgers University Press, 1999.

Gjerløw, Haakon, and Carl Henrik Knutsen. "TRENDS: Leaders, Private Interests, and Socially Wasteful Projects: Skyscrapers in Democracies and Autocracies." *Political Research Quarterly* 72, no. 2 (2019): 504–520.

Glaeser, Edward L., and David C. Maré. "Cities and Skills." *Journal of Labor Economics* 19, no. 2 (2001): 316–342.

Glanz, James and Eric Lipton. "The Height of Ambition." *New York Times Magazine,* September 8, 2002. https://www.nytimes.com/2002/09/08/magazine/the-height-of-ambition.html.

Global Construction Review. "Masts Made Shenzhen Tower Shake, Causing Panic, Experts Say." July 16, 2021. https://www.globalconstructionreview.com/masts-made-shenzhen-tower-shake-causing-panic-expe/.

Grant, Peter. "Blackstone Nears Deal Valuing Manhattan Office Tower at $2.85 Billion." *Wall Street Journal,* December 17, 2021. https://www.wsj.com/articles/blackstone-nears-deal-valuing-manhattan-office-tower-at-2-85-billion-11639737002.

Greenberg, Larry M., and Mitchell Pacelle. "TrizecHahn Will Pay $110 Million, Assume Debt in Deal to Buy Sears Tower." *Wall Street Journal,* December 3, 1997.

Grutzner, Charles. "A World Center of Trade Mapped off Wall Street." *New York Times,* January 27, 1960. https://nyti.ms/3RstcB5.

The Guardian. "Abu Dhabi Fund Buys New York City's Chrysler Building for $800m," July 9, 2008. https://www.theguardian.com/business/2008/jul/09/sovereignwealthfunds.usa.

The Guardian. "Carbuncle Cup: Walkie Talkie Wins Prize for Worst Building of the Year." September 2, 2015. https://www.theguardian.com/artanddesign/architecture-design-blog/2015/sep/02/walkie-talkie-london-wins-carbuncle-cup-worst-building-of-year.

The Guardian. "Turning off Building Lights at Night Cuts Bird Collisions, Study Shows." June 7, 2021. https://www.theguardian.com/environment/2021/jun/07/turning-off-building-lights-at-night-cuts-bird-collisions-study-shows.

Halpern, Dan. "Arabian Heights: How Does an Emerging Global Power Announce Itself? With the World's Tallest Building." *Architect*, May 7, 2007. https://www.architectmagazine.com/design/urbanism-planning/arabian-heights_0.

Hammill, Luke. "Schiff Hardin Extends Lease, Cuts Space at Willis Tower." *Crain's Chicago Business*, June 12, 2017. https://www.chicagobusiness.com/article/20170612/CRED03/170619996/schiff-hardin-extends-willis-tower-lease-with-less-space.

Hammoud, Mounib. "Kingdom Tower / Kingdom City: History in the Making." *Proceedings: 2015 CTBUH Conference* (2015). https://global.ctbuh.org/resources/papers/download/2383-kingdom-tower-kingdom-city-history-in-the-making.pdf.

Hammoud, Mounib. "Jeddah City & Jeddah Tower." Talk given at 2016 CTBUH Conference, October 18, 2016. https://www.youtube.com/watch?v=a6U-_LMdV2g.

Hartshorne, Richard. "The Significance of Lake Transportation to the Grain Traffic of Chicago." *Economic Geography* 2, no. 2 (1926): 274–291.

Heights of Building Commission. *Report of the Height of Buildings Commission to the Committee on the Height, Size and Arrangement of Buildings of the Board of Estimate and Apportionment of the City of New York*, December 23, 1913. (HathiTrust) https://babel.hathitrust.org/cgi/pt?id=nnc2.ark:/13960/t0dv3wd9r&view=1up&seq=40&skin=2021&qi=pay.

Heng, Cheryl. "Zoom's 400 per Cent Surge Propels 'Superman' Li Ka-shing Back to the Top of Hong Kong's Rich List." *South China Morning Post*, February 26, 2021. https://www.scmp.com/business/money/wealth/article/3123100/zooms-400-cent-surge-propels-superman-li-ka-shing-back-top.

Hepşen, Ali, and Metin Vatansever. "Relationship between Residential Property Price Index and Macroeconomic Indicators in Dubai Housing Market." *International Journal of Strategic Property Management* 16, no. 1 (2012): 71–84.

Hoeksema, Robert J. "Three Stages in the History of Land Reclamation in the Netherlands." *Irrigation and Drainage: The Journal of the International Commission on Irrigation and Drainage* 56, no. S1 (2007): S113–S126.

Home Insurance Company. *The Home Insurance Company: New York 1853–1903*. 1903.

Howarth, Dan. "'Chinese Architecture Will Benefit' from CCTV Building, Says Rem Koolhaas." Dezeen.com, November 24, 2014. https://www.dezeen.com/2014/11/26/rem-koolhaas-defends-cctv-building-beijing-china-architecture/.

Hoyt, Homer. *One Hundred Years of Land Values in Chicago: The Relationship of the Growth of Chicago to the Rise in Its Land Values, 1830–1933*. University of Chicago Press, 1933.

Hoyt, Homer. "After 150 Years Urban American Growth Has Reached a Plateau." *Real Estate*, August 24, 1940, 8–9.

Hsu, Jonathan, and Cynthia Chan. "Economics/Financial: The Emergence of Asian Supertalls." *CTBUH Journal* (2014): 28–33. https://global.ctbuh.org/resources/papers/download/1834-the-emergence-of-asian-supertalls-pdf.

Huang, Tianlei. "Why China's Housing Policies Have Failed." Working Paper 23-5, Peterson Institute for International Economics (2023).

Hubbard, Ben. "MBS: The Rise of a Saudi Prince." *New York Times*, March 21, 2020. https://www.nytimes.com/2020/03/21/world/middleeast/mohammed-bin-salman-saudi-arabia.html.

Hudson, Alexandra. "Architect of 432 Park Reveals Building's Design Inspired by . . . a Trash Can?" Viewing NYCV, June 3, 2015. https://viewing.nyc/architect-of-432-park-reveals-buildings-design-inspired-by-a-trash-can/.

Hughes, C. J. "In a Bid to Fill Office Buildings, Landlords Offer Kegs and Nap Rooms." *New York Times*, October 23, 2018. https://www.nytimes.com/2018/10/23/business/office-building-ameneties.html.

Huxtable, Ada Louise. "What's Higher than Highest? Wait and See." *New York Times*, December 3, 1972. https://nyti.ms/48uyxhB.

Ibrahim, Faudziah, and Phui Kuan Leong. "Petronas Towers and KLCC: Urban Catalyst" *Proceedings: 2015 CTBUH Asia and Australasia Conference* (2015). https://global.ctbuh.org/resources/papers/download/2425-petronas-towers-and-klcc-urban-catalyst.pdf.

Insurance Journal. "Miscellaneous Notes." *Insurance Journal* 14, nos. 7-8 (September 1886): 414–418. (Google Books) https://www.google.com/books/edition/The_Insurance_Journal/vOBAAQAAMAAJ?hl=en&gbpv=0.

Irish Builder and Engineer. "The Home Insurance Building." *Irish Builder and Engineer* 27, no. 634 (May 18, 1886): 143. (Google Books) https://www.google.com/books/edition/Irish_Builder_and_Engineer/NDhJAQAAMAAJ?hl=en&gbpv=0.

Janvatanavit, Kulvech. "Analysis of Factors That Contribute to International Competitive Advantage of Hong Kong Real Estate Developers." Master's Thesis, Massachusetts Institute of Technology, 1993.

Je, Haeseong, and Jaehyuk Lee. "A Study on the Impact of High-Rise Living on the Health of Residents." *Journal of Asian Architecture and Building Engineering* 9, no. 2 (2010): 331–338.

Jedwab, Remi, Jason Barr, and Jan K. Brueckner. "Cities without Skylines: Worldwide Building-Height Gaps and Their Possible Determinants and Implications." *Journal of Urban Economics* 132 (2022): 103507.

Jenney, William Le Baron. "The Construction of a Heavy Fire-Proof Building on a Compressible Soil." *Sanitary Engineer* 13, no. 2 (December 10, 1885): 32–33. (Google Books) https://www.google.com/books/edition/

Engineering_Record_Building_Record_and_S/o_EwAQAAMAAJ?hl
=en&gbpv=o.

Jing, Shi, and Wang Ying. "Shanghai Tower Rentals Reflect Confidence in
Country." *China Daily*, December 27, 2022. https://www.chinadaily.com
.cn/a/202212/27/WS63a9b022a31057c47eba63c0.html.

Johns, Adam. "Swiss Re Topples Millennium Tower." *The Times*, November 7, 1997.

Jones, Ben. "Past, Present and Future: The Evolution of China's Incredible High-
Speed Rail Network." CNN, February 9, 2022. https://www.cnn.com/travel/
article/china-high-speed-rail-cmd/index.html.

Jones, Christopher, and Daniel M. Kammen. "Spatial Distribution of US Household Carbon Footprints Reveals Suburbanization Undermines Greenhouse Gas
Benefits of Urban Population Density." *Environmental Science & Technology*
48, no. 2 (2014): 895–902.

Jou, Sue-Ching. "Domestic Politics in Urban Image Creation: Xinyi as the 'Manhattan of Taipei.'" In *Globalizing Taipei: The Political Economy of Spatial Development*, edited by Reginald Yin-Wang Kwok, 120–140. Psychology Press, 2005.

Kaika, Maria. "Architecture and Crisis: Re-inventing the Icon, Re-imag(in)ing
London and Re-branding the City." *Transactions of the Institute of British Geog-
raphers* 35, no. 4 (2010): 453–474.

Kamin, Blair. "50 Years Later, Lake Point Tower Is a Singular Achievement —
and Let's Hope It Stays That Way." *Chicago Tribune*, September 20, 2018.
https://www.chicagotribune.com/columns/blair-kamin/ct-ae-lake-point-tower
-anniversary-0923-story.html.

Kelly, Heather, and Rachel Lerman. "The Pandemic Is Making People Reconsider
City Living, Trading Traffic for Chickens." *Washington Post*, June 1, 2020. https://
www.washingtonpost.com/technology/2020/06/01/city-relocate-pandemic/.

Khan, Yasmin Sabina. *Engineering Architecture: The Vision of Fazlur R. Khan*.
W. W. Norton, 2004.

Kihara, Takeshi. "Hong Kong Pulled Closer to Mainland with Vision for New
Northern Core." *Nikkei Asia*, June 16, 2022. https://asia.nikkei.com/Business/
Markets/Property/Hong-Kong-pulled-closer-to-mainland-with-vision-for-new
-northern-core.

Killa, Shaun, and Richard F. Smith. "Harnessing Energy in Tall Buildings: Bahrain
World Trade Center and Beyond." *Proceedings: CTBUH 8th World Congress*
(2008): 1–7. https://global.ctbuh.org/resources/papers/download/464-harnessing
-energy-in-tall-buildings-bahrain-world-trade-center-and-beyond.pdf.

Kim, Jae-Ho, and Seung-Hoon Lee. "Application of High Performance Concrete
in Petronas Twin Tower, KLCC." *Age* 28 (2004): 700.

Knapp, Joseph G. "A Review of Chicago Stock Yards History." *University Journal
of Business* 2, no.3 (June 1924): 331–346.

Korom, Joseph J. *The American Skyscraper, 1850–1940: A Celebration of Height.* Branden Books, 2008.

Koster, Hans R. A., Jos van Ommeren, and Piet Rietveld. "Is the Sky the Limit? High-Rise Buildings and Office Rents." *Journal of Economic Geography* 14, no. 1 (2014): 125–153.

Krane, Jim. *City of Gold: Dubai and the Dream of Capitalism.* St. Martin's Press, 2009.

Krugman, Paul. "Wonking Out: Zooming and the Future of Cities." *New York Times*, June 2, 2023. https://www.nytimes.com/2023/06/02/opinion/cities -remote-work-economy.html.

Krummeck, Stefan, and B. MacLeod. "Capturing the Placemaking Potential of the New Skyscraper City." *Proceedings: CTBUH 12th World Congress* (2015): 26–30. https://global.ctbuh.org/resources/papers/download/2468-capturing-the-place making-potential-of-the-new-skyscraper-city.pdf

Kuhn, Gerald Wade. *A History of the Financing of Commercial Structures in the Chicago Central Business District, 1868 to 1934.* Doctoral Dissertation, Indiana University, 1969.

Lai, Lawrence Wai-chung. "The Leasehold System as a Means of Planning by Contract: The Case of Hong Kong." *Town Planning Review* (1998): 249–275.

Lainton, Andrew. "Floorspace Area Ratio–Making It Work Better," *Decisions, Decisions, Decisions,* July 1, 2011. https://andrewlainton.wordpress.com/2011/07/11/ floorspace-area-ratio-making-it-work-better/.

Lallanilla, Marc. "This London Skyscraper Can Melt Cars and Set Buildings on Fire." NBCnewscom, September 3, 2013. https://www.nbcnews.com/science main/london-skyscraper-can-melt-cars-set-buildings-fire-8c11069092.

Landau, Sarah Bradford, and Carl W. Condit. *Rise of the New York Skyscraper, 1865–1913.* Yale University Press, 1999.

Larson, Gerald R. "6.3. The Grannis Block." The Architecture Professor, September 6, 2020. https://thearchitectureprofessor.com/2020/09/06/6-3-the-grannis-block/.

Larson, Gerald R. "The Elevator, the Iron Skeleton Frame, and the Early Skyscrapers: Part 1." *International Journal of High-Rise Buildings* 9, no. 1 (2020A): 1–15.

Larson, Gerald R. "The Elevator, the Iron Skeleton Frame, and the Early Sky-scrapers: Part 2." *International Journal of High-Rise Buildings* 9, no. 1 (2020B): 17–41.

Larson, Gerald R., and Roula Mouroudellis Geraniotis. "Toward a Better Understanding of the Evolution of the Iron Skeleton Frame in Chicago." *Journal of the Society of Architectural Historians* 46, no. 1 (1987): 39–48.

Lee, Timothy B. "Tokyo May Have Found the Solution to Soaring Housing Costs." Vox, August 8, 2016. https://www.vox.com/2016/8/8/12390048/san-francisco-housing -costs-tokyo.

328   BIBLIOGRAPHY

Legislative Council Secretariat. "Major Sources of Government Revenue,"
November 6, 2020. https://www.legco.gov.hk/research-publications/
english/2021issf04-major-sources-of-government-revenue-20201119-e.pdf.
Leonard, Devin. "The Green Building That's Flunking New York's Climate
Law." Bloomberg.com, March 14, 2022. https://www.bloomberg.com/news/
features/2022-03-14/the-green-skyscraper-challenging-nyc-s-emissions-law#x
j4y7vzkg.
Leslie, Thomas. *Chicago Skyscrapers, 1871–1934*. University of Illinois Press, 2013.
Levine, Neil. *The Urbanism of Frank Lloyd Wright*. Princeton University Press,
2016.
Lewis, Lauren, and Wanyuan Song. "Luxury in the Clouds: World's Highest Hotel
with a Restaurant on the 120th Floor of a 2,000ft Tower Opens in Shanghai."
Daily Mail, June 24, 2021. https://www.dailymail.co.uk/news/article-9722001/
Worlds-highest-hotel-restaurant-120TH-FLOOR-2-000ft-tower-opens-Shanghai
.html.
Li, Sandy. "Beijing Bans Buildings over 500m in Height—Skyscrapers Topping 250
Metres Also Limited, but Analysts Say Ruling Might Not Have Much Impact
on Market as 180–200 Metres Is Optimal Range." *South Morning China Post*,
July 8, 2021.
Lin, Edith. "Hong Kong Needs Artificial Islands as Land Bank to Avoid Supply
Shortage in the Future, Government Says." *South China Morning Post*, Jan-
uary 20, 2023. https://www.scmp.com/news/hong-kong/society/article/3207635/
hong-kong-needs-artificial-islands-land-bank-avoid-supply-shortage-future
-government-says.
Liu, Crocker H., Stuart S. Rosenthal, and William C. Strange. "The Vertical City:
Rent Gradients, Spatial Structure, and Agglomeration Economies." *Journal of
Urban Economics* 106 (2018): 101–122.
Loss, Scott R., Tom Will, and Peter P. Marra. "Direct Mortality of Birds from
Anthropogenic Causes." *Annual Review of Ecology, Evolution, and Systematics*
46 (2015): 99–120.
Mafi, Nick. "New York's Chrysler Building Sells for Much Less Than It Was
Purchased for a Decade Ago." *Architectural Digest*, March 12, 2019. https://
www.architecturaldigest.com/story/new-york-chrysler-building-sells-less-than
-purchased-decade-ago.
Magnusson, Jon D. "A Remembrance: The World Trade Center Towers and the
Engineers who Designed Them." *Civil Engineering—ASCE* 92, no. 5 (2021):
52–53. https://www.asce.org/publications-and-news/civil-engineering-source/
civil-engineering-magazine/issues/magazine-issue/article/2021/09/a-remem
brance-the-world-trade-center-towers-and-the-engineers-who-designed
-them.

Maizland, Lindsay. "Hong Kong's Freedoms: What China Promised and How It's Cracking Down." *Council on Foreign Relations*, May 19, 2022. https://www.cfr .org/backgrounder/hong-kong-freedoms-democracy-protests-china-crackdown.

Makhlouf, Farah. "This Viral Video Shows How Secure the Burj Khalifa Residences Are." *Lovin Dubai*, September 11, 2022. https://lovin.co/dubai/en/latest/this-viral -video-shows-how-secure-the-burj-khalifa-residences-are.

Maki, Sydney. "New York to Developers: Stop Using Empty Space to Make Your Buildings Taller." Bloomberg.com, March 22, 2019. https://www.bloomberg .com/news/articles/2019-03-22/new-york-looks-into-voids-used-by-builders-to -bend-height-rules.

Maloney, Maureen, Tsur Somerville, and Brigitte Unger. "Combatting Money Laundering in BC Real Estate." *Report of the Expert Panel on Money Laundering in BC Real Estate* (2019). https://www2.gov. bc.ca/gov/content/housing-tenancy/ real-estate-bc/consultations/money-laundering.

Malott, David. "Case Study: International Commerce Centre." *CTBUH Journal*, no. IV (2010): 12–17. https://global.ctbuh.org/paper/11.

Mansharamani, Vikram. "Are Skyscraper Races a Warning of Economic Chaos to Come?" PBS.org, April 14, 2016. https://www.pbs.org/newshour/economy/ are-skyscraper-races-a-warning-of-economic-chaos-to-come.

Marcus, Silvian. "432 Park." *Structure Magazine*, July 2018. https://www.structure mag.org/?p=13350.

Mast, Evan. "JUE Insight: The Effect of New Market-Rate Housing Construction on the Low-Income Housing Market." *Journal of Urban Economics* 133 (2023): 103383.

Mathew, Shaji. "'Spectacular' Dubai Property Bounce Likely to Continue, Knight Frank Says." Bloomberg.com, March 1, 2022. https://www.bloomberg.com/ news/articles/2022-03-01/knight-frank-sees-spectacular-dubai-property-bounce -continuing#xj4y7vzkg.

McCue, George. "A Mile-High Building." *St. Louis Post-Dispatch*, November 18, 1956.

McNeill, Donald. "The Mayor and the World City Skyline: London's Tall Buildings Debate." *International Planning Studies* 7, no. 4 (2002): 325–334.

Meinhold, Bridgette. "The Incredible Story of How the Burj Khalifa's Poop Is Trucked out of Town." *Inhabitat*, November 29, 2014. https://inhabitat.com/ the-incredible-story-of-how-the-burj-khalifas-poop-is-trucked-out-of-town/.

Merchant, Brian. "Life and Death in Apple's Forbidden City." *The Guardian*, June 18, 2017. https://www.theguardian.com/technology/2017/jun/18/foxconn-life-death -forbidden-city-longhua-suicide-apple-iphone-brian-merchant-one-device-extract.

Morgenstern, Joseph. "The Fifty-Nine-Story Crisis." *The New Yorker*, May 21, 1995. https://www.newyorker.com/magazine/1995/05/29/the-fifty-nine-story-crisis.

Moretti, Enrico. *The New Geography of Jobs*. Houghton Mifflin Harcourt, 2012.

Mydans, Seth. "Malaysia Looks Down on World from 1,483 Feet." *New York Times*,
    May 2, 1996. https://www.nytimes.com/1996/05/02/world/kuala-lumpur-journal-
    malaysia-looks-down-on-world-from-1483-feet.html.

Nase, Ilir, Nick van Assendelft, and Hilde Remøy. "Rent Premiums and Vertical
    Sorting in Amsterdam's Multi-Tenant Office Buildings." *Journal of Real Estate
    Finance and Economics* 59 (2019): 419–460.

NBC.com. "World's Tallest Building Coming to Saudi Arabia." August 2, 2011.
    https://www.nbcnews.com/id/wbna43988244.

New York Times. "Chicago Skyscraper Limit," March 2, 1902, p. 10. https://times
    machine.nytimes.com/timesmachine/1902/03/02/issue.html.

New York Times. "Largest Office Building to Replace Waldorf-Astoria." December
    23, 1928. https://nyti.ms/3RjHnsf.

New York Times. "New Waldorf Site Sought for Year." March 10, 1929. https://nyti
    .ms/3PIFy76.

New York Times. "Waldorf Property Taken by Syndicate." June 4, 1929. https://nyti
    .ms/4651D5a.

New York Times. "Smith to Help Build Highest Skyscraper." August 30, 1929. https://
    nyti.ms/44VMwdh.

New York Times. "Enlarges Site for 1,000-Foot Building." November 19, 1929. https://
    nyti.ms/3sRDAYV.

New York Times. "Smith Skyscraper to Have Dirigible Mast Towering Quarter of a
    Mile above Fifth Av." December 12, 1929. https://nyti.ms/48jhoIK.

New York Times. "Airship Flies about Empire State Mast." December 17, 1930.
    https://timesmachine.nytimes.com/timesmachine/1930/12/17/112690295.html
    ?pageNumber=20.

New York Times. "Col. W. A. Starrett, Noted Builder, Dead." March 27, 1932.
    https://nyti.ms/45TYrcz.

New York Times. "L. G. Kaufman Dies; Ex-banker Here, 69." March 11, 1942.
    https://nyti.ms/45Vx6qA.

New York Times. "Empire State Sold; Price of Control Put at $50,000,000." May
    26, 1951. https://nyti.ms/3Peyuxo.

New York Times. "Floyd deL. Brown, Architect, Dies at 70; Designed and Built Air
    Terminals Here." November 8, 1955. https://nyti.ms/3RFxN3d.

New York Times. "Paul Starrett, Builder, 90, Dies." July 6, 1957. https://nyti.ms/3ZibWQO.

New York Times. "Andrew J. Eken, Builder, 83, Dies." June 12, 1965. https://nyti.
    ms/3PFhh1y.

New York Times. "New Sears Building in Chicago Planned as the World's Tallest."
    July 28, 1970. https://nyti.ms/3LoHMG7.

New York Times . "The World's Tallest: Saga of a Chicago Skyscraper." October 18,
    1970. https://nyti.ms/3LN6q3t.

New York Times. "MetLife Acquires Sears Tower from Trizec," August 29, 2003. https://www.nytimes.com/2003/08/29/business/metlife-acquires-sears-tower -from-trizec.html.

Ng, Cheuk Fan. "Living and Working in Tall Buildings: Satisfaction and Perceived Benefits and Concerns of Occupants." *Frontiers in Built Environment* 3 (2017): 70.

Nichols, Charles M. *Studies on Building Height Limitations in Large Cities with Special Reference to Conditions in Chicago. Proceedings of an Investigation of Building Height Limitations Conducted under the Auspices of The Zoning Committee of the Chicago Real Estate Board,* 1923.

Nissim, Roger. *Land Administration and Practice in Hong Kong.* Hong Kong University Press, 5th ed., 2021.

Officer, Lawrence H., and Samuel H. Williamson. "The Annual Consumer Price Index for the United States, 1774–Present," MeasuringWorth, August 2023. http://www.measuringworth.com/uscpi/.

Oldfield, Philip, Dario Trabucco, and Antony Wood. "Five Energy Generations of Tall Buildings: An Historical Analysis of Energy Consumption in High-Rise Buildings." *Journal of Architecture* 14, no. 5 (2009): 591–613.

Peck, Ralph Brazelton. "History of Building Foundations in Chicago: A Report of an Investigation." *University of Illinois Bulletin* 45, no. 29 (1948).

Petroski, Henry. "Engineering: Fazlur Khan." *American Scientist* 87, no. 1 (1999): 16–20.

Piketty, Thomas. *Capital in the Twenty-First Century.* Harvard University Press, 2013.

Poon, Alice. *Land and the Ruling Class in Hong Kong.* Enrich Professional, 2011.

Porter, Bernard. *The Battle of the Styles: Society, Culture and the Design of a New Foreign Office, 1855–1861.* Bloomsbury, 2011.

Powell, Kenneth. *30 St Mary Axe: A Tower for London.* Merrell, 2006.

Price, George M. "Statement by Dr. George M. Price, Director of the Joint Board of Sanitary Control, to the NYC Commission on Building Districts and Restrictions." *Commission on Building Districts and Restrictions: Final Report,* May 24, 1916. (Archive.org) https://archive.org/details/finalreportnewy/page/162/ mode/2up.

Pridmore, Jay. *Sears Tower: A Building Book from the Chicago Architecture Foundation.* Pomegranate, 2002.

Pristin, Terry. "Drake Hotel's Prime Space Remains Undeveloped." *New York Times,* November 17, 2009. https://www.nytimes.com/2009/11/18/realestate/ commercial/18drake.html.

Procter, Emma. "Flying Taxis, Robotic Avatars and Holograms—Saudi Arabia Pushes Ahead with Its Sci-fi City Vision." CNBC.com, October 25, 2022. https:// www.cnbc.com/2022/10/25/neom-saudi-arabia-pushes-ahead-with-its-sci-fi-city -vision.html.

Prynn, Jonathan. "All 25 Storeys of Office Space at the Shard Now Fully Let for First Time." *Evening Standard*, October 4, 2017. https://www.standard.co.uk/news/london/all -25-storeys-of-office-space-at-the-shard-now-fully-let-for-first-time-a3650096.html.

Qiao, Shitong. "The Evolution of Chinese Property Law: Stick by Stick?" In *Private Law in China and Taiwan: Legal and Economic Analyses*, edited by Yun-chien Chang, Wei Shen, and Wen-yeu Wang, 182–211. Cambridge University Press, 2017.

Quirk, Vanessa. "Rafael Viñoly on Walkie Talkie 'Death Ray': Consultants to Blame." ArchDaily, September 6, 2013. https://www.archdaily.com/425857/ rafael-vinoly-on-walkie-talkie-death-ray-consultants-to-blame.

Real Estate Board of New York. *Office Building Construction: Manhattan 1947–1967* (1964).

Reina, Peter. "UltraRope Lightweight Elevator System Can Double the Maximum Run to 1 Kilometer, Says KONE." *Engineering News Record*, June 10, 2013. https://www.enr.com/articles/512-ultrarope-lightweight-elevator-system-can -double-the-maximum-run-to-1-kilometer-says-kone.

Reisz, Todd. *Showpiece City: How Architecture Made Dubai.* Stanford University Press, 2020.

Ren, Daniel. "How Shanghai Tower Has Paid the Price of China's Quest for Height." *South China Morning Post*, May 19, 2018. https://www.scmp.com/business/ article/2146837/how-shanghai-tower-has-paid-price-chinas-quest-height.

Reuters. "Pride and Skyscrapers Cometh before the Fall: Report." January 11, 2012. https://www.reuters.com/article/skyscrapers-financial-correlation/pride-and- skyscrapers-cometh-before-the-fall-report-idINDEE80A0C320120111.

Richter, Wolf. "Glorious Effects of Money-Printing Bail Out Manhattan Luxury Housing Market in 2021, after It Fell on Hard Times." Wolf Street, December 24, 2021. https://wolfstreet.com/2021/12/24/effects-of-money-printing-washed- over-manhattan-luxury-real-estate-in-2021/.

Rithmire, Meg E. *Land Bargains and Chinese Capitalism: The Politics of Property Rights under Reform.* Cambridge University Press, 2015.

Robertson, Leslie E. *The Structure of Design: An Engineer's Extraordinary Life in Architecture.* Monacelli Press, 2017.

Robertson, Leslie E., and See Saw Teen. "The High-Rise Building—How High Can We Go?" *HKIE Transactions* 12, no. 4 (2005): 27–35.

Roeder, David. "Willis Tower Transforms into Friendly Giant to Keep Drawing Office Workers." *Chicago Sun Times*, May 24, 2022. https://chicago.suntimes. com/2022/5/24/23140296/willis-tower-transforms-into-friendly-giant-to-keep -drawing-office-workers.

Roudman, Sam. "Bank of America's Toxic Tower." *New Republic*, July 28, 2013. https://newrepublic.com/article/113942/bank-america-tower-and-leed-ratings- racket.

Russo, Gianpiero, Vincenzo Abagnara, Harry G. Poulos, and John C. Small. "Re-assessment of Foundation Settlements for the Burj Khalifa, Dubai." *Acta Geotechnica* 8 (2013): 3–15. https://link.springer.com/article/10.1007/s11440-012-0193-4.

Saini, Shivam. "'Death Ray' Skyscraper Is Wreaking Havoc on London." *Business Insider*, July 31, 2015. https://www.businessinsider.com/death-ray-skyscraper-is-wreaking-havoc-on-london-for-a-few-totally-insane-reasons-2015-7.

Sanderson, J. C., J. L. McConnell, and F. J. Thielbar. "Home Insurance Building—a Report on Types of Construction Used." *Journal of the Western Society of Engineers* 37, no. 1 (1932): 8–9.

Schaffer, Kristen. "The Early Chicago Tall Office Building: Artistically and Functionally Considered." *ICOMOS—Hefte des Deutschen Nationalkomitees* 54 (2012): 148–156.

Schatzker, Erik. "Prince Alwaleed Reveals Secret Deal Struck to Exit Ritz after 83 Days." Bloomberg.com, March 20, 2018. https://www.bloomberg.com/news/features/2018-03-20/alwaleed-reveals-secret-deal-struck-to-exit-after-83-days#xj4y7vzkg.

Schwieterman, Joseph P., and Dana M. Caspall. *The Politics of Place: A History of Zoning in Chicago.* Lake Claremont Press, 2006.

Sciocolone, Maria. "Developing Skyscraper Districts: La Défense." *CTBUH Journal* 1 (2012): 18–23. https://global.ctbuh.org/resources/papers/download/290-developing-skyscraper-districts-la-defense.pdf.

Sellar, Irvine. "Developing an Icon—the Story of the Shard." In *Proceedings: CTBUH 2015 International Conference* (2015): 138–145. https://global.ctbuh.org/resources/papers/download/2450-developing-an-icon-the-story-of-the-shard.pdf.

Shelton, Barrie, Justyna Karakiewicz, and Thomas Kvan. *The Making of Hong Kong: From Vertical to Volumetric.* Routledge, 2013.

Shen, Xiaofang, and Songming Xu. "China: Shenzhen Special Economic Zone as a Policy Reform Incubator." In *Untying the Land Knot: Making Equitable, Efficient, and Sustainable Use of Industrial and Commercial Land*, edited by Xiao Fang Shen with Xiaolun Sun. World Bank, 2012.

shenzhenshopper.com. "Must-See: Ping'an Finance Center & the 541m Freesky Observation Deck," n.d. https://shenzhenshopper.com/3032-must-see-pingan-finance-center-the-541m-freesky-observation-deck.html.

Shultz, Earle, and Walter Simmons. *Offices in the Sky.* Bobbs-Merrill, 1959.

Shuyong, Liu. "Hong Kong: A Survey of Its Political and Economic Development over the Past 150 Years." *China Quarterly* 151 (1997): 583–592.

Sinn, Robert. "Engineering Jeddah Tower—Robert Sinn Presentation." Institution of Structural Engineers and Thorton Tomasetti, September 23, 2020. https://www.youtube.com/watch?v=GJLjjTfJjWQ.

The SkyDeck.com. "What Do You Know About the Willis Tower?" Accessed September 15, 2023. https://theskydeck.com/for-kids/fun-facts/.

Smith, Adrian. "Burj Dubai: Designing the World's Tallest." *Proceedings: CTBUH 8th World Congress* (2008). https://global.ctbuh.org/resources/papers/download/1327-burj-dubai-designing-the-worlds-tallest.pdf.

Smith, Adrain. "Supertall/Megatall: How High Can We Go?" Skyscraper Museum Lecture, March 9, 2021. https://skyscraper.org/programs/supertall-megatall/.

Smith Rory S., and Stefan Gerstenmeyer. "A Review of Waiting Time, Journey Time and Quality of Service." Peters Research, November 17, 2020. https://peters-research.com/index.php/2020/11/17/a-review-of-waiting-time-journey-time-and-quality-of-service/.

Song, Chunhua. "Review of Shanghai Tower Design Consulting Activities." (In Mandarin.) Architectural Society of China (May 9, 2020). http://www.assc.org.cn/SocietyNews/306.

South China Morning Post. "Urban Legend: China's Tiered City System Explained." 2016. https://multimedia.scmp.com/2016/cities/.

Spector, J. Brooks. "Thomas Piketty: The Man and His Work." *Daily Maverick*, October 5, 2015. https://www.dailymaverick.co.za/article/2015-10-05-thomas-piketty-the-man-and-his-work/.

Stegmann, Claire. "Designing the World's Tallest Skyscraper." *Think*, August 1975.

Stengren, Bernard. "Biggest Buildings in the World to Rise at Trade Center." *New York Times*, January 19, 1964. https://nyti.ms/3EGfZwU.

Stiglitz, Joseph E. *The Price of Inequality: How Today's Divided Society Endangers Our Future*. W. W. Norton, 2012.

Story, Louise, and Stephanie Saul. "Towers of Secrecy: Stream of Foreign Wealth Flows to Elite New York Real Estate." *New York Times*, February 7, 2015. https://www.nytimes.com/2015/02/08/nyregion/stream-of-foreign-wealth-flows-to-time-warner-condos.html.

Summerson, John. "The Victorian Rebuilding of the City of London." *London Journal* 3, no. 2 (1977): 163–185.

Tang, Tony. "ICC–Rising High for the Future of Hong Kong." *Proceedings: 2016 CTBUH Conference* (2016A): 510–520. https://global.ctbuh.org/resources/papers/download/2916-icc-rising-high-for-the-future-of-hong-kong.pdf .

Tang, Tony. "ICC–Rising High for the Future of Hong Kong." Talk given at 2016 CTBUH Conference in Shenzhen (2016B). https://www.youtube.com/watch?v=EKo8Z6qe2KY.

Tauranac, John. *The Empire State Building: The Making of a Landmark*. Scribner, 1995.

Telegraphic Journal and Electrical Review. "Progress of Electricity in Western America" 17, no. 397 (July 4, 1885): 6–8. (Google Books) https://www.google.com/books/edition/The_Electrical_Review/VUA_AQAAMAAJ?hl=en&gbpv=0.

Thurber, Rawson Marshall. *Skyscraper,* movie script, version March 10, 2017. https://assets.scriptslug.com/live/pdf/scripts/skyscraper-2018.pdf.

Tomlinson, Richard, William Baker, Luke Leung, Shean Chien, and Yue Zhu. "Case Study: Pearl River Tower, Guangzhou." *CTBUH Journal* 7 (2014): 1–16. https://global.ctbuh.org/resources/papers/download/1629-case-study-pearl-river-tower-guangzhou.pdf.

Tri-state Transportation Campaign. *Road Pricing in London, Stockholm and Singapore: A Way Forward for New York City* (2018). https://tstc.org/wp-content/uploads/2018/03/TSTC_A_Way_Forward_CPreport_1.4.18_medium.pdf.

Tullis, Robert H. *The Home Insurance Company: Men of Vision during 125 Years.* Newcomen Society in North America, 1978.

Turk, Gregory. "World's 2nd-tallest Building the Shanghai Tower Opens with a Whimper after Delay." *Financial Review,* December 13, 2017. https://www.afr.com/property/commercial/worlds-2ndtallest-building-the-shanghai-tower-opens-with-a-whimper-after-delay-20171213-ho3jrm.

Turvey, Ralph. "Office Rents in the City of London, 1867–1910." *London Journal* 23, no. 2 (1998): 53–67.

Vogel, Ezra F. Foreword to *Learning from Shenzhen: China's Post-Mao Experiment from Special Zone to Model City,* edited by Mary Ann O'Donnell, Winnie Wong, and Jonathan Bach, vii–xiv. University of Chicago Press, 2017.

Watson, Howard. *The Shard: The Vision of Irvine Sellar.* Constable, 2017.

Watts, Steve, and Davis Langdon. "Tall Building Economics." In *The Tall Buildings Reference Book,* edited by David Parker and Antony Wood, 65–86. Routledge, 2013.

Weber, Rachel. *From Boom to Bubble: How Finance Built the New Chicago.* University of Chicago Press, 2019.

Weismantle, Peter, and Alejandro H. Stochetti. "Kingdom Tower, Jeddah: Meeting the Challenges of a One-Kilometer Tower." *CTBUH Journal* 1 (2013): 12–19.

Weiss, Marc A. "Skyscraper Zoning: New York's Pioneering Role." *Journal of the American Planning Association* 58, no. 2 (1992): 201–212.

Weiss, Marc A. "Astor, John Jacob" in *The Encyclopedia of New York City,* 2nd ed., edited by Kenneth T. Jackson, Lisa Keller, and Nancy Flood, 72. Yale University Press, 2010.

Wermiel, Sara E. "Norcross, Fuller, and the Rise of the General Contractor in the United States in the Nineteenth Century." *Proceedings: Second International Congress on Construction History* 3 (2006): 3297–3314.

Willis, Carol. *Form Follows Finance: Skyscrapers and Skylines in New York and Chicago.* Princeton Architectural Press, 1995.

Willis, Carol. "World's Biggest (Tall Buildings)." *Proceedings CTBUH 10th World Congress* (2019): 87–93. https://global.ctbuh.org/resources/papers/download/4263-worlds-biggest-tall-buildings.pdf.

Work, S. Isaac, and Shawn Ursini. "The World's Highest Pools: A Deep Dive." *CTBUH Journal* 2 (2022): 44–51. https://global.ctbuh.org/resources/papers/download/4580-the-worlds-highest-pools-a-deep-dive.pdf.

World Bank. World Bank National Accounts Data and OECD National Accounts Data Files for Iceland. Accessed April 26, 2023. https://data.worldbank.org/indicator/NY.GDP.MKTP.CD.

World Record Academy. "World's Skinniest Skyscraper: NYC's New Steinway Tower Sets World Record." April 8, 2022. https://www.worldrecordacademy.org/2022/04/world-s-skinniest-skyscraper-nyc-s-new-steinway-tower-sets-world-record-422169.

Wu, Weiping. "Proximity and Complementarity in Hong Kong-Shenzhen Industrialization." *Asian Survey* 37, no. 8 (1997): 771–793.

Xia, Jun, Dennis Poon, and D. Mass. "Case Study: Shanghai Tower." *CTBUH Journal* 2 (2010): 12–18. https://global.ctbuh.org/resources/papers/download/12-case-study-shanghai-tower.pdf.

Xue, Charlie Q. L. *Hong Kong Architecture 1945–2015: From Colonial to Global.* Springer, 2016.

Yang, Andrew. "Despite Sinking Economy, Work Begins on Super-Tall Shanghai Tower." *Architectural Record*, December 1, 2008. https://www.architecturalrecord.com/articles/4681-despite-sinking-economy-work-begins-on-super-tall-shanghai-tower.

Yu, Hong. "The Ascendency of State-Owned Enterprises in China: Development, Controversy and Problems." *Journal of Contemporary China* 23, no. 85 (2014): 161–182.

Yuen, Belinda, and Anthony G. O. Yeh, eds. *High-Rise Living in Asian Cities.* Springer, 2011.

Zhao, Renjie, Jie Chen, Chen Feng, and Shihu Zhong. "The Impact of Anti-corruption Measures on Land Supply and the Associated Implications: The Case of China." *Land Use Policy* 95 (2020): 104605.

Zuo, Mandy. "Chinese Government Bans Those 'Weird Buildings' That Xi Jinping Can't Stand." *South China Morning Post*, April 17, 2021. https://www.scmp.com/news/people-culture/article/3129880/chinese-government-bans-those-weird-buildings-xi-jinping-cant.

Photo Credits

p. xii: Keith De Lellis Gallery.

p. 3: Library of Congress, Prints and Photographs Division.

p. 13: Library of Congress, Geography and Map Division.

p. 18: Chicago History Museum, ICHi-017281.

p. 29: Courtesy of the author.

p. 38 (left): Waldorf-Astoria Office Building from the *Real Estate Record and Builders' Guide* (December 1929): p. 7.

p. 38 (middle): Wikimedia Commons.

p. 38 (right): Clark and Kingston (1930).

p. 46: City of New York Board of Estimate and Apportionment Committee on the City Plan, *Commission on Building Districts and Restrictions Final Report* (June 2, 1916): p. 259.

p. 47 (left): Milstein Division, The New York Public Library.

p. 47 (right): Esto Photographics Inc.

p. 49 (left): "King's Dream of New York." Moses King (1908).

p. 49 (right): Hugh Ferriss, *The Metropolis of To-morrow* (Ives Washburn, 1929): p. 87.

p. 51: American Society of Planning Officials, *Information Report 111* (June 1958). In the report the image was reproduced from H. M. Lewis, *A New Zoning Plan for the District of Columbia* (1956).

p. 55: Skidmore, Owings & Merrill, Architect, photograph by Balthazar Korab. Sears Tower, Chicago, Illinois. Exterior view from highway. Retrieved from the Library of Congress.

p. 59: Cmglee via Wikimedia Commons.

p. 70: HB-28864-F, Chicago History Museum, Hedrich-Blessing Collection.

p. 73: AP Photo/Ed Ford.

Index

Page numbers in *italics* refer to photographs or illustrations.

China (*cont.*)
   Three Brothers story and, 147–50
   urban ranking system in, 160
   urban workers and, 158
   urbanization in, 157–58
   zero-COVID policy and, 162–63,
     164
   See also Shanghai Tower
Chrysler Building (1929) (New York
   City)
   Abu Dhabi SWF purchase and, 90
   aspect ratio of, 241
   curtain wall facade, 9, 48
   height of, xiii, 32, 37
   land-lease system and, 90, 158–59
   rigid steel frame of, 8, 166
Citicorp Center (1977) (New York
   City), 169–70
Civil War, 23
Clark, W. C., 37
classical architectural styles, 17, 48,
   93, 151
climate crisis, 273–76, 277–81, 293
"Cloud Minders, The" (*Star Trek*
   episode), 182
cogeneration, 272
Commission for Architecture and the
   Built Environment (CABE), 83,
   88, 108
Communist Party, 137, 138, 141, 150,
   157, 160, 163
computer-based technologies, xvii–
   xviii, 64, 67–68, 102, 167–68
concrete. *See* skyscraper engineering
Condit, Carl W., 17, 20
congestion pricing, 261–62
"Consequences of Living in High-
   Rise Buildings, The" (Gifford),
   265–66, 267
constrained optimization problem, 63

Conventions for the Extension of
   Hong Kong Territory (Second
   Convention of Peking) (1898),
   132
cost-plus system, 31
Council on Tall Buildings and Urban
   Habitat (CTBUH), 149, 186,
   218–19, 299n
COVID pandemic
   China's zero-COVID policy and,
     162–63, 164
   Hong Kong's zero-COVID policy
     and, 289
   impacts of, 284, 289–90
   post-pandemic building amenities
     pressure and, 270–71
   returning to the offices and, 230
   Sears (Willis) Tower rental occu-
     pancy and, 61
   Shanghai Tower occupancy and,
     154
   skyscraper construction rate and,
     xvi
   as unforeseeable, 34
CTBUH (Council on Tall Buildings
   and Urban Habitat), 149, 186,
   218–19, 299n
Customs House (1927) (Shanghai),
   151, *151*

Daley, Richard J., 57, 58
damping systems, 75, 172, 240, 242
Davidson, Justin, 268
*Death and Life of Great American
   Cities, The* (Jacobs), 131
Deng Xiaoping, 138, 150
Dennis, Richard, 95
Dericks, Gerard H., 110–11
Destination Dispatching System
   (DDS), 172

Skyscraper Revolution, Third
  Asian country skylines and, 164
  Billionaires' Row benefiting from,
    240–41
  composite materials and, 166–67
  elevator technology and, 173
  foundation principles and methods,
    174–79
  geometry and, 164
  outrigger systems and, 168–69
  postmodern storylines and, 164–65
  sci-fi renderings/distinctive
    architecture and, 165–66
  wind engineering and, 169–72
skyscrapers
  architects and, 15–19
  as-of-right, 91
  bird strikes and, 276
  carbon footprints and, 276–81, 286
  clean energy and, 280, 281
  client-patron relationships and,
    xx–xxi
  as commercially oriented creativity
    hubs, 233–35
  computer technologies and, 64,
    67–68, 102, 167–68
  definition of, 6, 299n
  developers and, 15–16, 220, 227, 248
  economic rationality of, 123, 190,
    220–21, 244
  environmental concerns and,
    272–81
  future of, 292–93
  gentrification and, 243, 248–49, 253
  global competitiveness and, 234–36
  host cities and, 249, 254–55
  iconic corporate hives and, 63
  iconicity and, 227
  income inequality and, 243, 244,
    251–54

merit/demerit debates about, 39–43
money laundering and, 249–51
9/11 and, 60
psychological impacts and, 265–68
regulation and, 39, 252, 253–54,
  255–56, 258, 260
revenue streams of, 222
social science research and, 268–71
starchitect industrial complex and,
  227–28
technological design evolution of,
  xxi–xxii, 166–68
urbanism and, 268–72, 292–93
as vault delivery systems, 22
VEAM Principle and, 258–62
wind sway and, 76, 163, 243
zoning and, 40–41, 43–47, 46, 50,
  52, 57, 241
  See also Floor Area Ratio (FAR)
"skyscrapers follow urban growth"
  theory, 236
Smith, Adam, 16
Smith, Adrian, 148, 168, 185, 207
Smith, Al, xiii–xiv, 30, 35, 36, 37, 38
Smith, William Sooy, 10
sovereign wealth funds (SWFs)
  Arabian, 89, 90
  Dubai, 183
  Shanghai, 155
  trophy assets in global cities and, 89
Spatial Development Strategy (SDS),
  103
Special Economic Zone (SEZ), 138,
  139, 150, 157
St. Paul's Cathedral (London), 87,
  103, 263
St. Petersburg, Lakhta Center tower
  (2019), 124, 237
starchitects, 110–11, 227–28, 245
Starrett, Paul, 31, 32

About the Author

Jason M. Barr is a professor of economics at Rutgers University-Newark. One of the world's foremost experts on the economics of skyscrapers, he is the author of *Building the Skyline: The Birth and Growth of Manhattan Skyscrapers* (2016). His research has been featured in the the *Washington Post, The Economist, Curbed.com,* and *Architectural Record.* A Long Island native, Barr received his bachelor's degree from Cornell University, his MFA in creative writing from Emerson College, and his PhD. from Columbia University. His writings have appeared in the *New York Times,* StarTrek.com, Dezeen.com, *Scientific American,* and the *Irish Independent.* He currently writes the *Skynomics Blog,* a blog about skyscrapers, cities, and economics.